D1590430

MAD
JESUS

MAD

the final testament of a HUICHOL MESSIAH
from NORTHWEST mexico

JESUS

timothy j. knab

University of New Mexico Press
Albuquerque

Library of Congress Cataloging-in-Publication Data

Knab, T. J.
Mad Jesus : the final testament of a Huichol messiah
from northwest Mexico / Timothy J. Knab.— 1st ed.
p. cm.
Includes bibliographical references and index.
ISBN 0-8263-3204-8 (cloth : alk. paper)
1. Mad Jesus. 2. Huichol Indians—Biography.
3. Shamans—Mexico—Jalisco—Biography.
4. Huichol Indians—Religion.
5. Shamanism--Mexico—Jalisco.
6. Nativistic movements—Mexico—Jalisco.
I. Title.
F1221.H9M335 2004
299.7´84544´0092—dc22

2003023789

Printed and bound in the USA by Thomson-Shore, Inc.
Typeset in Bembo 11/14
Display type set in Disturbance and Trajan
Design and composition: Robyn Mundy
Production: Maya Allen-Gallegos

for my CHILDReN

CONTENTS

part ii: the gospel of mad jesus

part iii: resurrecting jesus

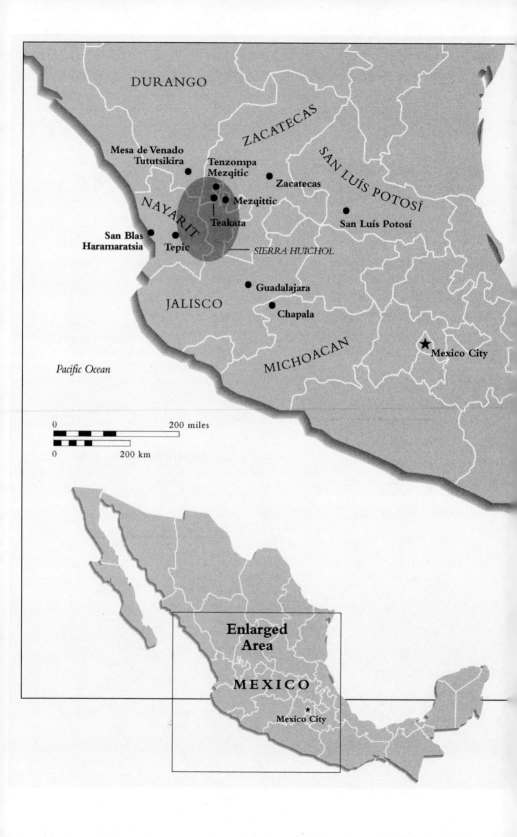

DURANGO

ZACATECAS

SAN LUÍS POTOSÍ

Mesa de Venado
Tututsikira

Tenzompa
Mezqitic

Zacatecas

Mezqittic

Teakata

San Luís Potosí

NAYARIT

San Blas
Haramaratsia   Tepic

SIERRA HUICHOL

JALISCO

Guadalajara

Chapala

MICHOACAN

★ Mexico City

Pacific Ocean

0   200 miles

0   200 km

Enlarged
Area

MEXICO

★
Mexico City

part I

MAD JESUS: SANTO CRISTO

true jesus

Jesus, *Jesús*, Mad Jesus, *Chucho Loco*: that was what he was called.[1] I never knew his Huichol name. A strange Indian Jesus, a redeemer condemned by shadows. He was stalked by dark deities of his remote homeland deep in the mountains of northwestern Mexico. *Jesús* was a Huichol Indian, an artisan, a shaman, a seer, a self-styled prophet, a mad messiah, a murderous mystic. His bloodshot eyes constantly darting about the room, his matted hair, his dark skin, and his baroque Huichol costume, all shimmer in my mind. His strident voice, his commands in place of questions, or requests, his tears, his pleas, his strings of disconnected words, all are as real today as they were thirty years ago.

Jesús came from a realm of scattered communities on high plateaus gashed by deep canyons where the Sierra Madre falls off precipitously to the Pacific; the Sierra Huichol, a region of refuge isolated by geography. This was his Mother-Father land, a terrain of myth and magic, the domain of his gods to which he could never return. An exile from his homeland, he became the quintessential Huichol artisan, a mystic shaman for his patrons, and father for his native flock. His bewildered band of dispossessed followers attributed to him messianic stature. He saw himself as a savior, a redeemer of his people, yet all but his most ardent followers knew him as Mad Jesus, Chucho Loco.

Jesús was assassinated by Mexican police in the name of public safety, sanity, and Mexico's never-ending "war" on drugs. Greed, jealousy, revenge, and ineptitude were the real reasons behind Chucho's demise.

For the few left who followed him, he remains a martyred messiah, a man of compassion and hope, a prophet of a new age for his people. For others who knew him, he was a madman, best forgotten.

As any good narrator knows it may take ten, or twenty, or even thirty years before a tale can be properly told. What are anthropologists but tellers of tales, tales of social and moral philosophy, tales of the past as we see it from excavations and monuments, tales of the world of man and mind, language and culture? Juan Rulfo in his reading of the tale of Mad Jesus more than twenty-five years ago saw a dark, mythic, and forbidding tale, a messiah shadowed by the evil sorcerer Kieli. This is assuredly part of the tale of Mad Jesus, but the man was more than a haunted psychopath. He was a successful artisan and broker. He was a careful and caring shepherd for his flock for many years.

The psychiatrist and psychoanalyst who helped me try to understand Mad Jesus saw the troubled and tortured life of this man. They did not see his long years of striving to learn the basics of our civilization: reading, writing, law, and economics. They did not see his business acumen, or the power his visions held for his followers.

Over the years I have struggled to tell the tale of the man I knew: *Jesús*. His tale cannot be set off from the text with dry anthropological commentary. It is not just his story. I have tried to weave together the threads of one man's life with the culture and context of his world. To do this I have constructed a narrative using many different sources: tapes, interviews, field notes, and documents, as well as techniques from fiction, biography, history, and travel writing. My own role in the story as protagonist and narrator is as much a narrative device as it was a part of the way events unfolded. The plot has been constructed to drive the narrative and hopefully reveal something of the man I knew as Mad Jesus, the true *Jesús*.

COLOR aₓainst the sky

Long before I ever imagined anyone like Mad Jesus, I met his brother, the first of his tribe I knew. He was but a flash of color in the great sea of humanity that is Mexico City.

Cold gray clouds hung over the city. A *norte* had come in from the coast. Mexico City was then home to six million, a village compared to the vast sprawl of humanity that it is today. The Metro was new; it was an underground labyrinth of marbled arcades with swift, orange French-made trains. At least the Metro was warm.

From the Metro, there were *peseros,* aging vehicles cobbled together with Mexican ingenuity, communal taxicabs that charged a peso. Josh and I searched for a pesero heading up the hill to the village where I had just rented an apartment. Josh at least spoke Spanish. I had been lost in Mexico City since I arrived a few weeks before. A Chicago cop's billy club in front of the Hilton at the height of the Democratic Convention had convinced me that I wanted nothing more to do with the United States. That was really why I was in Mexico.

As each pesero arrived, the crowd surged toward it and piled in. Josh, wrapped in a dark pancho, looked like an American movie image of Zapata's minions. I was freezing in a light sweater as we waited. There was a flash of color in the crowd. I stood about a head taller than anyone and was looking at two strange hats; broad brimmed and flat, woven of straw with red felt borders and red-felt x's sewn on to them. One was decorated with what appeared to be squirrel tails, and the other with a halo of feathers and woven bangles of beads. I motioned to Josh and edged toward the two bobbing hats.

Another pesero arrived and we flowed into it with the two young men in bright hats. The door closed, and we were off.

The two young men had costumes that would have been the envy of anyone in the Haight; three-quarter-length white pants with multi-color patterns cross-stitched into them, peacocks and stars, flowers and sunbursts. They wore multicolored flower-print shirts open at both sides and tucked into heavy wool belts; they wore necklaces with thousands of tiny red beads, beaded earrings, and chokers, and they carried shoulder bags in a whole array of rainbow colors.

"Who are these guys?" I asked Josh.

"I think they're Indians from somewhere, maybe Chiapas."

"Eh, ask 'em where they're from, Man!" I told Josh. "If everyone there looks like this, it's someplace I want to go."

The two young men were speaking with each other in a language that rose and fell with singsongy tones. Maybe they are asking the same things about us, I thought. Josh started talking to them in Spanish, and the heavier one answered him.

"They're from the mountains somewhere in Jalisco," Josh told me.

The one near the window was struggling to get one of his shoulder bags out and was jostling everyone around as the pesero sped up the hill in a cloud of smoke. He brought out a handful of beaded jewelry and said something to Josh.

"He wants to know if we want to buy some of this stuff," Josh told me.

The young man sitting next to me reached into his handful of beads and pulled out a red, blue, and white band, which he proceeded to tie on my wrist; then he showed me his wrist. He had six wristbands and two watches on.

The other one then said something to Josh.

"He wants to know where you are from."

"Tell him I am from near Chicago, but that I am going to live up in the village of Leones now."

Words went back and forth in languages I didn't understand, and then Josh asked, "Do you have a pen? He wants your address. They are going to visit someone near Leones, and when they are finished they'll stop down to visit you."

"That sounds great!" I told Josh.

Josh proceeded to write the address on a piece of paper and handed it to the guy next to the window. He even drew a little map.

Meanwhile the young man next to me was fishing through the beads in his hand and found a ring which he put on my index finger. He had rings on every finger and even his thumbs. He smiled, showing me his hands full of multicolored bands. I was really beginning to like the guy.

We got out of the pesero in the village of Leones, paid the driver and the young men, and they proceeded farther up the hill.

"Do you think we'll ever see them again?" I asked Josh as we made our way to the landlord's house.

"I don't know," he said. "I've never met any Indians like that."

"They're Indians, you're sure of that?" I asked.

"They're Indians all right!" Josh assured me.

We got the papers for the apartment signed and we got a big load of firewood.

While Josh was building the fire, an old man came to the kitchen door with deep furrows and a stubbly beard. I couldn't understand a word he was saying, so I got Josh. They talked for a moment.

Josh turned to me and said, "Well, it looks like your Indians are back. They're down in this man's store asking how to get here. He didn't want to send them up here without asking first. I don't think he trusts Indians too much."

Josh went with the man to his store and left me to start the fire. The fire was essential in that damp cold. I was freezing.

When he came back with the two Indians, he told me they were looking for a place to stay. I had been fumbling ineffectively with the fire the whole time Josh was gone, with just some smoke to show for my efforts. The young man who had been sitting next to me in the pesero went right over to the fire, and in a few seconds had a roaring blaze going. That did it, if I had ever had any doubt: they could stay.

Josh spoke to the older one and found out their names, Pedro and

Juan. I didn't know that Huichols also had names in their own language that they generally preferred, but the pair turned out to be Matsiwa and Neyaucame. Matsiwa was the elder brother of Mad Jesus, and Neyaucame, though he spoke no Spanish at the time, became one of my closest friends.

Josh and I went back to the boarding house to get my things. The Huichols went down to the center of town for their things. We were getting ready to leave the boarding house when Little Jack, a tall, blond Swede from Minnesota who had been in Mexico only a few days longer than I had, walked in with two other guys, obviously also of Nordic descent.

"Eh, ya got your apartment, eh?" Little Jack asked. He punctuated most of his speech with, "Eh."

"Yea," I told him, "it's a done deal and I also just got a couple of roommates in the deal. Two Indians we met in the taxi."

"Indians! Are you crazy?" one of Jack's friends piped in.

"This is Einar," Jack said. "He's lived here since he was three, eh. He should know something about this country an' ya should listen to him, eh."

"Well, what's the matter with Indians?" I asked.

"First of all, they're stupid," Einar said.

Neyaucame and Matsiwa didn't seem stupid to me, I thought. But Einar just went on.

"Only a dumb gringo would invite Indians he met in a taxicab to his house. You are really looking for trouble. Where are these little Indians from?"

"Someplace I think called Halliscoo," I said. They wear big hats with feathers and they gave me these," I said showing him my wristband and ring.

"They must be Huicholes," Einar said. "They're the Peyote People. You're going to get busted if you don't get rid of them fast."

The Peyote People, I thought. Now, I was really fascinated! I had plenty of experience with hallucinogens in the sixties. Einar had convinced me that I had, perhaps, just made the best move of my life inviting Matsiwa and Neyaucame to my new apartment, but I didn't want to tell him that.

When I got back up to my new apartment in Leones, Neyaucame and Matsiwa were waiting for me with two women and a toddler. These were two of Matsiwa's wives, I would learn, and his son.

As we were all just starting to settle in, one of the women came into the bedroom to offer me a big cup of something that tasted like very sweet tea. I came out into the main room. Everyone was huddled around the fire and sitting on the sofa. The women had the old coffeepot right on the fire perched on three stones.

This would never do, I thought; so I reached for it, burning myself and swearing up a streak. One of the women began to cry, and I felt terrible. I grabbed a rag and took the pot off the fire and took it over to the stove in the kitchen. Then I motioned to everyone to come into the kitchen. I lit the stove and put the pot on it. This was our first lesson in living together.

I could see things would be difficult. I had to start studying Spanish right away. The next day I went to the Universidad de las Américas, which was a couple of kilometers down the hill. While asking about Spanish classes, I found out there was an Austrian linguist in the Department of Anthropology, Dr. Karl Heidt, who might be able to help me with the Huichol language. Bill Sweezy, the dean, also suggested I take a course on Mexican Indians. I enrolled for the next semester and never looked back.

Karl inspired in me a lifelong fascination with linguistics, and Sweezy passed along his euphoric love of Mexico. Within a year I was hooked and became an anthropologist. My house became the Casa Huichol with an ever-changing population of indigenous friends, up to eighteen or twenty at a time. I found my Huichol friends, with their vibrant costumes, their constant use of peyote, their strange tales, and their incessant rituals fascinating. I had been forced to learn their language just to survive in my own house, just to tell them simple things like "Don't put the fire in the middle of the living-room floor!"

Finally, as that first year waned, I took another apartment in Mexico City. The constant demands of my Huichol guests and the constant fighting, their sometimes abrasive nature and arrogant ways, had worn me down to a frazzle after a year. My studies were too important to me now. I began to value my solitude. I was always very careful not to tell more than one or two of the Huichols where my new apartment was in Mexico City.

After more than a year living with my Huichol friends, I thought I knew something about them. But one Huichol was about to invade my life, and he would haunt my mind for years to come: *Jesús*.

HUICHOLaND

Jesús was so unlike all of the other Huichols I had known, yet he was so much a Huichol. How do I speak of "The Huichol"? No one individual can represent the totality of a people, and *Jesús* was certainly not the prototypical Huichol. He was dark, different, haunted by the gods he had left behind; an urban creature, not a man of the Sierras; sometimes tearful, sometimes incoherent; in his soul he was Huichol.

At first I knew nothing of "The Huichol," yet I knew a lot about my Huichol friends. Some were haughty, demanding, difficult, secretive; others were the quintessential sarcasts, poking fun and making the most obscure jokes out of everything. Men would cry easily and women were stoic, but laughed with great spontaneity. They all had their own way of doing things, their own way of telling a tale, or talking about their relationships with their gods and each other. Each individual had a personal ideological stance, derived from experience, religion, myth, and ritual, his or her own fundamental philosophy. No two of my friends were the same, yet they were all Huichol.

Stacy B. Schaefer and Peter T. Furst have observed, "What this sometimes striking ideological diversity reflects, perhaps more than anything else, . . . is the freedom of each Huichol to travel his or her own trail along the common road to the divine."[1]

For my friends from the Sierra, religion never was based on any kind of institutional dogma; it was a part of everyday life, whether putting a new peso next to my bathroom sink for the Spring Mothers, or making an arduous pilgrimage to the sea.

Lumholtz, the Norwegian explorer who spent considerable time in the Sierra at the turn of the century, noted, "Religion is to them a personal matter, not an institution, and therefore their life is religious from the cradle to the grave wrapped up in symbolism."[2]

Unknown Mexico, Lumholtz's two-volume tale of his travels and adventures in northwestern Mexico, was the first work that I read on "The Huichol." The region of the Sierra Madre my friends called home is still, almost a century later, "Unknown Mexico," an area of not more than 50 by 100 miles where the states of Jalisco, Zacatecas, and Durango converge. It is an area of high mesas and deep canyons. The Chapalagana Canyon, which bisects the region, dwarfs the Grand Canyon. There were virtually no roads in the region until a few years ago, and even now what are called "roads" are but rutted trails that challenge even the roughest vehicle. Today Huichols in dilapidated, but sturdy pickups ply these roads. In Lumholtz's time the only way into the region was with pack animals.[3]

My first journey into the Sierra—into "Unknown Mexico"—was a revelation. The bus could only get as far as Jeréz de la Frontera in Zacatecas. From there we had to walk with pack animals, first to Mezquitic, and then into the Sierra Huichol. It was a hot, dry, rugged land. Not a leaf, not the slightest sign of life. Everything was tinder dry. It was a hostile land for both man and beast, so sun-parched that it was hard to imagine any life in the region, yet at the base of deep canyons where there was still water, there was bamboo; there were bananas, sugarcane, and pineapples growing in little patches of tropical abundance. The high mesas were windswept with forests that looked more like the Colorado Rockies, or northern New Mexico, but so much drier. Snow was not unknown in winter. How anything could survive in that hostile climate was a mystery. It was the height of the dry season when I first visited the Sierra Huichol.

My brightly clad friends walking through the deep dry canyons and across the desolate mesas added color to the hostile environment. On subsequent trips in the rainy season, and shortly after the rains, the Sierra was a verdant paradise with an exuberance of growth. It was a land of stark contrasts. It took nearly five days on that first trip into the Sierra to reach the first isolated Huichol *rancherías*. I was discovering Lumholtz's "Unknown Mexico."

We were greeted like long-lost family in the Sierra. Everyone came from the surrounding rancherías to get a look at the strange character their friends had brought. We were offered sweet hot tea made from the bark of local trees. Food was scarce; corn, beans, and squash are the mainstay of the diet in the Sierra, but there had been little rain the year before and most supplies had run out weeks ago.

The women gathered what they could: roots and the sweet hearts of local *agaves*, fruits and seeds. Children hunted small birds and lizards. Many of the men who hadn't gone either to the coast to work or to the cities to sell their handiwork were out hunting with little to show for days on the high mesas. Women ground, squeezed, kneaded, and boiled the strange seeds and roots we found into delightful little morsels. Most of the cattle looked like emaciated skeletons, not worth even considering as food. The few chickens and pigs left were in about the same shape; even the dogs barely moved.

My friends had brought corn and beans from Zacatecas, but there was little else. Working as urban artisans, my friends could amass far more in a few months than others who spent the whole season working on the coast as hired farm laborers. There was a ready market for their vibrant handicrafts in Mexico City, Guadalajara, Guanajuato, and Ciudad Juarez. Many Huichols were becoming permanent urban artisans who visited their homeland only occasionally. This was already beginning to have a profound effect on their remote Sierra stronghold.

At the turn of the century when Lumholtz, Diguet, and others visited the Sierra to amass vast collections of purloined artifacts for major museums, art was far more utilitarian and rarely produced for an external market. It was for adornment or religious offerings, but as their art became ever more popular new forms evolved that were never seen in the Huichol homeland. Huichols began to produce large paintings of wool yarn pressed into wax for sale. The same technique that was used to make beaded votive bowls, pressing small glass beads into wax, began to be used to decorate carved jaguar heads from Guerrero and horses from Guanajuato. With the popularity of their art, and the economic success it brought them, many of my friends began to establish permanent and semipermanent urban enclaves in Mexico's major cities.

Today, Huichol art is vibrant, exuberant, and in some ways almost baroque. Woven bags, belts, and heavily embroidered costumes in iridescent colors accented by long necklaces and earrings of complicated multicolored beads transform Huichol men into peacocks, walking advertisements for Huichol art. Both Lumholtz and Zingg, who titled his ethnography of the Sierra *The Huichols: Primitive Artists*, recognized the artistic vigor of Huichol traditions. More recently Furst, Schaefer, Valadez, and many others have discussed Huichol art.[4] There have been exhibits of Huichol art in San Francisco, Los Angeles, Santa Fe, Houston, San Antonio, Chicago, and New York. The Mexican government has sent Huichol artisans to the major capitals of Europe and Asia to exhibit their art. Since the early sixties Huichol art has become increasingly popular, earning considerable sums of money for urban artisans, especially those who could establish their own name and reputation among dealers and collectors.

There are not more than twenty thousand people living in small, widely dispersed settlements throughout the Sierra, and there are perhaps another five thousand on the coast of Nayarit, as well as those in major urban centers. In the Sierra most people live in extended family groups on widely separated rancherías. Kinship is of paramount importance in the mountains, and my Huichols friends can spend days discussing distant relations.[5] Often they reminded me of my maiden aunts interminably gossiping about distant relatives, dissecting family relationships and cousins so far removed I could not even imagine them as kin.

In the Sierra each family group pertains to a particular temple center, or Kaliwey.[6] The Kaliwey centers each consist of a single large circular or oval structure with a high, thatched roof.[7] This is the Kaliwey itself, or *tuki*, in Huichol, the great meeting house, the Huichol temple. In front of this building is a large, well-swept patio for dancing, and all around the patio are sometimes dozens of *shiriki*, shrines for gods and ancestors pertaining to particular families.

The Kaliwey is the center of ceremonial and social life in Huichol communities. A council of elders, the *kawiteros*, who dream appointments of the shamans, singers, and dancers for annual ceremonial activities, orchestrate the ritual year. They help to organize the annual pilgrimages and labor parties and to adjudicate local social disputes. The kawiteros are generally the shamans, the *mara'acames*, who have held numerous posts within the religious hierarchy, are esteemed for their vast knowledge of traditional lore and their ability to chant for days on end the mythic basis for the Huichol world, and are adept at organizing complex rituals.[8]

The Sierra is organized politically by a *gubernancia* system of Hispanic origin. The three major Huichol *comunidades* are San Andrés, San Sebastián, and Santa Catarina. As Diguet observed in the early twentieth century, "This subdivision of the Huichol territory is of some interest from an ethnographic and linguistic point of view. It shows the evolution that each tribe underwent through the course of time. Confined to their respective territories where they live under a communal regime, the Indians of each district have contact with their neighbors only at certain times of the year for religious practices. This situation has created certain differences not only in their customs but also in the language. The language has been progressively modified in each tribe and results in the three dialects spoken today."[9]

Guadalupe Ocotan and Tuxpan were incipient Huichol comunidades at that time. Now, as a result of the Cristero revolts shortly after the Mexican Revolution and subsequent hostilities between Huichols and their mestizo neighbors, the hated *tewalis*, there are numerous small Huichol communal ranches of the dispossessed on the coast of Nayarit and in the drainage of the Rio Lerma. Although they are not in fact *comunidades indígenas* in official terms, many try to imitate the social and political structure of their homeland. Each comunidad indígena is headed by a *gobernador,* or *tatoani*, with his secretary and a staff of minor officials, as well as a tribunal of judges. This system was probably transmitted to the Huichol by Tlaxcaltecan troops stationed around the edges of the Sierra shortly after the Mixton wars in 1541.[10] The region did not come under complete Spanish control until the eighteenth century.

Unlike so many indigenous Mexicans who readily surrender their language and their native costume and try to blend in with Mexican national culture, my friends were different, proud, even disdainful of Mexican national culture. The Norwegian explorer Carl Lumholtz observed, "Never for a moment will a Huichol allow that any other race may be superior to his. Even when far away from home, among the whites, the Huichols bear themselves as if they had never known masters."[11]

There were repeated attempts to missionize the region throughout the seventeenth and eighteenth centuries, but as the ruined churches in San Andrés, San Sebastián, and Santa Catarina attest, the missions had little success. Lumholtz noted that the Huichol commitment to Christianity was tenuous at best: "The most civilized of them know how to make the sign of the cross and are familiar with the names of María Santisima, Dios and Diablo. Many are clever enough to put an external show of Christianity toward people from whom they expect some favor. All of them observe the leading Christian feasts, which offer occasions for prolonged eating and drinking, and they worship the saints as so many gods."[12]

For my friends from the Sierra there is an overwhelming confidence that they, as the first people of this world, are the rightful stewards of all that they may see. The fact that other peoples may possess more than Huichols, or may have an easier life, is simply due to larceny, or sloth. They are satisfied that their complex rituals are the will of the gods and part of the proper way for human beings to behave on this earth.

My friends quite clearly were not a pristine and untouched people. Their pilgrimages take them across vast stretches of Mexico. They have been in constant contact with Mexican national culture since the time of the conquest and probably long before.[13] They have assimilated, absorbed, and subsumed into their worldview the traits of many cultures. Some are in fact quite sophisticated, having traveled to the major capitals of Europe and performed at the Kennedy Center in Washington, D.C. Recently in the Sierra, I spent an entire afternoon with friends comparing passports and swapping stories about trips to Europe and Asia. They had just returned from two months in Southeast Asia and Europe and were all busy working on filling the orders they had taken from folk art shops.

Each community in the Sierra is different; in fact, almost every ranchería has its own version of Huichol traditions. As Lumholtz noted, "The different districts naturally have slight diversities of customs; even in the same temple there may be variations in regard to religious rites, according to the orders of the shaman."[14] Phil Weigand attributes this to what he calls "differential trends in acculturation," that is, the different historical and social patterns that have shaped each region of the Sierra, but it is more than that.[15]

Much of their religion is linked to their intimate relationship with the sacred cactus, *hikuli*, or peyote. The peyote cactus is the focus of annual pilgrimages to the deserts of San Luís Potosí, ritual deer hunts, planting rituals, medicine, rain ceremonies, human and animal fertility, and much of what can be called "common intellectual culture" of the people from the Sierra Huichol. "Among the Huichols, peyote engenders a living complex of myth and symbol and ritual that they consider vital to their existence and survival as a distinct people."[16] At Huichol rituals often vast quantities of peyote are consumed for days on end, and even outside of ritual contexts some Huichols will regularly consume considerable quantities of peyote.

On my first journey to the Sierra, my host, a well-known shaman of considerable esteem in the community, would often leave his ranch compound at four or five in the morning and make his way through the darkness to the nearby Kaliwey where he would sit with the kawiteros, the elders, eating peyote until eight or nine in the morning. On his return, my host would often stop at the blackened old cookhouse where I was staying to tell me of his morning activities.

There he would recount his visions and the myths they recalled for him, instructing me to look at them with him on the blackened walls of the hut. He would describe how various deer and birds were connected by lightening bolts, which were hallucinogenic allusions to the myths that linked such things. My host regularly instructed me in the proper hallucinations one should have when eating hikuli. Toward the end of my sojourn in the Sierra, my host would insist that I accompany him in the early morning to the Kaliwey where we sat with the elders, eating vast quantities of peyote, giddy with glee at the most mundane things and impenetrable remarks.

People from the Sierra Huichol feel that direct contact with the gods is an essential part of life. This is a part of reality. It should come as no surprise that in some regions of the Sierra up to 80 percent of the men, and a large percentage of the women, are shamans, or mara'acames.[17] A shaman is constantly seeking new methods and techniques of direct contact with the supernatural. The mara'acames are masters of the methods of ecstasy, and each has his or her own particular view of the supernatural.

Despite individual variation there is a common thread that all Huichols share. It is part of being Huichol. It is a part of the essential participation of every individual in Huichol culture. Zingg observed, "The most important conditioning of the Huichol individual comes from the functionally polygynous family. Into this group the child is born and lives until marriage. The extended family kinship group of the ranchería has important economic and ceremonial functions which train the child in the technological and religious lore of the tribe. Formal education does not exist except as a by-product of the ceremonies. Here from the time he is half grown, the Huichol must stay awake during the long drawn-out singing of sacred myths. Thus by the time the Huichols are adults they know by heart the philosophy of the tribe which is all contained in the mythology."[18] Although many others have noted the differences among individuals and regions in the Sierra Huichol, there is a similarity of shared beliefs in myth and ritual, as well as the Huichol attitude in everyday life.[19] As Bronislaw Malinowski has noted, magic and myth are the science and theory of the primitive world.[20] Ritual is its technology. Any individual brought up in the Huichol world, as Zingg could see, knows this.[21]

Although the myth may vary and the rituals may change, the basic role they hold in affirming the fundamental tenets of Huichol society remain the same. The gods are the Mothers and Fathers of the Huichol. Tatewali (our Grandfather), the old fire god, sits in his diminutive Huichol shaman's chair, his *uweni*, supervising ritual activities in every Huichol Kaliwey. Takutsi Nakawe, the goddess of creation whom Lumholtz called "Grandmother Growth," still stands with her serpent cane above the springs of Teakata, the Huichol center of the world near Santa Catarina. Together these two primordial deities are the Mother and Father of the Huichol. They represent the wet and dry seasons, playing primary roles in what Zingg distinguished as the wet- and dry-season myths. In rituals of both seasons, their acts in the creation of the world and in bringing Huichol culture to its present state are reaffirmed. Among myriad Huichol deities there is none perhaps as important as Kauyumali. He is the culture hero who established the present world order for the Huichol and brought them the things that distinguish Huichol culture from all others. Kauyumali is the deer, the shaman's patron and the first peyote pilgrim. He is the patron of the peyote pilgrims and the "proper" Huichol way of doing things. His evil brother Kieli is the "Tree of the Winds," the patron of sorcery and malfeasance. The embodiment of Kieli is *Datura*, or *Solandra*, two plants containing dangerous and potent hallucinogens with nearly identical pharmacological action.

Being sophisticated and cosmopolitan, my Huichol friends had of course adapted Catholicism to their worldview. However, theirs was quite a different Christ than the redeemer I had learned about in catechism. R. M. Zingg observed, "The personality of Christ that emerges from Huichol mythology is a far cry from His Christian prototype."[22] They subsumed Christianity into their own system of myth and ritual. They have their own vision of Christ as culture hero and now have little need, or tolerance, for priests and missionaries who talk of a Christ few can recognize. Even today priests in the Sierra must often be accompanied by hired gunmen.

What Zingg called the "Christian myth cycle" explains fundamental differences between Huichol and Mexican culture: "The Christian myth cycle of the Huichols is an extraordinary document in that it gives a rationale for every non-Huichol trait, both within their culture and those observed in Mexican life on their trips. The differences between the two cultures have impressed the thoughtful Huichols who go on pilgrimages for peyote, or seawater. The curiously naive and mystical rationale of these differences has become incorporated into the solid corpus of the Christian myth cycle."[23]

In the Christian myth cycle that explains how the world outside the Huichol homeland came to its present state, Santo Cristo is the culture hero and the equivalent of Kauyumali in the wet- and dry-season myths. Kauyumali though does play a role in the Christian mythology just as do Tatewali and Takutsi Nakawe. Zingg noted, "Though Nakawe made the world, Santo Cristo improves on it at the command of the sun-father.

Thus the fundamental opposition between the sun-god (dry season) and rain goddess (rainy season) also involves Santo Cristo."[24] This maintains the basic Huichol structure of Christian beliefs and integrates those beliefs into an intelligible system for the Huichol.

The Jesuits and then the Franciscans and the Josephines tried to missionize the Huichol.[25] Perhaps before that, the Huichol used their own version of the Christian mythology as an overlying explanation for the fundamental differences between Huichol society and the outside world. Zingg argued, "In this Christian myth cycle which accounts for all things foreign to Huichol culture it is fitting that the culture hero Kauyumali, who established most Huichol ceremonies and all pagan customs, should have written the customs for the saints (gods, the myth says). The myth reveals that he was powerful, even if half-bad. He told the people what to do (the saints) and that the woman should be named Santa Guadalupe, according to the command of the sun."[26]

The "Christian" rituals that have become a part of the annual ceremonial cycle in the Sierra begin in early January with the investiture of the Hispanic officials of the gubernancia system.[27] Carnival is celebrated in different regions in different ways, or not at all in some cases, but usually involves a hilarious burlesque of Mexican customs and traditions. Its main actors include the lecherous priest, corrupt officials, greedy police, lazy schoolteachers, sadistic doctors, thieving landowners, wicked bosses, perhaps a pompous general or colonel, and recently even the figure of Mexican president Carlos Salinas Gotari in prisoner's stripes with a sack of ill-gotten money.

The Holy Week ceremonies are the most widely celebrated of the Christian rituals in the Sierra.[28] These ceremonies usually last from Palm Sunday to Holy Saturday. They involve hundreds of people, all the members of the Hispanic gubernancia, three to five officiating mara'acames, dozens of dancers, and bull sacrifices.[29] On Good Friday Santo Cristo is interred at sunset, and with great festivities singing and dancing his vigil is kept until he reappears as the rising sun on Holy Saturday. Easter Sunday is anticlimactic as the saints and ritual paraphernalia are returned in their god's houses to await the celebrations of the coming year.

Although the Christian rituals of the Huichol ceremonial cycle are ancillary to the more important Kaliwey ceremonies, they are never-

theless extremely significant for they define the way in which the
Huichol view the outside world. The role of Santo Cristo as the culture hero of the non-Huichol world is essential for defining the basic
differences between Huichol and non-Huichol society.

Lurking beneath the texts of the Christian myths is the notion that
Santo Cristo somehow shortchanged the Huichol and the deeply held
feeling that someday this slight will be redressed. In a way the Huichol
are awaiting the return of Santo Cristo, the messiah, who will restore
the Huichol to their proper place as preeminent masters of the world
around them.

For some, Mad Jesus represented that hope to restore the Huichol
to their proper place in the world, a hope that the yoke of domination
would be lifted, the world restored to proper order. For the displaced
urban Huichols who clung to *Jesús* as a father, broker, provider, and
redeemer, the notion of a new world and a new age was the glimmer
of hope they needed. And this band of sycophants was just what *Jesús*
needed to empower his vision. I had little knowledge of that, though,
when I first met him. It was his name that I knew, and little more.

a PROPOSITION

At first I did not realize who *Jesús* was, or how he identified himself with the "Christian" culture hero, Santo Cristo. When Matsiwa, his half brother who was one of the first Huichols I had met, approached me with a proposition to record *Jesús's* life story, I barely knew Mad Jesus. He was a very successful artisan, a shaman, and much more. Yet most of my Huichol friends referred to him as Chucho Loco, Mad Jesus.

They related tales of him twirling like a dervish when he was drunk and told tales of his infamous peyote fire dance. Once while in Wilikuta, the Magic Peyoteland of the Huichol, *Jesús* managed to set the back of his pants on fire while doing the peyote dance. He continued dancing while periodically dropping to the ground to extinguish the flames, providing other Huichols with great merriment and a new version of the peyote dances, which they thought was hilarious.

But there was always something strangely malevolent about *Jesús*. It was never actually mentioned, but it was always there. Even Matsiwa, his brother, had warned me not to invite *Jesús* to my house.

The morning Matsiwa arrived at my house in Leones outside of Mexico City with his proposition, he wore full Huichol regalia, a bright blue shirt with red piping that was open up the sides and at the sleeves, folded and tucked like a tunic into his woven belts. He had on thick necklaces of tiny glass beads, a wide-brimmed, flat straw hat like the Franciscans used to wear, ornamented with blue and red tufts of wool, the feathers of a red-tailed hawk, and four squirrel tails. He had a brightly embroidered triangular cape edged with red felt. There were three shoulder bags that completed Matsiwa's outfit; two were hand-woven and another that was embroidered in multicolored hallucino-genic zigzags.

Matsiwa was obviously not at the house just to visit with the other Huichols who were staying there. He had come to visit for a reason. As soon as he arrived he announced to Kukucame, one of the other Huichols staying at the house, that he wanted to see me. I no longer stayed at the house outside Mexico City very often, but I had come up to visit early in the morning. I was usually at the Casa Huichol on Fridays, and Matsiwa knew that. Kukucame told me immediately that Matsiwa wanted to see me.

I greeted him in Huichol and told him to come in. It was a cool morning. There was already a fire in the fireplace. My friends still did not like using the fireplace, but it was far better than having them set the fire in the middle of the living-room floor. I sat down on the sofa, but Matsiwa pulled down one of the Huichol chairs, an uweni, that I had hanging on the walls Huichol-style around the living room. I knew he had come to ask a favor, and that was the first thing he did when he sat down.

"Don Timoteo, I have a favor to ask of you," he said, getting right down to business. "I want one of those little tape recorders you have."

"Well, I don't just give those away," I told him. "They are for people who do work for me, a lot of work."

"Oh, it's not for me," he said. "It is for my brother *Jesús*. He wants it."

"Well, what could he do for the tape recorder?" I asked. I had given small cassette tape recorders to a number of Huichol friends for them to record stories, songs, myths, music, and legends for me. In exchange I let them keep the recorders and gave them cassettes of Huichol music and stories, but they usually preferred ranchero music.

His brother *Jesús* would, Matsiwa explained, tell me his life story in exchange for the small cassette tape recorder, and Matsiwa would of course be willing to give me any help I needed translating it.

Matsiwa had often helped me with translations, but as my Huichol became better and better I had less need for his assistance. I was fascinated by the idea of getting a life history from *Jesús*. I had been working on the life histories of several other urban Huichol artisans, so *Jesús*'s tale would make a nice addition to my collection. I had not an inkling of how this strange man would change my views, or how long his tale would haunt me.

Mad Jesus would be a perfect subject for a life history. I had heard about him for years from the other Huichols. My Huichol friends warned me to be wary of *Jesús*. They alluded to violence and madness without ever saying anything concrete. I knew that *Jesús* couldn't go back to the Sierra, but I never knew exactly why. Passionate vendettas, drunken brawls, and machete fights were not unusual in the Sierra. There were allusions to witchcraft, too. The other Huichols often commented that *Jesús* knew quite well "how to place an evil arrow," that is, to do witchcraft. All of my Huichol friends harbored a deep fear of witchcraft.

Matsiwa had warned me about his brother. *Jesús* could get "crazy," he told me and then there was no knowing what he would do. The couple of times I had seen *Jesús*, each time from a distance with other Huichols, I had not noted anything unusual about him. I was not prepared for what was about to happen.

Matsiwa arranged for me to meet *Jesús* at the Plaza de la Veracruz across from the Alameda Park and the Palacio de Bellas Artes in downtown Mexico City. Recently the Mexican government had converted several rooms in one of the old monasteries at the Plaza de la Veracruz into rent-free accommodations for Huichol artists, through the National Folk Art Bank. Matsiwa often stayed there rather than at my house because transportation was cheaper and there were dozens of other Huichols around. Matsiwa had come to Mexico City with both of his wives and three of his children. I looked forward to seeing them.

La Plaza de La Veracruz

The Plaza de la Veracruz, sunken, and still sinking in the heart of Mexico City, joins the primordial ooze of Lake Texcoco on which most of the city was built. With its twin churches, skewed bell towers, and buckled buildings, the great monastery looked down on the sunken plaza of the True Cross.

There was construction everywhere, in an attempt to reconstruct, restore, reinforce the monuments sinking into oblivion before the next earthquake could raze the square completely. In the plaza, there was a tourist market for *ex votos*, devotions, kitchy icons, and plaster saints, cheap curios, leather bags emblazoned with the Aztec calendar, exuberant iridescent folk art and gaudy paper flowers. I walked purposefully straight through the market with my tape recorder under my arm.

There was a young Huichol coming out of the side entry to the old church. It was Neyaucame. He too was one of the first Huichols I had met. We had learned Spanish together as I learned his language. We always got some rather strange stares in Mexico City. A tall, bearded gringo with a short, dark Huichol dressed in a traditional costume carrying on in the Huichol language. He often stayed at the Casa Huichol, but now these lodgings in the center of the city were preferable. Neyaucame had quite an eye for the ladies, and at nineteen he was definitely looking for a wife. Even for a Huichol, Neyaucame was quite a dandy. Since he was on the lookout for a wife, he wore rather more jewelry than most. In addition to the usual earrings and bracelets he also wore a choker of many strands of tiny bright red beads and had about thirty bead earrings hanging from the brim of his hat at just about eye level. The Huichol quarters at the Plaza de la Veracruz were far better hunting grounds for a new wife than the house in Leones.

Neyaucame made sure that he looked his best every time he went out into the Plaza de la Veracruz. Although he didn't seem to like being stared at, he would never part with his Huichol finery for Mexican street wear.

As we strode past the stalls selling cheap trinkets that tourists love Neyaucame told me, "You know that Chucho, Matsiwa's brother, is a crazy one. Be careful of him."

He had already heard via the Huichol grapevine that I was coming to see Mad Jesus. Huichol gossip is often a more rapid means of communication than a telephone. He seemed concerned and offered to come in with me.

"I am not sure that I can recognize *Jesús*," I told Neyucame. "You will have to point him out," I said.

"I will, but you will know who he is. He is there with Matsiwa and the others. Chucho just came down from Guadalajara. Maybe he did something crazy there again."

"Like what?" I asked.

"Well maybe he's in trouble with the *mordilones,* the cops, again."

"For what?" I asked.

"Well, I don't know, I don't think he hurt anyone again. Maybe he was just being crazy. Maybe he was drunk. They've thrown him in the can for that before."

"He drinks a lot?"

"Well, once in a while, but he usually just passes out. Sometimes he just gets, well . . . uh, crazy," Neyaucame intimated.

We walked behind the stalls into the rather ruined colonial part of the building and entered what had been the central courtyard of the monastery. The buildings were crumbling beneath the smog and neglect of the city.

We meandered through the courtyard to a door on the far corner of the patio behind the church. The stones above the lintel were loose, and it looked as if the passageway were ready to fall at any minute. We entered what was obviously the refectory of the old monastery. There was a pulpit at the far end of the room that ran the entire length of the building. Huge, barred windows with little glass left and high ceilings kept the room from looking like a cavern.

Throughout the room there were small groups of Huichols. Each group had their own space cordoned off by chairs, bolts of cloth, old tires, wooden windowsills. Inside were *petates*, straw mats for sleeping, neatly rolled up; outside sat Huichol chairs, uweni for the high-status men and *upali* for the women.

Each little grouping represented a single extended family just like in the Sierra, and there was probably the same animosity that existed from ranchería to ranchería in the Sierra there too. I could see there was very little contact among the groups when I walked in. Huichols were like that: if they were not related by blood, preferably closely related, then people weren't worth even knowing. They were suspicious, distrustful, and blatantly hostile to someone unrelated by blood. This was obvious as we walked through the old refectory, which had now become a virtual model of the hostilities of the Sierra, controlled hostilities, but hostilities nevertheless.

I saw Matsiwa at the end of the room with his two wives and a few other Huichols whom I imagined must be part of the clan as well. They waved us over like long-lost relatives despite the fact that Matsiwa had visited my house just a day before. I figured that Matsiwa's crazy half brother, Chucho, was among this group.

"It's that one over there," said Neyaucame, pointing with his lips in the Huichol manner to Chucho.

Chucho's thick shoulder-length black hair was knotted and disheveled. There was dried mucous under his nose, and when he looked up at us, his eyes seemed about to bleed. I suspected that he had quite a hangover. *Jesús* was outlining a design for a *nealica*, a Huichol wool painting made by pressing yarn into wax. He formed the figures with great confidence while one of Matsiwa's wives and her son filled in the designs. This was a typical Huichol studio in the old refectory room of the monastery. *Jesús*'s work was not as refined as his brother Matsiwa's, nor as colorful as Neyaucame's, but he kept outlining design after design with long strands of yarn on 40 by 60 centimeter sheets of plywood coated with beeswax.

I went over to watch him. He kept on, taking no notice of me in the Huichol manner. I began talking with Matsiwa's son Tutuwari, who was about seven years old at the time. Tutuwari had been a part of our extended Huichol household for nearly two months when Matsiwa first came to Mexico City. The boy was always bright and cheerful.

"Long worms, huh," I said referring to the yarn that he was pressing into the beeswax.

"Yes, twisty worms," he replied making a pun about the way he was twisting the yarn into the wax, "twisty long worms, unending worms that crawl into the wax. I'm making the worms walk on the wax," he said playfully squirming around, making like a worm.

"I'm making the worms take a walk. I'm making the worms take a walk," he began singing as he worked.

"You're becoming a little worm," his mother admonished him, and he went on singing.

"I'm a little worm, a little worm crawling around on this little man," he sang as he filled in the outline of a man that Chucho had done.

"You are the little worm in the poor man's belly," Chucho joked, coming over and putting a squiggle of yarn in the center of the figure of the man to suggest a worm.

The boy outlined the squiggle and filled in the rest of the figure rapidly leaving the worm in the figure's belly.

"This is really a little worm child," I joked to Chucho.

"Sure is," Chucho smiled.

He looked up at me with his red eyes.

"You're the 'Watermountain,' the one they call Tiimoteeeo," Chucho said, singing out my name as my Huichol friends often did.

I could see that his eyes were not red from the night before, but from what appeared to be a rather serious infection.

"Yes, I am Timoteo, the one they call the Watermountain." That was one of my Huichol names. "And you are Don Chucho," I said, trying to flatter him with the honorific title of Don, "the brother of Matsiwa." Establishment of kinship relationships was always an important first step in opening a conversation with a Huichol.

"You just came to Mexico City?" I asked him.

"Yes," he said, looking off into space.

There was something strange about Chucho when he spoke. He never looked at someone, but around them, around the room, and around the area. His eyes darted about the room constantly. It was as if he was looking for someone who wasn't there.

"You came from Guadalajara?" I asked.

"Yes, I was in Guadalajara many years," he replied.

"You were staying with Padre Cerillo?" I asked.

"Me? I wouldn't stay with that thief. He stole my work and sold it to the tourists."

"What kind of things did the padre steal?" I asked.

"Anything he could sell," Chucho replied with an angry rasp that told me I should go no further with this conversation.

I was always interested in anything about others who lived and worked with the Huichol. Padre Cerillo was someone I had heard much about, but never met. The man was in charge of the Franciscan mission to the Huichol outside of Guadalajara. He had ventured into the Sierra several times, I was told, to take photographs. He was said to be a great friend of the Huichols and to admire their culture—not a usual thing for a priest.

"Your nealica, your paintings, are quite nice. You must sell a lot of them," I said, trying to flatter him.

"Yes, he sells lots of them," said Tutuwari, "a lot of them."

"You want to buy one?" Chucho asked.

"Well, if there is one with a special story," I said, "I might be interested if you could tell me the story and explain the things in the painting." I had done this with many paintings and found it an excellent way to extract information from my normally secretive Huichol friends.

"Well, they all have stories," he said. "What kind of story do you want?"

"Well, do you know anything about the Kieli?"

"Theee. Eeevil. Ooone," he replied, drawing each word out and punctuating it. There was something malevolent about the words and the way he said them.

"Yes, the sorcerer, Kauyumari's evil brother," I said.

"Wheew, yes, do I know Kieli. He almost got me once. My grand-father, the old man José, the witch, was using him for evil things, but I got him. I got him right there. . . . Kieli, the evil one, the tree of the winds, the hunter of men, the sorcerer lives on the cliff in the rocks above the houses in Taimarita."

His speech was becoming incoherent, confused with memories and perhaps unpleasant experiences, so I asked, "Is that the one up near my father Pedro's house?"

I called Pedro my father as he had taught me to speak Huichol. When I was in the Sierra Pedro was my sponsor and defender. I had thus taken to calling him my Huichol father, because in a sense he was. This solved a lot of problems with kinship. People could relate to me through Pedro.

The Kieli that sat perched on a cliff near Pedro's house was well known, and many times Huichols would stop there on their way back from Teakata, the Huichol center of the world, where the Huichol gods lived.

"That was the one. That was where I got that evil old one, right there, at the home of Kieli. On Kieli's doorstep, in the patio of the evil one's house, that's where I stopped him with his sorcerer's arrows and his evil songs," Chucho said, glancing around.

He was becoming agitated, looking for an escape like a trapped animal. His eyes were darting all about the room and his words poured out so fast that they almost cascaded into a pool of Huichol gibberish. His knotted hair flew about as he went on looking around in every direction shaking his head. Chucho was disturbed, incoherent, ranting in a paranoid way.

I had heard that he had been involved in several murders. I didn't think that I would be in any danger there in the old monastery. There were plenty of other Huichols around, no one was too drunk, and it was nearly midday. I looked around for safety's sake. There was nowhere to go.

It was clear that I wanted another opinion about Chucho's agitated state of mind. At that moment I decided I was going to see if I could get a couple of friends who were experienced psychologists to meet him. Perhaps they could tell me about the demons haunting *Jesús*.

Matsiwa saw me and came over. He spoke to Chucho. He reminded

his distraught brother of the plan to tell me his life story. Chucho's babbling ceased and he became very clear. His eyes focused on me.

"Sure, I'll tell you the whole thing from the time I was a little one,
the time that I could just walk. Maybe we can make a deal for a *wewia*
or a nealica," two different kinds of wool paintings, "and maybe you can
make a—what do you call it? —a tape of it for me. I wouldn't have to
tell them about it again. Every time I tell it they all come back. They
do. They are still trying to get me," he said, his eyes now focusing on
blank space in the middle of the great room. "I want that recorder, the
one that eats the worm and speaks"

"And wha', what good would a tape recorder do?" I stammered,
trying to figure out what Chucho was after.

"Well," he replied, "when the tape recorder speaks I don't have to
speak. It says my words as if I were saying them. Then those evil ones,
the bad ones like old José, and the Kieli ones, those sorcerers, the
ones that speak to the Kieli, and the ones that speak when the Kieli
speaks, will think it is me. They will get that *grabadora,* that tape recorder
of yours. They will go after it. They will destroy it. They will think it
is me."

"Well, you think that you need a tape recorder then," I said, trying
to figure out what he was talking about.

"Well, yes, but just for a little while." A little while with a Huichol
could mean forever. Their concepts of time are vastly different from
our own.

Most Huichols were very reluctant to speak of the Kieli. But
Chucho did not seem to have any reluctance talking about it. Even if
it did take giving him a small tape recorder, I had three left at the time
for just that purpose, the life history would be worth it.

I wondered if Chucho would really tell me his whole life story, or
if I would have to extract it from him, or if he would just disappear
when it came time for him to tell his story. Perhaps I could just get him
to give me a brief idea about his life, I thought. But seeing how upset
he was already just talking about the Kieli made me hesitate. Some neu-
tral topic would be better. Kinship was something all of the Huichols
could spend hours talking about, so I switched the conversation, asking
Chucho, "If I call Pedro my father, then are we distant brothers?"

Huichols always like figuring out proper kinship terms for distant relatives. That way they can easily incorporate them into the proper place in their network of relationships. Given that Huichol kinship recognizes generational differences I always found it entertaining to be called someone's father, brother, son, or grandfather.

"No," Chucho replied. "I think that makes you a father for me," he said, calculating the generational differences from his grandmother's father's side of the family. I was also making a mental calculation and Chucho was right, despite the fact that I was quite a few years younger than he was.

"Well, my son," I joked with him, "are you going to tell me all about the things that have tied your threads together, the way your thread has been spun, the way that your tale has been woven and painted?"

I enjoyed using the elegant and metaphorical phrases that old Pedro had taught me to describe the telling of a story, and I hoped it would put Chucho at ease. He replied in the same manner.

We spoke for a while, and I set up my tape recorder so that Chucho could begin his tale. While I was testing the volume, though, Tutuwari couldn't resist warbling loudly so that he could hear his voice on the recorder too. Once he heard his own voice other Huichols from the other groups came over and wanted to hear their own voices too.

I could see that I was not going to do much recording that day. I asked Matsiwa what he thought about inviting Chucho over to my apartment the next day. He agreed that it would be a good idea and promised to come along to see that Chucho behaved himself.

I walked out of the vast cavernous refectory hall into the dusty courtyard and through the market out to the plaza. *Jesús* was a very unusual character, even for a Huichol, and I could see that I was going to need some help if I was ever going to understand him. A friend of mine, José Amparo, a Frommian analyst, might just be able to help. I stopped at the Sanborn's restaurant in the blue-tiled colonial mansion in front of the Latin American Tower, the only place there were telephones, and gave him a call. His first client wasn't due for a while, so we would have plenty of time, he told me.

José was a man with heavy, long black hair and a thick jet-black goatee. He was about twenty years older than I was, but we had always gotten on as colleagues. I met him at a seminar on Mexican culture and personality and found out that he was my neighbor's analyst. José was a very thorough and insightful psychoanalyst. That was why I wanted to speak to him about Chucho. His deeply humanistic view of the mind might help bridge the gap between Chucho's world and my own. I was quite pleased with our conversation and went back my apartment in the Colonia Napoles.

JESUS: SANTO CRISTO

VI

Early the next morning Matsiwa arrived at my little apartment on Calle Nueva York with *Jesús*. We settled the terms of the agreement.

At first his tale had been pretty much a standard formal Huichol tale that began with the origin of the world, the Mothers and the Fathers of the Huichol, their gods, and all the other peoples of this earth. This was the proper way to begin an important tale. It was the way marriage proposals began, and it was the way the kawiteros, the old men, the Huichol council of elders, asked someone to take an important office in the community. There were variations on themes I had already heard, and *Jesús* was a fine narrator, but there wasn't anything really interesting in the first day or so.

On the third morning I began to get an inkling into the life of Mad Jesus. I heard a banging on the door and knew it had to be the Huichols. They never used the bell.

I got up from my desk. The early morning sun streamed into the apartment, bathing the sofa and the low coffee table that my tape recorder sat on in the clear light. It had stopped raining; fresh air was blowing in through the open courtyard windows. When I opened the door *Jesús* and his brother stood before me, grinning.

"*Ke'aku,*" I greeted them, and we exchanged greetings in Huichol.

The two Huichols strode in and sat down. I went into the kitchen for some beers and cigarettes. As the *patrón* it was my duty to provide such things, even at nine in the morning.

"Give me the beer," ordered *Jesús*.

Jesús grabbed a bottle and drank it in one gulp. I went back into the kitchen for something to nibble on while we spoke, and when I came back *Jesús* was already nearly finished with the second beer. Matsiwa took the last one. *Jesús* took one look at the chips I brought and said, "Tomorrow get something else, some tortillas and a salsa maybe, or some nice refried beans."

"Or some chocolate cookies. They go better with beers," Matsiwa chimed in. That was Huichol taste, chocolate with a beer for breakfast.

Huichols can be very abrupt and demanding. This was something I had learned, but *Jesús* was different. Even other Huichols seemed to find *Jesús* "a little strange."

While most Huichols lived in extended family groups even here in the city, he lived alone. He had a little band of followers who produced the artwork he sold, but he didn't stay with them either. From what Matsiwa had said, he was staying with one of his *patrones*.

He motioned me to turn on the tape recorder. I was using my big reel-to-reel machine to record his tale and transferring it to cassettes for *Jesús*. Finally he began his tale:

"It was after the time that I talked about yesterday when the first Hewi were born," he began.

The Hewi were the ancient ones for the Huichol, not quite gods, but ancestors and revered elders. The Huichol gods all bear kinship terms. They are the Mothers, Fathers, Elder Brothers, Younger Brothers of the Huichol.

"They came after the Fathers and the Mothers, the Brothers and the Sisters and the Aunts and Uncles of the Huichol had come forth from Teakata, the navel of the world. They showed us the way to live, as I told you.

In the waters at Haramaratsia, in the sea at San Blas, lived the Kuwe Eme, the two great green poisonous Sea Snakes who lay in coils around the sharp white rock. They lay there quietly sleeping, not moving.

The Hewi came to that spot. More Hewi were born. The second Hewis were the mother and father of the Coras, our neighbors. The third were the first parents of the Tepehuanes, and the fourth were the father and mother of the Mexicans. The fifth was the beginning of the Chinese, the Blacks, the Whites, and the Americans, and all the others that live in the world.

One day, however, a Virgin dressed in blue, the color of the sea, came from the south to Lake Chapala where all the Hewi were living together. Her name was Guadalupe. She came to them and asked, 'How are you going to live? Which one of you will build my church?'

The fourth Hewi, the father of the Mexicans, stood up and said, 'I will build your church.' But while he made the church, the others only looked on and did nothing. When he had finished, the Virgin Guadalupe went up onto the roof. Everyone looked up at her.

She called down to the Hewis, 'Tell your sons to play me some tunes and I will dance.' The sons of the Hewis played, but they did not play well. They did not do it right.

Then a shepherd boy in the fields heard the music and said, 'Who is playing the violin? I have to know this.' He dressed himself in white and went walking toward the church. His name was San José and he sat down outside the church and watched everything.

When the sons of the Hewis saw him, they stopped playing, but the boy thought he heard a violin inside the church. His own violin, which was inside his bag, started to answer. The two violins played together and then they stopped.

The boy played four songs and before he played the fifth, the Virgin called for him to come up to the roof. They danced together while he played.

Meanwhile, down below, the Hewis started complaining. 'What is this? The Virgin promised to dance to our music and now she is dancing to his!'

Many of those people got angry and took out knives. They began to fight among themselves. These were the Judios, the Jews."

Jesús looked up at me from his seat. His voice rose. He went on.

"This is true. This is how the *padres* told it to us many years ago," and *Jesús* went on.

"So the Virgin ordered the fourth Hewi to stand guard at the church door. 'You will have a club and will be known as the *alguacil*, the executioner,' she said. 'You will guard us and keep us.'

The next morning, the Virgin then came down from the roof and started to sweep the church to greet the Sun. On the floor of the church, in the center, she found a white flower that smelled very good. She put it in her skirt, and when she had finished sweeping, she found it had disappeared. A little while later, she felt something move inside her stomach. She went back up on the roof to the boy. He said she looked like she was carrying a child.

At five the next morning Santo Cristo was born. He was born in the dawn, with the first light.

The Judios came to the church and asked the Virgin, 'Where is that baby? It's name is Santo Cristo and we have to look for it and kill it. We have heard that baby has to die.'

Santo Cristo blew up a strong wind that took Him to all of the five directions.

The Judios shot arrows at Him as he flew overhead," *Jesús* said, pointing upward with his lips. The Huichol point with their lips.

"They tried to kill Him. Five arrows hit Him. Here! Here! And here!" *Jesús* shouted, pointing to his hands and feet and heart.

"Making wounds on his hands, feet and chest!" Matsiwa added.

"But the wounds were cured by Grandmother Growth! Takutsi Nakawe saw all this and Teayau, the Sun, helped her," *Jesús* went on.

"Then Takutsi Nakawe said, 'See, our poor son is naked. He has no clothes, although otherwise he is beautiful and shining. He is large and strong and well endowed. I will send Him white Mexican *calzones* because his privates are exposed. He cannot go about unclothed, or He would be torn apart.' She said, 'Now He can go and instruct the world, especially the Mexicans.'

"Then Santo Cristo met the Mexicans. They were planting with sticks but nothing grew. Nothing grew at all! So Santo Cristo blessed the fields and named the things that would grow there for the Mexicans. He showed them how to plant seeds and harvest crops and how to use machetes and hoes. He showed them how to grind wheat and make bread. But the Mexicans ate the first crops from their fields without giving thanks to the Sun and to Grandmother Growth. Now they live a life without ceremonies. They are like the animals, and not the Huichols, who do the proper thing."

Matsiwa nodded.

"The Judios were still chasing Santo Cristo because they thought they would turn from boys into men by killing Him, which is what they do now in the Sierra. This is what our neighbors, the Coras do, just like the padres taught them.

Santo Cristo hid. He hid sometimes in the pine trees, which were his trees, and then in church towers.

The Judios searched everywhere for Santo Cristo, so He made liquor and established cantinas where they got drunk and passed out while He continued His work.

While they were drunk Santo Cristo went into the Sierra, and He taught the Huichols how to build churches. He made whipping posts, stocks, and jails, and named six old men as kawiteros who would listen to Him in dreams and communicate His wishes to the people. He then commanded the saints to come down to the churches and live in little colored boxes of the five colors. They did this and now we take them out once a year, so they can look around.

By now, however, even though He had sworn never to be with a woman, He was becoming tired.[1] He didn't like to walk up and down the mountains so He didn't give as many things to the Huichols as to the Mexicans.

Now it was almost time for Santo Cristo to die," *Jesús* commented. *Jesús*'s voice became suddenly sad in tone.

"He was in his tower and the Jews were all around Him. He ate only by breathing in clouds of copal incense."

Jesús breathed in his cigarette smoke, savoring it and looking at the cigarette before exhaling. There was a tear in his eye. He buried his head in the crook of his arm and began a ritual type of weeping.

"Then He leapt from his tower causing an earthquake! He went toward Mexico City. He passed through the Mexican towns and blessed the people and stopped to perform miracles. Around Him gathered the sick, the wounded, and the drunks, and He blessed them all. But when He encountered a blind man, He could not cure him.

Along the way there were Judios who tried to grab Santo Cristo. Finally, He got to Mexico City and greeted the crowds there. He Himself was the mara'acame, the shaman, the holy one, and He began to sing the songs of Semana Santa, the 'Holy Week Celebration.' We Huichols still do this in the mountains.

The work of Santo Cristo was finished. Father Sun was tired of Him so Father Sun sent the Judios an order that they could catch Him, but Father Sun said they must not kill Him. The Judios grabbed Him and Santiago, San Pedro, and El Rey de los Rayos didn't defend Him, though they had said they would.

The crowd was yelling, 'Let's see what is going to happen.' Half of them hated Him. Half of them loved Him. Half knew He had shown them all these things because He was a good man.

Finally Santo Cristo called out to a man, 'Do me a favor. Go to the carpenter because I want a cross. Here is money.' And He said to others to go buy Him five nails, tinfoil for the cross, and some clothing so He would be beautiful. Others brought candles, chocolate, and cookies to offer to the sea.

Then Santo Cristo asked for a young bull to be killed for his sake.

Finally, Santo Cristo had all He needed. He said, 'Now you have me. I was thinking you wanted me to live with you, but you did not give me your permission. Now it is four in the afternoon. Take me to the plaza and nail me up on the cross.'

After they did this, the people who loved Him wept and were very sad.

The great Mothers of the Sea could not bear to see Santo Cristo suffering. They sent the blind man that Santo Cristo could not cure to the city. They gave him a knife and told him, 'If you want to see, if you want to live, push this knife into the tree that is growing in front of the church.'

Everyone was shouting when the blind man pushed the knife in. Then a gush of blood came into that man's eyes and then he saw that he had killed his god!

The heart-soul of Santo Cristo left his body and flew to heaven, but the blood and the body stayed here on earth. At the same time all the other saints died!

When they took his body to the church, all the children offered chocolates, cookies, and candles on the way. All night we watch the way they did then.

Of course, everyone is eating peyote at this ceremony, and the mara'acames are smoking the strong tobacco and drinking tequila and *aguardiente* to help them with their singing. They do this every year. The blue flashes of Peyote are traveling between the nodes, combining with the reds and oranges of the fires, and the yellows of the candles.

Finally, toward dawn, the singing and the dancing stops. Suddenly, all the mara'acames are rushing toward the church and the altar. The Sun is coming up, and they must help Santo Cristo, who is now Teayau, the Sun, to rise out of the grave. It is time to begin to sacrifice the bulls. Great singing and shouting is going on! It is getting brighter.

It was at this ceremony, in the spring, in the Sierra, that my mother brought me forth as a baby. She could feel Sister Niwetuka giving me a *kupuli*, a soul!

My mother stayed in the kitchen. She told me this. Her sister, my father's other wife, and my grandmother helped her. They tied a rope to an old beam overhead and put a bull's hide under her as the mara'a-cames started to welcome the Sun.

I started to come out. I began to leap forth. I was yelling! My father came in with a mara'acame. The blue lights of Peyote were dancing off the feathers on his broad-brimmed hat. The fire crackled in just the right way. They told me I was a Child of the Sun. They told me I would be well endowed. There were flashes from the fires and peyote flowers burst into the air. There were lightening bolts flying from my father's hat and my mother saw more flowers on the hard mat beneath her. I was a Child of the Sun. They all said I appeared when the first light burst forth.

A Child of the Sun," *Jesús* paused, catching his breath, and repeated the phrase, giving me time to interject an anxious question.

"How did they do that when you were born?" I asked.

"I do not know," *Jesús* replied, "because I was just born. Five days later, the mara'acames named me. After they had named me, they washed me, and my mother hid my birth-coat in a tree, but that tree was hit by lightening and it burned down.

"A year later, my father took me to the priest in Tenzompa, and because I was born in Semana Santa, the priest called me *Jesús*."

aftermath

As soon as he had finished, *Jesús* turned to his brother. He said something in Huichol. It was very rapid. I didn't understand except that the word "Kieli" came up again.

"What are you two talking about?" I asked. I was ignored.

Then Matsiwa said suddenly in Spanish, "He wants his tape recorder, now! Give him the worm and the machine that eats it! He wants to use it. He wants to listen to it tonight!" He was agitated, demanding; that was unusual for Matsiwa; he spoke in Spanish.

Jesús suddenly stood up and grabbed the reel-to-reel recorder. He pulled the plug right out of the wall. He made a move for the door.

"Wait, *Jesús*!" I yelled.

"You can't have that. It is mine!" I tried to grab *Jesús*. A floor lamp next to the table toppled over and crashed.

Jesús spun around, clutching the recorder, and yelled back at me with a hiss in his voice: "Thisss worm, thisss ssssnake hasss my wordsss."

"It's mine!"

"Matsiwa told me it would be mine and He could hear it. Then He will not come after me," *Jesús* paused, out of breath.

He shouted, "Then He will not be angry with me!"

Jesús's eyes were wide and bloodshot. Although I had given him some antibiotic for his eyes, he probably was not using it.

"Who needs it, *Jesús*? Who is *he*?" I said, realizing that *Jesús* wasn't talking about Matsiwa and, in fact, wasn't listening at all.

He was about to make a break for the door with the recorder clutched in his arms.

When he darted in that direction, I was already ahead of him.

"The tape recorder is mine. Mine!" I shouted.

I backed up to block the door and pleaded with *Jesús*.

"*Jesús*, PLEASE be careful!" I said, trying to hold him back.

"You are going to break it!"

"Matsiwa! Stop him!" I shouted over *Jesús's* shoulder.

"Please, be careful! Make him stop, Matsiwa!" I yelled.

"Chucho! *Jesús*! It's me, your brother!" Matsiwa shouted. He was trying to help.

"Stop! I will show you how to work it! You can't do anything with that grabadora now. You have to push buttons to make it work. You don't know how," Matsiwa loudly persuaded his brother.

Jesús looked around at his brother. Chucho stopped. He was a little unsteady on his feet. He looked frightened.

Then he snarled, "You heard what I said. You heard my words. Why do you need the snake? It has eaten my words and I want them back! They are my words!"

"I need it for my work," I pleaded. "I need that tape. I will give you a little recorder that you can take with you."

Jesús shouted back, "I want this one! I won't let you have it! You will change it. You will give me one that breaks!" He was out of breath.

"You want my words! You will sell my words. You will make plenty of money and give me none. Wordthief!"

"*Jesús*," I said, "You have to tell me more, tell me the whole story, not just the beginnings." His heart was pounding. I could hear it from where I stood blocking the door.

"Matsiwa," I turned to Chucho's brother and said, "Tell him what our deal was. You brought him here!"

Matsiwa started talking in rapid Huichol to *Jesús*, staccato bursts of words to head him off, to convince him, to calm him. They talked excitedly for a few minutes.

Matsiwa turned to me and said, "He says for you to give him that small machine now. The one he can carry around in the mountains."

"I can't. I have to make a copy of the tape for him," I explained.

"Where is his machine, then?" Matsiwa demanded.

I went to the closet and showed *Jesús* one of the cassette recorders. I promised to bring him a copy of the tape that evening at the Plaza de la Veracruz.

"He must finish his story," I said. "I will bring the small recorder to the plaza this evening with a copy of the tape for it, but he must finish."

Jesús defiantly handed back the recorder, hissing in my face, "You have agreed."

"So have you," I hissed back at him.

Matsiwa and *Jesús* left.

I copied the tape, cleaned up the apartment, picked up the broken glass.

I also called Luís Mendez. Luís is a neurophysiologist who specializes in psychopharmacology. Luís had worked for many years at the Clinica Santa María on the southern edge of Mexico City and was used to dealing with some rather dangerous schizophrenic patients. I was hoping to get Luís to help me deal with *Jesús*, or at least tell me how to deal with someone like *Jesús*. He agreed to come downtown with me.

We entered the refectory together and went straight toward Matsiwa's cordoned off little world. Several Huichols detected a potential customer and came up to Luís with bags and embroideries to sell. He started to negotiate for a bright red and blue handwoven bag while I talked to Matsiwa. *Jesús* sat alone in an uweni, staring off into space, murmuring something. He took no notice of us.

"He's been sitting there since we returned," Matsiwa told me.

"He's singing to some of Them, waiting for you to come with his words. Have you brought them?"

I showed Matsiwa the recorder and the four cassettes to which I had transferred Chucho's tale.

"Let's see if he will listen," Matsiwa said as we walked over to where *Jesús* was seated. I bent down in the growing darkness, took the recorder out, loaded a cassette, and turned the machine on. One of the other little groups of Huichols had a gasoline lantern that they were just lighting. Its white glow cast strange shadows over the great hall. There was only one naked bulb at the far end of the vast room, but the Huichols didn't seem to mind. It probably made the place seem more like their homes in the Sierra. There is no electricity in the mountains.

I put the tape on fast-forward, knowing the batteries wouldn't last long, and then played another section of the tape. I turned the tape over, played some more, and put in the next tape, but still Chucho did not move.

"No!" he finally cried out when I put the tape on fast-forward again, "I must hear the Mothers, the Sea Mothers, Kuwe Eme, twisting turning clouds and water before the first deer, the first hikuli, the first corn."

He had stopped murmuring his song. His eyes were darting about. "Who is this?" he asked in Huichol, pointing with his lips to Luís.

"He's my friend. He's a doctor," I explained to *Jesús*.

"I don't need a *meeedico*," he replied. "What does he want?"

I explained that Luís was a friend who just came along to meet *Jesús*.

"Well then let him hear my words, how I was born like Santo Cristo. You tell him what I am saying. He cannot speak the words of the People, the *Wishalica*."

I reversed the tape and found the section that Chucho wanted to hear. I translated for Luís and the batteries began to give out. Chucho's words began to be drawn out, rising and falling as the batteries gave their last to the motors of the recorder.

"Stop it!" Jesus commanded, and he began to tell the tale again in Spanish, but this time in the first person. He got up from the Huichol chair, took his shaman's bundle, his *takwatsi*, opened it, and took out a *movieli*, a shaman's wand with eagle or hawk feathers hanging from it. He began pacing as he told his tale of Santo Cristo, waving his wand. He was Santo Cristo, the shaman and redeemer of his people.

As he finished the tale and came to the part about his own miraculous birth during Holy Week he began shouting in Huichol.

"Know me, KNOW me, know MEEE! I came to take what you have, your medicine, your monastery here, your cars, your trucks, your underground orange worms," which was what the Huichols called the trains of Mexico City's subway system. He was ranting incoherently.

Now Chucho was silent. He sat back down in his uweni. Staring at the candle one of Matsiwa's wives had put in front of him. He began once more to murmur his song.

We waited to see what would happen, but *Jesús* just sat there. Luís told me he had to leave.

As he was leaving he said to me in English, "Careful with this character. He could be dangerous. I don't need to see any more of this to know that. Be careful!" He paced out of the shadows in the refectory hall, leaving me to deal with *Jesús* and the other Huichols.

Jesús, Mad Jesus, Santo Cristo, Jesus Christ, and Chucho Loco merged in the myth he had told. It was a tale about a bizarre Jesus and about himself, his own miraculous birth, his own Santo Cristo, his vision of himself, his own view, his role in the world. It was a strange tale that combined the Christian myth with *Jesús*'s own birth. I wondered just how this man saw himself. I turned to look at him sitting there in the refectory as I left.

Matsiwa's children were playing on the mat next to *Jesús*, but he paid them no attention. He was lost in some sort of vision, or delusion, as I left in the darkness.

LittLe jesus of tHe peyotes

When the two brothers did not show up the next day, or the day after, I went in search of Matsiwa. I had no trouble finding him with the other Huichols at the Plaza de la Veracruz. *Jesús* was not there, but Matsiwa sent a Huichol boy out to see if he could locate him. Matsiwa said that his brother wanted to continue the tale. They were working on a nealica down in the old refectory, so I should bring my equipment there. I took a pesero back home for my recorder, some tape, and a long extension cord. Electricity would be a problem.

By the time I returned, *Jesús* was there. Both of them were working on the large Huichol yarn painting that *Jesús* had designed. By now I could quickly identify his style. They were twisting brightly colored threads into the wax to fill in the outline that Chucho had made.

There was a low table where Matsiwa said I could set up the tape recorder, and while I did so, half the women and children there came over to watch. I put on a little tape of Huichol music just to test the machine, and some of the children immediately began to dance to it. It was great fun. Then I set up the microphone and let them hear their own voices. That was even more fun. Finally *Jesús* came over and asked if everything was ready. He shooed the women and children away, pulled up an uweni, and sat down a few feet from the microphone while I adjusted the volume. The Huichols were more used to the tape recorder unlike the first day at the monastery.

"Is it ready?" he asked. "Can I begin?"

"And now, while Matsiwa works here, I will begin to tell you of the way my thread was spun," he said. "How my *iyari* has been formed, my soul spun. How the yarn has been twisted and the course that my river, my life, has followed. I will tell you how the net has been woven and the design has been set. You will not forget it. No one has heard this story. And remember, at the end, a machine is mine, isn't that so, Matsiwa?"

"It is," Matsiwa answered.

"Chucho will tell you the truth, the one true story, how his thread has been spun, but he isn't telling this for you. He wants the 'Other,' the One who is the Wind, the Nightwind to hear it. The Brother of the Deer will hear it, then perhaps he will be safe," Matsiwa said, still working on the yarn painting.

I still did not understand for whom Chucho was telling his tale, but Matsiwa's reference to the Wind, the Nightwind, should have been clear. It was Kieli, the Sorcerer, the "Tree of the Winds," the Nightwind. I was more interested in just getting the story at that time than in Chucho's motivation for telling it.

"Matsiwa, wait a minute, you are doing that wrong," *Jesús* said, turning toward his brother, who had begun to fill in the black-and-blue sky designs on the painting. "Put these on the way I made it. Let me show you."

Jesús got up and went over to where Matsiwa was working. He began speaking rapidly in Huichol as he showed Matsiwa how to fill in the yarn painting. I couldn't quite hear them but something was said about Kieli. He came back to his seat, but continued talking to Matsiwa.

"Can you speak into the microphone, *Jesús*?" I asked. "I cannot hear what you are saying unless you speak into the microphone. The tape will not have anything on it."

"I will speak and you will listen," *Jesús* said rather gruffly. "And I don't want any more of your words in that snake," he added.

"I will tell you about my mothers and where they came from," he started out. "They were sisters and they lived on the rancho of José Santero, who was their father. José's ranch was on the mesa beyond La Colonia above Mesquitic, and he had four wives. He moved to Pochotita when the tewalis took our land on the mesa. Everything even beyond Tenzompa and Mezquitic was once a part of the Huichol territory. From the time when the first tewalis came, they took more and more."

🦌   🦌   🦌

Jesús told a tale of conflictive family relationships. His paternal grandfather Juan had ridden with the Cristeros and was heavily involved with the cattle trade in Guadalajara, as was his father. His maternal grandfather, José, was a well-known mara'acame and also a sometime witch. His mother was his father's second wife and her sister became his father's third wife. Chucho's maternal grandparents were never really happy with the match, and the sisters were never fully trusted on his father's ranch. Everyone knew José's reputation for witchcraft and his dissatisfaction with the match, so the sisters too were suspect as potential witches.

When Chucho's father was gone, which was quite often because he regularly drove cattle to Guadalajara with his own father, both his mother and her sister were treated like outsiders on his father's ranch. They would often return to José's ranch when his father was gone. His maternal grandmothers were constantly trying to find a new husband for their daughters, and every time families gathered for the festivals and ceremonies that are so much a part of life in the Sierra, they were busy matchmaking.

Jesús explained that one day, just before embarking on his first peyote journey, "Over there on grandfather's rancho, all José's family had come down. The ranch was just below the mesa in a little canyon. It was well protected. The brothers and the sisters, the fathers and the mothers, the old man, José, and all the others were there. My father had gone off to Guadalajara with grandfather Juan and the *arrieros*. My grandmothers were asking everyone if they knew of a good man who did not go off with the tewalis for my mothers.

"At José's they were all preparing for the journey to Wilikuta; they were going off to find their lives. Every year we do this to go and hunt the peyotes. It is our way. They were all discussing who would go to the

Magic Peyoteland and who would stay. Grandfather said that they all had to go to the tuki to talk about these things with all of the others who wanted to go to find their lives. My grandmothers liked this. They were sure they could find my mothers a new husband there. Everyone from the community would be there. 'There will surely be a man looking for two strong wives there,' they said.

Everyone went with grandfather José to the tuki, the temple, there. In the Kaliwey, the tuki, is where Tatewali has His seat. He watches over us all there and makes sure that we do all the proper things. There were other families that came to the Kaliwey, too, and there were many people there while everyone decided who was going to make the journey to Wilikuta. Grandfather spoke to everyone of the journey to Wilikuta....

Grandfather announced to everyone that Shiraulime would lead the journey. He said to them all, 'This one, this man this will be the first one. He will be our Brother. He will lead the way. He will take us to the place where the sun rises. He is Kauyumali. He will show all of you the way to the first light.'

Grandfather would be one of the ones who stayed in the Kaliwey and sang the songs so that we could hear them there on the way to Wilikuta. This is a very important thing, maybe even more important than leading the pilgrims, for the head mara'acame must talk to Tatewali all the time. Grandfather had me sit behind him when he sang to Tatewali that we were going to go in search of the Blue Deer.

There were others there who were going to go, but my mother did not want to go on the journey. Her sister wanted to go, but she did not. Her sister said they would find another husband if they went on the trip.

Grandfather said it would be good if she went along on the journey, and he told me that I was to go, too. Grandfather said that he had dreamed that I would be a mara'acame and that I must go on the journey. I was a child of the Sunfather, Teayau, and I would find my life there in Wilikuta.

Each night I listened as grandfather and the others discussed the journey and I wanted to go. I pleaded with mother to go, so that I could accompany the pilgrims.

Finally we all knew who was going to go. Only mother was undecided. We knew what offerings had to be made and we knew what we would need to take along on the journey. The old men had told us all this.

Everyone at the Kaliwey was busy preparing things for the journey. The men who were not in the temple made arrows or gathered things for offering bowls. They showed us how arrows are made and told us what each one was for. Each one carries a message. They made things for their sacred bundles, their takwatsi, too. Shiraulime even showed me his takwatsi and all of the wondrous things he had in it.

There were feathers and crystals and frozen lightening. There were arrows and his movieli, his wands of power, decorated with eagle and hawk feathers. There were little animals of stone, and there were pieces of cloth with animals that he told me were alive in his dreams. He said all of these things helped him when he dreamed, so that he should see things more clearly, like when we eat the hikuli, the peyote. 'You see things more clearly when you have eaten the peyote,' he told me.

You never tire. You can dance the peyote dance all night," *Jesús* said and asked me, "Have you ever seen the peyote dance, Timoteo?"

He must have known that I had accompanied my Huichol friends twice on the peyote pilgrimage, but I think that this was a good excuse for taking a break from the story.

"It is like this!" he said, bounding out of his seat and going over to his brother Matsiwa, who was still diligently working on the painting.

"Let's show him how we dance with the hikuli!" *Jesús* said, putting his arm around his astonished brother's shoulder.

"Like this!" he shouted, holding on to Matsiwa and beginning to dance by jumping up and down to some imaginary tune; three steps forward and two steps back.

Matsiwa immediately began to jump up and down with his brother. Some of the children joined in putting their arms around each other's shoulders following *Jesús* and his brother. They danced around the table and then up and down the refectory with more and more people joining in. Tutuwari grabbed my arm, and we joined the dance, moving clockwise around the great hall. The brightly colored shirts were flapping in the early afternoon light. It was about to rain as everyone bounced around the room, arms around each other's shoulders.

Jesús and his brother began to sing, as they swung around the room.

After a few minutes everyone was exhausted; we all stopped.

"You must have some hikuli," Matsiwa said, "then you can dance like this for hours, for days."

"The hikuli will teach you how to dance. The hikuli can teach you how to see things clearly too," *Jesús* declared, sitting back down in his seat in front of the tape recorder.

tHe maɡical way to peyoteLaND IX

Matsiwa, still panting, went back to work on the painting. The women and children sat around us giggling and laughing. *Jesús* sat down and continued on as if nothing had happened.

"It was then that grandfather told me that I must go to Wilikuta," Chucho said. "Grandfather told me I had to fly to Wilikuta with the other children. He was going to assist Shiraulime. He was going to take us on the mythical journey to the Magic Peyoteland right there in the kaliwey. He would lead us to Wilikuta right there in the kaliwey. It would be a magical journey.

"We were all gathered there in front of the Kaliwey; it is called a tuki in Huichol. Shiraulime, the mara'acame, came out with grandfather and Pablo. They had made paint, *usha*, for our faces, and everyone helped us to paint our faces. Mother painted peyote flowers on my face and Shiraulime's sister had the 'Rivers of our Mothers' in Teakata painted on hers. Shauleme had the 'Eye of the Deer' painted on his face. Everyone else also had bright yellow patterns painted on their faces just like the real pilgrims who go to Wilikuta.

Shiraulime, old Pablo, and grandfather then took their movielis and brushed each of us from head to toe before taking us into the Kaliwey. They did this to clean us and to be sure that we were prepared to see Grandfather Fire in the Kaliwey. Then they brought each of us into the center of the Kaliwey where the fire burns.

The fire was just smoldering and grandfather began to sing. He began to sing to Tatewali. He asked Tatewali to help us on our journey to Peyoteland. He gave us each a small candle, and we lit them. He sang to Tatewali, but Tatewali did not answer him. Shiraulime and Pablo began to sing to Tatewali. Then grandfather told us to call on Tatewali and he gave us things to feed the fire. We all called out, 'Tatewali, we have things to feed you!' We all began to call out to Tatewali together and we threw our things into the fire.

The fire began to smolder and then it leapt forth. Grandfather said Tatewali was there.

He was in his seat there in the Kaliwey on the ridge pole above the fire. That is where Tatewali sits so that he can watch that we all do the proper things.

Grandfather said that Tatewali asked him, 'What do you want? Why do you call me?'[1]

'We have these little ones here. We have these young eagles, these little hummingbirds, these hawks, these butterflies who wish to go to see the Land of the Blue Deer,' grandfather said.

'It is a long and dangerous journey to Wilikuta,' Tatewali said. 'Are they going to make the trek afoot?' he asked.

'They want to fly with us there to the Land of the Blue Deer,' grandfather replied. 'They want you to guide them through the dangers on the Path to Wilikuta.'

'Is that why you have called me from my home, from my shiriki, from my place in Teakata, to lead them to the Land of the Sun and the Land of Life? I am busy,' Tatewali replied.

'I led the first ones, but there are others who can lead these little birds better than I. I will call out to them and I will search them out for you,' Tatewali said. 'Kauyumali!' he called out.

There was no answer. . . .

He called out twice more. 'Kauyumali!' 'Kauyumali!' . . .

There was still no answer and they told us to call out. 'Kauyumali!' we all shouted.

There was still no answer.

'He is sleeping,' said Tatewali. 'I will fly to where he sleeps and call him to lead you to Wilikuta. I will fly to the Hill of the Dawn in Wilikuta and call him out, but you must all call him too.'

Grandfather passed us the horns and the rasps the peyoteros use and told us that he would tell us when to use them. We had to help Tatewali awaken Kauyumali. Shiraulime and Pablo would make the drum speak. They sat in front of the drum.

There was no answer and grandfather told us to blow the peyotero's horns and call out to Kauyumali. We did this and shouted and made all kinds of noise.

'What is it you want?' he asked, grandfather told us.

'We want you to show these young birds, these young eagles, the Path to Wilikuta,' Tatewali said.

'Is that why you have awakened me?' Kauyumali asked. 'I am busy. I have my woman here and I am occupied with her,' he said.

'I am not the one to take them to the Land of the Blue Deer. There is another who is near to you there. Ask Him! I am occupied! Seek out my brother Mashakwashi,' he said.[2] . . .

'Perhaps if you all call out to Him he will hear you,' Tatewali said. 'He is near you there, and I must return to my house. I will help you call Him out.

'Mashakwaaaaaashi!' he called out.

'Mashakwaaaaaashi!' we all called out. We blew the horns.

'What is it you want?' Shiraulime told us He said.

'We want you to take these little ones to find their lives,' Tatewali said. 'I must return to my house, but they want to see the Land of the Blue Deer, the Magic Land of the Peyote.'

'Very well,' Mashakwashi said. . . .

Grandfather gave us tufts of cotton that we tied together and placed in our head bands for the clouds, and Shiraulime passed a long cord around us.

Grandfather gave us each a bit of ground peyote. We rolled it into little balls and ate it. Then he gave us each a piece of the peyote from his own peyote garden, the one he keeps at his ranch. Grandfather said that the peyotes always sing sweet songs to him from there. Grandfather gave me several pieces of the hikuli. I ate them all.

After a short while I began to see the flowers and the lightening bolts. I was on the Path of the Flowers.[3] . . .

Shiraulime told us that we were hummingbirds; we were young

eagles, young hawks, *Uruacas*, Golden Finches, Birds of the Sun. We gathered there in front of the fire and grandfather told us what Tatewali said.

'Fly up. Fly out of here. Fly to the clouds, oh little ones,' he said.

Tatewali instructed us there how to seek the Blue Deer. He told us to pay careful attention to Mashakwashi, who would instruct and protect us on the journey.

'Come now we must fly,' Mashakwashi told us. 'Hold on to the cord and we will see how to seek the land of the peyotes.

'Now you must look into the fire and give to Grandfather Fire the things that He needs,' Mashakwashi said.

Shiraulime passed us bits of chocolate and twigs of *ocote*. He gave us *atole* and tortillas for Grandfather. We could eat only hikuli now, he warned us. We all watched the fire and fed Grandfather and laughed. It was great fun watching the lightening bolts and swirling flowers there in the fire.

Then the fire leapt up and Tatewali said, 'You will follow this One. You will follow Mashakwashi. He will be the first in line. He will lead you through the Gate and over the Mountains, past the Pools to the Mountain of the Eastern Sun. . . . Over the Mesa, past the Gate, through the pine river, over the mother stones, the deer's flash, the white tail we followed it, the Blue Deer.'

My soul! My soul, iyari, my heart, its heart was mine!" *Jesús* shouted out.

"The Deer spoke to me! 'Come, come, follow me! Follow me, follow the path, follow the white flash, follow the hikuli!' he said. . . .

We finally arrived there in Wilikuta, the Magic Land, the Peyoteland. We called out to Him, 'Kauyumali! Kauyumali!'

Finally grandfather said that He answered, 'What do you want now with all these little birds? I am busy with my woman making the ground shake. We are busy enjoying each other.'

'These little birds have come to find the Blue Deer,' Mashakwashi said, 'You must help us to see Him. Go to the place of the Drum Mother, and there at dawn on the ridge you will see the Blue Deer. The peyotes are the tracks of the deer. If you wish to see the Deer you must have the help of the hikuli, the peyote.'

Inside the Kaliwey grandfather passed around more peyote for each of us then and we ate it.

'I see the Blue Deer,' I told everyone, and Shiraulime showed me where to shoot the arrow, then he shot another arrow. We had shot the Blue Deer, and grandfather said only a mara'acame can do that. He gave me more peyote.

I saw Him and I spoke to Him. He said I would be a mara'acame, a singer. I wanted to learn this. I wanted to become a great singer, a great mara'acame.

When they had finished their songs Mashakwashi called out that we must fly home again.

'We have returned! We are back! We bring the offerings from the Blue Deer and the clouds from the Mothers!' We called out when we had returned. Everyone came back into the Kaliwey and welcomed us there. Shiraulime took the cord that had bound us and offered it to Tatewali, the fire.

Everyone celebrated. They all congratulated us on our return just the way they congratulate the real pilgrims with singing and dancing. My mothers and grandmothers had food for us with salt and sugar. On the pilgrimage we cannot eat salt.

That was the first time that I knew I had to go to Wilikuta. I knew then that I would be a mara'acame.

That was my first trip to Wilikuta.

That one was the best.

I spoke to the Deer," *Jesús* said with some finality.

He was finished. He got up and went to see how his brother was progressing with the wool painting. I turned off the tape recorder.

intimations of the "evil one"

Jesús wandered back to where I was seated next to the tape recorder and motioned for me to turn it back on. His hand traced circles in the air like the recorder's reels spinning. I checked the volume and turned the machine back on. Jesús continued his tale without even a pause, as if he had never left off. There was something driving him on. I looked over to where he sat murmuring a low chant before beginning. I should have probably gone back to my apartment hours ago. Matsiwa was still twisting wool into wax. Chucho's design was beginning to come alive.

"Back there in the Kaliwey, while everyone was feasting, I sat down with Tuturica and Shauleme, and we talked about what our first trip to Wilikuta would be like.

I had to go to Wilikuta that year. I just had to go! The Deer had spoken to me! He had called me. I would one day be a mara'acame! That I knew.

Tuturica, Shiraulime's little sister, said they were both going to go.

I knew that I would go to Wilikuta that year. Mother had to take me 'to find our life' there.

Shauleme said that my mother would not go. He said the only reason my 'other mother' would go is that she was looking for another man.

'She will go,' I told him.

'She will not!' Shauleme said smugly, 'Your father must go too, or she will not go.'

'You had best find another father, or you will not go,' he said. 'Your "other mother" is looking for another father. Tell your mother she must do the same, or you will not go. Your "other mother" says your father is always off with the tewalis, that is why she is looking for another man. If your mother does not find you another father who is a good Huichol, you will not go.'

Shauleme told me, 'Your grandfather, José, is not going. He is too old. He follows another path. He knows the Whirlwind. None of your uncles, or your elders want to go, and your father is nothing but a tewali like his father. They are not good Huichols. They follow the tewali path with their cattle. They just follow the path to Guadalajara, not the Path to the Magic Peyoteland.'

'She will go. She will go with me because I will be a mara'acame. The Blue Deer said so,' I told him.

'She won't go! Your father is a tewali!' he shouted.

'He is not a tewali!' I shouted. 'He's not! He's NOT!'"

Chucho's voice became childlike, reliving the futility of the fight, the boy's anger.

"*Así era*," he wheezed and fell silent. Then he began again.

"And grandfather came over to see what the matter was. Otherwise I would have pushed Shauleme right into the fire and let Tatewali punish him. Shauleme was not my friend any more!" Chucho still had the voice of an angry little boy. . . .

"Grandfather asked me which of the pilgrimages to the four sides of the world I would like to make. I told him I would like to go to the sea, to Haramaratsia, to San Blas, and he agreed that that was a good place to start, but he said, I would have to go to the North as well.

"That was the most dangerous spot. He said he would help me to get there. The North is the place of the Evil One, the Tree of the Winds, the Evil Brother of Kauyumali, Kieli. Grandfather knew well of the 'Evil One.'"

🦌 🦌 🦌

The "Evil One" is Kieli, a god, a plant, a powerful hallucinogen, a sorcerer, a sorcerer's familiar, and an exacting patron. Few will speak openly about Kieli. *Jesús* was intimately involved with the Kieli, and it haunted him throughout his life.

R. M. Zingg first recorded a myth about Kieli and identified Kieli as the "Datura Person."[1] *Datura* is a plant known throughout most of Mexico as *Toloache* from its Aztec name *Toloatzin*. It has been used as an intoxicant for centuries among native peoples of California, the Great Basin, and the American Southwest. In the Puebla Valley *Datura inoxia* is still used ritually in life-crisis situations.

The pharmacological action of the plant is for the most part due to scopolamine, a devastating, toxic compound in large doses. Andrew Weil is correct in classifying the compound as a deliriant rather than a true hallucinogen. Under its effects hallucinations are so overpowering that they become reality. "Because Scopolamine usually leaves you with some amnesia, it is often hard to remember these hallucinations clearly when the drug wears off."[2]

The *huey yohualli*, or great night rituals in the Puebla Valley, utilize this effect of *Datura* to help resolve life-crisis situations, but practitioners must be extremely careful with *Datura*. The alkaloid content of the plant can vary immensely from one plant to the next, and there is considerable variation in the potency of different parts of the plant. Avoiding a fatal overdose is one of the practitioner's primary preoccupations.

In the 1960s Peter T. Furst and Barbara Myerhoff recorded a far more extensive version of the Kieli story from Ramón Medina Silva, but still identified Kieli exclusively with the *Datura*.[3] They correctly maintained, I believe, that Kieli had a cultural historical dimension among the Huichol with *Datura* use representing an earlier ritual complex supplanted by the peyote cult. Furst has since modified and expanded on his work concerning Kieli to take into account the natural history of the cult.[4]

By the early 1970s it was clear to me from the myths concerning Kieli, the descriptions of the plant by my Huichol friends from Santa Catarina, and their depiction of the Kieli plant in traditional Huichol art, that the plant, the "Tree of the Winds," was not in fact the low herbaceous Datura. Colette Lilly first correctly surmised that the Kieli of the region of Santa Catarina was a species of *Solandra* rather than *Datura*. Colette and her husband, John Lilly, a cinematographer, obtained the first botanical specimens of the Kieli for Dr. I. Matuda at the National University of Mexico who identified it as *Solandra guttata*. I pointed out that mythic descriptions of the Kieli plant, both among the Huichol and the Tepecano, fit *Solandra* rather than the *Datura*.[5]

The most important pharmacological component of *Solandra*, like *Datura*, is scopolamine. Yasumoto has recently added another genus—*Brugmansia*—which also contains scopolamine, to our list of plants identified with Kieli.[6] *Brugmansia,* a recent import from South America, is quite similar to the *Datura* and was considered until a few years ago an arboreal form of *Datura*. The Japanese researcher asserts that all three genera are in fact identified as Kieli, and he is most probably correct.

But what of Kieli Tewiali, the sorcerer, the "Tree of the Winds," the evil brother of the Huichol culture hero Kauyumali? My Huichol friends were very reluctant to talk of Kieli, partially due to His association with sorcery and partially due to the fact that knowledge about Kieli is not generalized. It is the province of but a few shamans.

Susana Valadez has recently pointed out that Kieli is intimately associated with Huichol wolf shamanism, a very specialized type of esoteric knowledge.[7] J. Fikes also reported wolf nagualism and shamanism in Santa Catarina, but I never heard much about such matters while I was in the Sierras.[8] I paid little attention to wolf and coyote lore among the Huichol.

There were, in fact, no wolves to be found in the Sierra at that time, and the coyotes were nothing but scruffy little dogs that might steal a tortilla or two on the trail. I thought such things insignificant. I never asked my Huichol friends about them. Perhaps I should have, but the questions one asks are a product of one's own curiosity about others. The Huichol are in general loath to divulge sacred or esoteric lore. All such knowledge is considered a secret to be learned.

I had often asked about Kieli, but most of the information I got was second- or third-hand, and none of my Huichol friends would admit to having actually used the "Tree of the Winds" as an intoxicant. In fact such an admission would have been tantamount to an admission of sorcery.

Pedro, whom I called *notat,* my father, among the Huichol, had taken me to one of the Kieli god plants near his ranch, a *Solandra* lodged in the rocks on a precipitous cliff ledge. Pedro helped me lower myself down to the Kieli to photograph it. There were hundreds of offerings, arrows, votive bowls, miniature Huichol violins, and patches of embroidered cloth tied to the plant. Pedro told me that people would come to the plant with offerings, sing to it, and ask it for favors in their endeavors, but he knew nothing about anyone who had actually used the plant as an intoxicant. He was very wary and distrustful of the Kieli and refused to actually go near the plant, fearing its evil magic. When I came back up the cliff after photographing it he took out his movieli, his shaman's wand, and brushed its feathers all over me to remove any trace of ritual pollution which might have tainted me while I visited the plant.

The cliff ledge where Kieli, the god/plant, lived was so narrow that it would have taken great courage to simply leave offerings there much less spend an entire night on the cliff singing to the plant, yet Pedro assured me that that was what people did. There the god/plant spoke to people in their dreams, Pedro explained. Kieli was a powerful yet dangerous ally, he said, but he would tell me little more.

I was elated about the idea of getting more information about the Kieli from *Jesús* as he continued his tale. But I was not sure how much he would be willing to tell me about the plant in front of other Huichols.

He went on without mentioning much more about Kieli. It was not a subject to be discussed in public among other Huichols in the refectory. Was his tale told for me or for his compatriots there in the great hall, or was it for another, an unseen, unheard audience? I do not know. He continued just where he had left off.

fathers and forefathers

As the tale went on, the influence of José, *Jesús's* grandfather, was clear on the young man. He was a substitute for his absent father. Neither *Jesús* nor Matsiwa ever spoke much about their father.

"Grandfather called everyone together to come to the Kaliwey, those who would go and those who would stay.

"He said to them, 'The Mothers, the Fathers, the Ones who led the way must be asked, They must be beseeched there in Teakata to help us, to aid us, on the way, on the way to find our life.' . . .

Teakata is a very special place. It is where all of the Mothers and Fathers live. It is the Heart of the Earth. It is the Womb of the World where the first spark of life leapt forth onto this earth. It is where Tatewali came forth.

For the trip to Teakata, grandfather José was the singer. . . . He was the one who would speak to the Mothers and the Fathers there. He was the most important mara'acame in the whole area. He knew all of the songs and he knew how to make offerings to all of the Mothers and Fathers there in Teakata.

For many days before we actually left, José had us make *ulus* and *shokolis,* the arrows and bowls that carry our messages to the Mothers and Fathers, the Ones on the other side.[1] Both the gods and mara'acames can read the feathers and the markings on the arrows and the designs on the bowls. They know what each of them is for.

Grandfather José began to teach me the way to make the arrows and what each of the designs means. 'Each arrow is different and the design is very important. It is how we talk with "Them." It is how They talk with us,' grandfather told me. 'The feathers say some things and the lines on the shaft say other things. For special things we tie little things on the arrows. If you want cattle, you tie a cow made from bread on the arrow, and if a woman wants to weave or embroider something special she ties a piece of cloth to the arrow.'

'The colors are very important on the arrows,' he explained.

Grandfather said, 'Come, you must follow me to find the bamboo and the nice hard woods for the arrows.'

I went with him into the canyon and *barrancas* to find those things, and he told me about each of the Mothers and Fathers, Brothers and Sisters at the springs and in the rocks. They are everywhere. We gathered the things we would need to make the arrows that would take our messages to Them.

When you take an arrow and place it in front of this Mother or that Brother it is like shooting it off into the air. It takes a message to Them. Once the arrow has been 'shot' the message is sent."

Huichol arrows, thousands of them, entombed in a vault, hidden in the far reaches of the Museum of Natural History on New York's Central Park West, all bear hidden messages of their makers. Carl Lumholtz collected the arrows for the museum at the turn of the century; some Huichols might say he stole them, from the mounds of ritual offerings left for the gods of the Sierra. Lumholtz was under considerable pressure from his museum patrons to produce from his long expedition some tangible results in the form of objects for the museum's collection. He shipped back thousands of objects to that great storehouse on Central Park and made detailed studies of the objects he brought back, especially the arrows.

"The Arrow," Lumholtz observed, "as an expression of prayer, answers to all the wants of the Indian from cradle to grave. There is no symbolic object in more common use, either by the private individual and the family or by the community represented by the officers of the temple. No feast can be imagined without the presence of arrows. Whenever an Indian wants to pray his first impulse is to make an arrow."[2]

The arrows, the prayers, that Lumholtz collected were so numerous that the Museum of Natural History has traded them over the years with other institutions. The Smithsonian, the Field Museum, and other institutions now have Huichol arrows, Huichol prayers, some a hundred years old, displayed for an uninterested public, or hidden for scholars in cabinets, or cases.

Each arrow is a prayer. From gathering bamboo of just the right size for the shaft, to finding the fine hardwoods for the tip is an act of prayer. The feathers, the "wings" of the arrow, are called "precious jewels" that make it pleasing to the god and help the maker's message fly to the world of spirits. Lightning bolts are painted the length of the shaft to help the arrow reach the Mothers and Fathers. Colored bands are painted around the shaft for each god so that the arrow will be recognized. Feathers, bits of cloth, tobacco gourds, and diminutive models of ritual objects are tied to the arrow to make the prayer's intention known.

Then the arrow is offered. It is left for this god, or that god. The mounds of offerings at some of the caves and springs where the gods of the Huichol Sierra reside are so immense that they cascade from the sites down steep ledges into the canyons and streams of the Sierra. Lumholtz and others have gathered these spent prayers and deposited them in the collections of great museums, where they are devoid of meaning except as curious artifacts.

Once the arrow has been offered, the prayer has been said, its message sent, it is but an artifact of intention and devotion. Lumholtz, Diguet, Preuss, Zingg, and others have gathered hundreds, perhaps thousands, of these artifacts of intention unaware of the words and messages of their makers. Scholars have classified and analyzed Huichol arrows without ever hearing the prayers and chants, the real supplications that the arrows represent, that went into their making.

Votive arrows, arrows for the gods, for offerings are very different from hunting arrows, even the ritual arrows used to hunt the peyote in Wilikuta. They do not have the sharp hardened tips of hunting arrows, often even the nock is missing. They will never be shot at something. They are messages, intentions, petitions sent to the other world, which every Huichol must learn to make.[3] *Jesús* was learning his first devotions from his grandfather, just as all of his forefathers had.

to teakata: the center of the world

"The women were all weaving belts and bags to take on the journey to Teakata, the center of the world. It is the Huichol treasure house of offerings. Everything that anyone has ever offered Them is there."

Jesús turned aggressively and said directly to me, rather than to the tape recorder.

"All you tewalis try to get us to take you to Teakata, where the river gives its seed to the caves so that we may live.

Our Mothers, our Fathers, our Grandmothers, our Grandfathers, our Sisters, and our Brothers, the Ones who watch over us, live there. It is the Navel of the World. But all you want to do is take the *things,* the arrows, the bowls, the little seats, the shields, and the cloud paintings that we leave there.

These are things that we have already given to Them; they are spent, the arrows have already been shot, and they are no longer worth anything. But nevertheless, tewalis want these worthless things. They do not know that once these things are given, they are worthless. Worthless!

There are many caves in Teakata, and they are full of the arrows and the things that we have given Them," *Jesús* said angrily. "In those caves are our ancestors who used to talk to us and guide us. There are no bundles there with masks so that we can see their faces painted like pilgrims, adorned with fine cloth and beads. All the bundles were stolen by tewalis, destroyed. The priests took them and burned them. The *Federales* held them for ransom and stuck them in the *juzgado,* but they still speak to us, they still tell us things in dreams.

They are still there! The Mothers and the Fathers still live there in those caves in the place we call the Womb of the Earth, in Teakata.

They speak to us as I speak to you."

"What do they say to you?" I asked.

"You wouldn't understand, tewali," *Jesús* declared, turning toward me and making the word tewali an obvious insult.

A tewali is a non-Huichol. The word is sometimes glossed as "Christian," but it refers to all the nonindigenous neighbors of the Huichol. It is a Huichol depreciative, and it was intentionally used as such.

"They speak to you in dreams. They speak peyote talk. They speak in visions."

Jesús turned back toward the tape recorder and went on as if nothing had happened.

I wondered if his outburst was really for the benefit of his Huichol audience, or if it was for me. He must have known that I had visited Teakata and that I had accompanied my Huichol friends on the peyote pilgrimage twice by that time. Was this anger, or was it a warning?

"Everyone gathered in the Kaliwey. At dawn we left for Teakata to leave our offerings and tell Them we were off to hunt the peyotes. Everyone danced out of the Kaliwey single file all in the proper order as if they were going to go to Wilikuta. Grandfather gave us the things to carry for him to Teakata, very special things that help us find our life and death too."

"*Jesús*, these are not things for this man!" Matsiwa blurted out in Huichol.

Jesús replied, "I will tell him what I like. I will tell him how we die. I will tell him how we live, how Our Mothers and Fathers came forth from the center of the world in Teakata and how we find our life on the hill of the dawn in Wilikuta," he continued.

"It is like that when someone is very ill. Very often they will know when it is their time to die, and they will just lie there and wait. Sometimes they do not know that it is time to die, and they will try to ward off death. They will struggle and fight, but finally it will come to them that it is their time, and like the deer they will give up their breath so that others may live. That is how it is. All things have a time to die.

They must know when it is time to die. They must also know how we find our life.

We all danced in single file to Teakata to find our life, following grandfather. You can see Teakata from Santa Catarina. The music of grandfather's violin and the little guitar, the rattles and the rasps echoed through the canyons as we danced on the way to Teakata. Under the oaks and along the stony paths we danced, across the mesa and down the canyons we danced following grandfather.

From far off we could see the great virile shaft that guards the Womb of the Earth. It rises erect over the great gash that is the Womb of the Earth. The Womb of the Earth is at the edge of the great deep canyon. From Teakata the waters of our Mothers fill the Chapalagana Canyon and then fall thousands of feet. The Chapalagana is so deep that it takes two days to cross and the bottom of it is like the *tierra caliente* where bananas and pineapples grow."

Teakata, the navel of the Huichol world, is much as it was when Lumholtz visited it. In his notes at the Museum of Natural History from Sunday, May 8, 1898, he describes his excursion to Teakata:

At the entrance to the right there were some arrows put under the root of a fig tree. The god worshipped here is *kupeméte*. Other arrows were lying on the ground.

Now we enter the passageway, a huge crack in the rock called *tetatzaiwa* which means "A crack in the Rock."

On the right there is a projecting rock over 100 feet high. The road leads downward. A small quartz crack to the left, about midway, is dedicated to *Nakawé*. Then follows a stone: *mükí* (dead). Then at the exit is the same god as at the entrance *Kupuméte*, with arrows.

First Cave. Name— *Nakawé Kia* (*Nakawé* house) on the river about thirty yards from the cave *Tealuta*, where visitors sleep. Here parents leave bits of cotton on the rock as described on my first expedition. . . .[1]

The diary that Lumholtz kept of his Huichol expedition reveals more about what he was really after in Teakata than his notebook does.

The entry for May 8, 1898, reads: "At last the Indians were ready to take me to Tæakata. Successful day. The *Tæpali* of *Tatévali* was covered with earth and there was no doubt that the ancient idol is not here any longer, but the Indians have not been willing to allow that the rumor I had heard was true, until today. It disappeared and nobody knows how. Manuel Velasquez no doubt stole it for Diguet."[2]

Lumholtz did bring back an immense trove from Teakata, including the image of Takutsi Nakawé. He claims that a shaman made "a similar representation of the goddess with all of her paraphernalia."[3] Yet some Huichols claim that the actual image of Takutsi was stolen. The effigy that Lumholtz shipped to the Museum of Natural History in New York has graced exhibits from San Francisco to New York.

The Huichol are justifiably wary of non-Huichol visitors to Teakata. His description of the journey to the center of the world was very much like my second visit there, when we went with the peyote pilgrims from Pochotita.

Teakata, the canyon of the gods, center of the world, place of emergence, is a wondrous place. Perched on the peaks overlooking the Chapalagana Canyon, Teakata is a place where the gods surely live, a place where the natural and supernatural merge, where myth is woven into the landscape of every spring, crevice, and cave.

I never fully understood Teakata until my last journey there just over five years ago; I had not seen the Sierra, its pine-covered mesas, the rocky trails, the rancherías of the Huichol homeland, for more than twenty years. I had taken the Huichol cooperative bus emblazoned with the shield of the deer, the peyote, and the maize from Heujuquilla to Pueblo Nuevo and trekked across the high mesa to Pochotita. I no longer remembered the paths, so a local schoolteacher helped me to engage a boy to show me the way. As I walked down the steep stony path from the mesa to the Kaliwey I wondered if anyone would remember me there after so many years. I could see a man doing wash on the ranch of Kukutemai who had been my host there many years ago. I walked to the gate of the ranch and yelled out a greeting in my broken Huichol. I asked if this was the ranch of Kukutemai. Without looking up, the man doing wash said gruffly that it was. As he came toward the gate I identified myself by the Huichol name I had been given many years ago. The man looked at me up and down, and a glimmer of recognition came over both of us. It was Kukutemai.

He greeted me like a long-lost friend. I had never expected to see him alive again. He was older than my father, tall, gaunt, and muscular. He was a Huichol of dignified taste in all of his finery, even while doing the wash. Now he dyed his waist-length hair black rather than let anyone see his age; at the roots it was mostly white. His high cheek bones, smooth skin, and rounded face did not reveal his years either. He had been a model for Diego Rivera's painting of a Huichol boy in his youth. He still retained the joyous countenance of the painting.

I asked about his vast family. He told me of his children, wives, grandchildren, and great-grandchildren. He had just returned from Washington, D.C., he told me, and the year before he had been to Madrid. He brought out his passport to show me the stamps. According to his passport, he was seventy-eight years old. His sons Kukucame and Mashawali had accompanied him to Madrid two years ago for an exhibit of Huichol art, so had his fifth wife. He had danced at the Kennedy Center less than a month ago with his sons and their wives.

Kukutemai had two other ranches, one on the high mesa and another overlooking the Taimarita Canyon. He was a wealthy man by anyone's standards, owning more than four hundred head of cattle and three ranches. Kukutemai was a shaman, a singer, an elder of the local temple, and paterfamilias of one of the largest clans in the region. Three of his wives, two of his sons by his first wife, four of his children by his third wife, sixteen of his grandchildren, and four of his great-grandchildren lived with him on the ranch in Pochotita in a protected little hollow looking out across the deep canyons of the Sierra.

His fourth son, Kukucame, came down to the gate to see what all of the commotion was about. I was overjoyed to see him again. Kukucame had accompanied me on my first peyote pilgrimage many years ago. We had been quite close. He was only a few years younger than me. We reminisced about our wives and children. His first wife who had gone with us to Wilikuta was killed by lightning in front of his house as she sat weaving. He showed me her soul, a frozen lightening bolt.

He complained that his son wouldn't even accompany him on the peyote pilgrimage any more. I had tried to give my son the arrows I used on that first peyote pilgrimage, I told Kukucame, but the boy showed no interest. Children must find their own paths, we agreed.

I mentioned to Kukucame that I wanted to go to Teakata again before leaving the Sierra. I wanted to fill in the gaps in my notes from my trips there in the 1970s. I thought I could publish a short monograph or a long article about Teakata, but I also simply wanted to see once again that awe-inspiring place where the gods lived. He was planning a trip there with his newborn daughter after the *peyoteros* returned that week.

In the years since my first peyote journey, Kukucame had become a knowledgeable mara'acame. Twice he had been the singer of the rains in Pochotita and one year he had led the peyote journey. We had danced the peyote dance arm in arm, up and down, three steps forward, two steps back, for what seemed like hours around the fire in the deserts of San Luís Potosí on my first journey to the Magic Peyoteland. Kukucame had continued on the "path of the flowers," the path of the peyote, to become a very knowledgeable man.

He began to tell me what we would have to make to take to Teakata; as he did so, he told me the story of the center of the world as I had never heard it before. His tale was complex blend of myth, magic, reality, and symbolism. I spent two afternoons listening to Kukucame's tales of Teakata while we made arrows and decorated votive bowls.

I went with Kukucame, both of his wives, and three of their children to Teakata. We visited the gods there, bathed his newborn daughter in the waters of life, left arrows and offerings. Kukucame instructed his nine-year-old son about the center of the world; he spoke to the Mothers and Fathers of that place and had dreams I could never have.

I knew that I could never write an article or a monograph about that place. He took me to the secret places and showed me the gods themselves, the ones that had not been carted off to museums.

He told me explicitly where the earth and fire, the rainy and dry seasons, the clouds and the parched earth met to give his land life. We visited the primordial couple Takutsi Nakawé and Tatewali, Grandmother Growth and Grandfather Fire. We saw where their union was consummated. We visited the abodes of the gods, the caves, the springs, the ledges, and gullies where the Mothers, the Fathers, the Brothers, the Elder Brothers, the Younger Brothers, the Sisters, the Aunts, the Wives, the Uncles, the Grandfathers, and Grandmothers of the Huichol lived.

Kukucame spoke to me, to his son, his newborn daughter, his wives, and his gods of the wonders of Teakata.

There are some things that should never be fixed on the printed page, things a father must show his son, a shaman must show an apprentice, things a mother must nurture in her newborn. With Kukucame, I finally began to understand Chucho's trip to Teakata, the said and unsaid mysteries of the center of the Huichol Universe.

at the earth's axis

Chucho began to describe his journey to the center of the Huichol world. "When we arrived at the entry to Teakata, when we arrived at the Gate of Stone, the great rock that Kauyumali split apart to show us where the Mothers and Fathers live, José said that we had to purify ourselves. He sent the women and children to gather leaves. He made a movieli and attached the leaves, then he cleaned each of us of the filth of life.

As he cleansed each of us he told us to pass through the Gate of Stone. He instructed us how to pass the Gate and what we would see there when we entered the Womb of the Earth. Tuturica and I were blind-folded as this was the first time that we had entered the Womb of the Earth. Shauleme and some of the others were blindfolded too. . . .

Tuturica and I came through the Gate with grandfather after every-one else. José instructed us all the way through the gate to the other side where we removed the blindfolds. Shiraulime was waiting for us there. We were in a huge grotto with a stream flowing through it. Along the walls were the shrines of our Mothers. Shiraulime pointed to the shrine of Takutsi. I could see her image with her staffs. He told us where each of the Mothers and Grandmothers lived in the Womb of the Earth. He told us of their Snakes that lived in the pools, and we even saw one. He told us of their staffs and how they release the waters that give us life.

Tuturica asked if each of the Mothers had Snakes, and Shiraulime replied that they did. The Snakes are the ones who bring the first rains and the waters. . . .

Grandfather brought us all to the pool in the very back of the cave. That was where we saw the Snake. . . .

Finally we reached the end of the valley of the Mothers and Fathers. Grandfather stood there and sang as the sun set on the deep red rocks, and then everyone began to descend in the dusk as the sun disappeared behind the mountains. The path is treacherous and narrow to where the home of Tatewali is.

Many did not go, but waited above, for the place is small and dangerous. Grandfather insisted that I accompany him. Tuturica went with me down the cliff to the home of Tatewali. Mother came too, but she was not well. Grandfather told us where to leave offerings, and when we got to the shirikis he began to light the fire for Tatewali. Grandfather tried to help mother by searching for her soul. He brushed her with his movieli and spit magic water from the Spring of Life on her. Grandfather, old Pablo, and Shiraulime sang there all night. We sat in front of the shirikis, the houses of the gods, of Tatewali, and listened all night.

I was there for the fire ceremonies, and I listened while grandfather sang. José told us of all the things that we would have to know along the way to the desert. . . .

This was when they all told mother that she had to come on the peyote journey that year. It was there in front of the house of Tatewali. It was there that they all told her that she had to go to Wilikuta. That was the only way she would be cured, everyone said. She had to find her life on the way to Wilikuta. I implored her to take me to Wilikuta. They all told her that she would find the 'Way to Life' there on the Path to Wilikuta. They told her that she must come with them to where the Blue Deer brought the sun forth and where we get our antlers. . . .

Grandfather said mother was to be the Squirrel Sister. I was to be the Little Squirrel and she was the Squirrel Mother. Her brothers had the squirrel tails for her hat and the bag she would have to take to Wilikuta. The Squirrel Sister darts through the trees and warns the rest of them—the Armadillo, the Rabbit, and the Deer. She listens to the *witsi* birds and helps us pass the Gate of the Clouds and the Hill of the 'People Eaters.' My mother's sister, my 'other mother,' would be the Armadillo. José said the peyotes told him this. He sang to her all night of the deeds of the Squirrel. All of the pilgrims told mother that she must join them. . . .

Grandfather kept telling my mother that she must go to Wilikuta, but she did not want to go. All the others said that they needed the protection of Sister Squirrel. Grandfather told her she must 'complete' herself—that is how we say it. . . . He told her that she must take me to the Magic Peyoteland. He told her she must go, and I implored her to go. I wanted to be a mara'acame too. Mother was ill, and they all said that she would find her life on the Path to Wilikuta.

She did not want to make the pilgrimage without my father. She knew my father would be furious. We have to be pure on the journey. We have to abstain, but some people just can't do that, especially the women; they are always hungry for men. They are always looking for men. They always want men.

My father thought most men really went on the pilgrimage just to have a good time and find a wife. My father had only been to Wilikuta once, before he was married. He was not really even a mara'acame, nor was his father, old Juan. Juan was almost a tewali. He and father made their pilgrimages to Guadalajara with the arrieros. They laughed at Huichols who went to find their life in the Magic Peyoteland.

Grandfather and my 'other mother,' though, convinced my mother that she would have to make the journey to Wilikuta. It was the only way she would find her life. The only way that she would be cured. . . .

"On the way back from Teakata was the first time that I saw that José followed another path. He knew the 'Evil One.' Grandfather pointed out the Kieli plant to me there in Taimarita and another one near Santa Catarina. Not the little one with the white flowers that they use on the coast. This was the tall one that lives on the cliffs and in the trees. This one was truly the 'Tree of the Winds,' the 'Evil One,' the 'Evil Brother of Kauyumali.' It lives near José's rancho in the trees there in the forest. There is another one that was banished to the cliff there in Pochotita where José went to sing. His rancho was not far from there. He told me then that he would teach me of the Kieli when I returned.

He said that there were many other Kielis in the Sierra and that at one time one of them was as powerful as Kauyumali. He knew the places where they lived and he knew Tututsikipa, the home of the five Kielis of the five colors. I believed him. I was just a *nunutsi*, a little one. I thought perhaps Kieli is more powerful than Our Brother, the Deer. I did not know that he was the Evil One.

The Kielis are different, you know. The little ones, the ones that become horns like the deer we call the Kielisha, the bad Kielis, but they are not the ones that the mara'acames use. The ones that the mara'acames use are the 'Trees of the Winds.' They sing to Them. They ask Them for things. They seek Their help. And if they are not careful, the Kieli will take them, and the Kieli will not let them go. The Kieli will just keep on singing to them so that they can never escape its evil song. When the Kieli sings, I sing back to Him, and the Evil One leaves, but sometimes He makes me drunk and crazy."

"When does he sing to you?" I asked *Jesús*.

"I will tell you more when it is time, tewali," *Jesús* said gruffly and got up.

Kieli was not a topic that most Huichols would even mention in ordinary conversation, yet *Jesús* seemed obsessed by Kieli. Or perhaps better said, as his brother had observed, he was haunted by Kieli in some strange way.

Jesús went over to see how his brother was doing on filling in the design that had been roughed out on the wax. I decided to see if I could get him to continue by asking about the peyote pilgrimage.

"Did you see the deer the first time in Wilikuta?" I asked *Jesús*. "Will you tell me about that first trip to Wilikuta?"

"I will tell you that when it is time," he said.

"How old were you when you went to the Magic Peyoteland the first time?" I asked just to stay on the topic.

"He was a small child then and he went with his mother," Matsiwa said.

"Please do not ask him about that. That is something that you should leave. You must not ask those things," Matsiwa implored.

"Chucho, you will tell me about Wilikuta, won't you?" I insisted.

"Don't ask him that!" Matsiwa insisted, again.

I foolishly ignored him.

"I will tell him," Chucho said, "he must know these things if he is to know the whole true story."

"Chucho, you must not speak of these things," Matsiwa still insisted.

"I will tell him," said *Jesús*. "Now Listen! Get that machine of yours going."

Jesús sat down in front of the microphone. Matsiwa scowled at me and continued twisting yarn into the wax.

the journey to madness XIV

"When I went with my mother to the Magic Peyoteland the very first time it was very different. I was very small, no more than six or seven. Is that not so Matsiwa?" *Jesús* was trying to answer my question, but did not want to deal with the matter of age. Huichols find very little value in chronological age. One is a child, a youth, a man, or an old man.

"My mother did not want to go to Wilikuta. She was sick, she was afraid, but her sister and her father, my grandfather José, insisted. Everyone said that she should join them to find her life. Then she would be well, they all said. But she knew that father would be mad if she went with the pilgrims to the Magic Peyoteland. Isn't that so, Matsiwa? Am I telling the truth?" *Jesús* asked, looking over at his brother.

Matsiwa looked up, "You are saying the truth. I was not there. I was with father. I had arrived at the ranch just before father left for Guadalajara again, but he was mad. . . ."

Chucho continued, "Everyone gathered in the Kaliwey after we returned from Teakata. Everyone was ready to depart.

We all left with mother. Mother was not well. She was coughing and she was weak, but everyone said she would find her life in Wilikuta. She had to eat peyote, plenty of it.

Peyote is the only medicine we use, and it can cure anything," *Jesús* said with an assuring nod.

"Grandfather did not accompany us beyond the Gate of the Mountains. He was not going along, but he would speak to us all the way through the deserts to Wilikuta. Every time we stopped he would come and tell us things on the path and at night in dreams. He warned us there was a witch about and told me especially to take care of mother. I saw him there in my dreams. He spoke to me there on the way when we stopped for the night. Grandfather said he would care for me. . . .

We were walking, and mother could not keep up. We arrived at the Ocote Place and burned sticks of ocote for Tatewali. She kept falling behind, and all the people had to wait for her because we were not allowed to get out of order. Every time we stopped, her sister went for her and helped her. She prodded her to keep up. I could do nothing. I was too young. I stayed at the front of the line with Shiraulime.

Finally we arrived at the Gate of the Clouds where we must all be purified. Shiraulime gave each one of us a cord, and we were to make as many knots as people we had been with. The children tied no knots, but some of the old men had to tie knots for every five, or ten, or twenty they had known. Mother tried to remember them all, but I am sure she did not. She was coughing, and I was afraid that she would not pass the Gate of the Clouds. She was very ill.

We were all blindfolded and told how to pass the Gate. All of those who have never been to Wilikuta before are blindfolded. Shiraulime sang for us and helped us through the gate. We stayed there at the Gate to the Clouds all day the next day because mother could not go on. We had passed the most dangerous part of the journey.

She rested, but everyone said that she would be cured if she got to the place where children were bathed, the place where the kupuli, the soul, is made whole. First we had to pass to where the Corn Mothers were. They would feed mother there and would give her sustenance and strength to go on to the place where her soul would be made whole again.

She fell way behind everyone when we got to Hawuletameima, the carrier rocks beyond Zacatecas. They all had to go in the same order as the first ones who went there. I was in the front, and I could not see mother. She was very weak, and they had talked about carrying her past the rocks."

Chucho's voice changed; he was almost crying. These were not ritual tears as he had shed for Santo Cristo. His voice was choked and uneven.

The memories brought forth all the heartfelt sorrow, loss, and isolation that he had probably felt as a boy.

"My mother was weak and she could not walk and she could not dance past the rocks. She was no longer dancing," he began weeping loudly.

I looked over at Matsiwa. I was about to interrupt *Jesús*, but Matsiwa signaled me to remain seated.

"They carried mother all day," he wept.

"Shiraulime sent his little sister off for water. Mother was very thirsty. Tutu had to go twice for water just for us. Mother insisted on walking the next morning, but we had to go very slowly.

I was in the front of the line. I was the Squirrel Child, and I could not see mother. We stopped many times because mother could not stay in line. Her sister kept telling her that she must push on, that she must find sustenance with the Corn Mothers so that her soul could be purified.

I dreamed, I dreamed, I saw, I saw there, there, that she was next to me. She was walking there next to me. She was there with me on the way to Wilikuta, but she was not. She was behind us. Behind. Far Behind. . . .

A little witsi bird, a hummingbird, a buzzing bird, a darting bird, the one who comes from the Mothers and the Fathers, the one who comes from the clouds, was saying, it was saying, 'Tsurrrrru!, tsurrrrru!' It was saying, it was chirping, it was speaking, it was calling out, 'Help her, help her! There she is, there she is!' That was what it said. It said that. That was what it said!

Then the witsi bird said, 'Get up! Go! Hurry up! Find her!'

She was cold. She was so cold there in front of the fire.

The fire had not warmed her heart.

It had not given her the spark, the spark of life.

The sparks did not crackle in the fire!

The fire was speaking to me.

The fire was telling me she was gone, gone! GONE!" He wept now, speaking partially in Huichol and partially in Spanish.

"The fire no longer warmed her heart.

It no longer warmed her.

She was gone!

She no longer saw the way, the Path to our life.

The Path!"

Jesús was starting to yell. He upset the chair and stood up suddenly, sweeping a beer bottle that held a candle to the floor where it broke into a thousand sharp pieces.

He staggered a little. He was uneasy on his feet.

I was about to get up, but Matsiwa motioned me to remain seated.

"I was looking for her!

Looking for her!"

"What is he talking about?" I finally asked, looking at Matsiwa.

Jesús was whirling about, yelling incoherently, faster and faster.

Both Matsiwa and I got up quickly as *Jesús* dropped to all fours. His hands and knees were ground into the broken glass.

He was shouting and then looking up.

Rolling on the floor with the glass everywhere, screaming.

He had cut his face, his hands, and his knees. There was blood everywhere.

Matsiwa was suddenly on his feet on one side of *Jesús* and motioning wildly for me to go around to the other side of *Jesús*.

"Grab his legs! Professor, grab them!" he shouted. "Twist them! Get him off the floor! Ummph. Yes! Grab him!

Into there! Yes, Lift!

Carry him! Lift!

Get him up!" Matsiwa shouted at me.

"Get him into there!" He yelled trying to hold on to *Jesús*'s flailing arms while I attempted to hold his legs.

"Don't you understand anything?" Matsiwa snarled, struggling with *Jesús*'s arms.

I came out of my shock at the whole scene and followed orders.

"Yes, that's right! Over there in the back!" We carried *Jesús* out of the refectory into what must have been the monastery kitchens.

There was a huge open fireplace on one wall and a series of low metal doors on the other. Matsiwa motioned toward the doors.

Jesús was still yelling nonsense syllables and crying at the same time.

Matsiwa finally got the door open and, holding tightly onto *Jesús*'s shoulders, pulled him into the little vault.

He loosened his grip, and *Jesús*'s head hit the floor with a thud as Matsiwa turned and made his way out of the door.

He helped me force *Jesús*'s kicking legs into the vault and then said, "Slam the door! There! Now lock it!" and pushed the door shut with me.

"What is going on here! What do we do?" I asked. I was in a state of shock. I had no idea what to do.

The screaming, crying figure that was *Jesús* was sealed in the darkness, twisting and turning. The trauma, the emotion, the tears, and the blood were a twisting blur. Adrenaline coursed through me, my heart a drum in my chest. The confusion and blood everywhere brought the other Huichols around. Shocked onlookers stared at us.

Matsiwa turned to me and said, "He will stop, *amigo*. He always does! The dark will calm him down."

Several minutes of banging and then it began to slow.

"See," Matsiwa said, "he's getting quieter. We've always had to do this with him. That's why he is so 'Mad.' Sometimes we just tie him up with some ropes. Leave him in for a while! He will sleep. Then it will be safe. Then we can open the door. He will continue the story. It's always like this when he remembers our mother."

"He is often like this?"

"Oh, he is even crazier if Kieli is after him. Sometimes he can go on like that for days, and he is not right again until he starts to sing the songs of Kieli."

RETURN from DARKNESS   XV

Once he was locked away in his little dark cell, there was no need for me to stay. I wanted to leave, but Matsiwa convinced me that there would be no more trouble. Chucho would continue his tale in a bit. I told Matsiwa I would return shortly and went out to wander aimlessly in the city.

Walking among the crumbling colonial monuments at the center of Mexico City, I tried to sort out what had happened. His mother's death had been traumatic, but if that had set him off, what other things could set him off? Just how unstable was *Jesús*? Was he dangerous? There was Matsiwa's constant reference to Kieli. I wanted to know about Kieli, but I did not want to go through another bout like this with *Jesús* to find out more about it.

It was late afternoon when I returned; the shadows were getting long. I went over to Matsiwa, who was nearly finished with the painting *Jesús* had outlined. It was indeed spectacular; the brilliant colors on the dark background pulsated. Matsiwa would probably finish the painting shortly. Matsiwa had brought his brother out from his prison cell. He was quiet now, nursing the cuts, which were not as bad as they had first appeared.

Jesús was seated in his uweni, staring off into nothingness, chanting. I asked Matsiwa if *Jesús* would be all right, and he assured me that he would be. He motioned to me, and we both went over to see *Jesús*. Matsiwa began speaking gently to his brother, and immediately *Jesús*'s chant ceased. He looked around the room and then at both of us.

"He got me again," *Jesús* said, "the 'Crazy One,' the 'Nightwind.'" As if that were a perfectly logical explanation of what had happened that afternoon.

"Do you want to hear about the rest of the journey?" he asked.

I actually did not want to hear anymore that day from *Jesús*, and I suggested that we continue another day, but *Jesús* insisted.

I set up the tape recorder again. Once I had everything arranged, *Jesús* started talking, but his voice was distant and sounded hollow. The other Huichols paid us no heed. His head was slumped down. He spoke only for the microphone and the machine. It was as if there was no one else there in the great hall. There was great sadness in his voice.

"It was over. It was over. They buried her out there in the sands at the place we call Shaltoca, the place of the Hewi, the Ancient Ones. They placed her sandals on top of the stones they piled on the grave so that the animals would not eat her, so that she wouldn't return, and so that she couldn't follow us, but they gave her all the things of the Squirrel Sister that she had carried with her. Shiraulime sang over her. We stayed there for two days before we went on to Wilikuta. Shiraulime would find mother's soul, the *ulucame*, he told me.

"I knew that she was still with us there on the path to the peyote-land. She was still seeking her life there with the Blue Deer. Mother wanted to see the sun rise from the Eastern Mountain, the one where we put on our face paint to greet the sun. She would follow the path from there to Wilikuta, that I knew."

"*Jesús*, perhaps you want to rest. Can I come back tomorrow?" I said.

Jesús just kept on talking. He was lost in his own tale.

"We continued the trek to Wilikuta. My 'other mother' refused to speak. She said not a word to me or to anyone else until we got to Wilikuta. I thought perhaps she was angry with me, but she spoke to no one.

I was all alone there. Both my mothers were now gone. I tried to speak with her, but she said nothing. It was as if I was not there. She was not my mother.

I went on with the little sister of Shiraulime, the mara'acame. She stayed with me there in Wilikuta, and Shiraulime found me a lot of peyotes to listen to when we got to Wilikuta. He made sure that I knew each place where we stopped. His sister and I were blessed by the Corn Mothers. . . .

Then we went to Tatematenieli, the Spring of our Mothers, there in the desert. We camped there for two days. That was where I last saw mother. She was wandering in the brush. She had her hat covered with squirrel tails and she carried the squirrel bag. This time the Squirrel had failed to warn the pilgrims. The Squirrel was gone. Mother followed us no more after that. . . .

When we got back, I went with the pilgrims to Shiraulime's ranch. He called me 'younger brother' there and said I might even be a brother-in-law someday. Then we went to the Kaliwey in Pochotita. We all danced in the Kaliwey. We were welcomed back from the journey by everyone and especially old José. Grandfather already knew about mother's death. He said, though, that she had found the Sun. Mother now helped Teayau, our Sun Father, grandfather told me. Grandfather and Shiraulime and Pedro sang me the songs of our Sun Father, and grandfather carefully brushed my soul clean with his movieli, just in case some evil thing that had gotten my mother had fallen on me. I was not the one, though, who needed to be cleaned of evil things. They had fallen on another.

Shiraulime's little sister, the one who was with me, was already getting sick. She couldn't breathe and was coughing until there was blood. She could not dance with the rest of us there in the Kaliwey. She stayed in one of the shirikis, the god's houses. I brought her atole and big fat beans, but she did not eat. Shiraulime tried to cure her, so did grandfather. Nothing helped. I think that she knew that it was her time to die."

Jesús wiped a tear from his dirty face with his cut hand. He began to weep ritually with his face buried in the crook of his arm.

"They thought that maybe the same witch that got my mother got her. She left us there at the Kaliwey.

I didn't want to stay there if that witch was still around. My father was in Guadalajara, so I went with my 'other mother,' my mother's sister and her children, to José's ranch. She still wouldn't speak to me. Only grandfather and grandmother would speak to me at first. My 'other mother' didn't want to live at grandfather Juan's rancho with my father anymore. I was also afraid to go back there because they were all saying that old Juan must have been the witch. He didn't want my mother to go to Wilikuta. He didn't think that it was right for her to go without my father.

I knew that old Juan just didn't want her to go to see the magical Deer. Old Juan never liked those things, and he wasn't even a mara'a-came. He had only been once to Wilikuta and that was on the train. Grandpa Juan was just jealous of us there in the Magic Peyoteland. That was the problem.

But he did know witchcraft, or so they said. At least everyone at José's ranch was convinced that it was Juan who had put an evil arrow out to get mother. They all knew he was furious.

He must have been the witch," *Jesús* declared. . . .

"Well, finally, I heard my father had come back from Guadalajara with Matsiwa. I wanted to go back. I wanted to see him. I wanted to see Matsiwa. But they never came for me.

One time I even heard that one of my father's brothers had ridden up near the ranch, but he didn't want anyone to know he was there. My uncle Tutupica, José's son, saw him.

The Rain Festival passed and the Corn Festival passed, but no one came to the ranch for me. Matsiwa was too young to come by himself. José would have witched him.

It was dry season, there was never enough to eat, and my brother and sister always got everything. They would steal my food, and when I shot a little bird with my slingshot so I could eat it, they would take it from me.

When I went with grandfather to the Kaliwey in Pochotita, they would even wear the clothes that my mother had made for me. They were jealous because grandfather told everyone I was on my way to becoming a mara'acame.

The time I was living with José after my mother died was not easy. There was very little there, and my mother, my brother, and my sister would give me nothing. Matsiwa was off riding with my father. They would not come over to get me, and I was too afraid to walk through the mountains myself. They did not come. . . ."

"That is true," Matsiwa said. I had just stepped over to the table to see Matsiwa's work. Matsiwa was finishing the yarn painting by meticulously twisting the last threads into the wax.

"I couldn't come. Father wouldn't let me," he said. "I couldn't defend myself from José's arrows. Father could not defend himself against José's arrows. If he said he couldn't, how could I?" Matsiwa looked over at his brother. Perhaps he was simply justifying his inaction.

He began speaking directly to *Jesús*. Chucho, however, just kept speaking to the tape recorder. He ignored his brother.

"I tried to find the way to Juan's rancho myself," said *Jesús*, "and I was stung by a scorpion in the canyon. I almost didn't make it. It was a little one, dark yellow, the kind that try to kill you, but don't. You swell up and get thirsty. You stagger around. It was dusty, but there was a little stream nearby or I would have died. I put mud on the sting and dried 'yellow bush' leaves. I was there for days, and I could not find my way out. I finally had to go back to José's ranch. I could not find father's ranch on my own.

"Everyone there had been celebrating, especially my stingy brother and sister. They thought I was dead, and that I would never be found again. I told them about the scorpion, but I didn't tell them I was trying to find my father's rancho."

venGeaNce
XVI

"A year went by and after the Peyote Pilgrims had returned again, we all went to the Peyote Festival. There were Peyote Dancers there with their long black feathers from the Uruaca that stuck straight up from their heads; they danced all night around the fires, and there were all the people who had been on the journey. I had wanted to go with them, but there was no one to accompany me.

José sang the songs of Kauyumali, the Elder Brother of the Huichols. Just as the fiesta was over and we were packing up our things to carry back to the ranch, my grandfather Juan came into Pochotita where the Kaliwey was and rode up to José.

He had a gun. My father and his two brothers were with him, but they rode from behind the Kaliway. They had extra horses, and Matsiwa was with them, too.

'My son wants his wife back,' he told José.

'She is my daughter. She cannot go off with a bunch of witches like you,' José said.

'Witches?' old Juan said. 'The only witch around here who places the evil arrows in front of the Mothers and Fathers is you. I don't know about those things.'

Juan and José had a huge fight.

My father came in behind the two old men who were standing in the patio in front of the Kaliwey. My other mother's sisters were helping her load the mule with her things for the return to José's ranch. My father and his brothers jumped down and grabbed my mother's sister, my 'other mother.' She was screaming that she would not go, but they pulled her up onto the horse and tied her there and rode off. His brothers grabbed my half brother and half sister, who were hiding in a shiriki, and Matsiwa told me to get on his horse."

"Oh, I remember that!" Matsiwa declared to no one in particular.

"I climbed on and we rode off toward the mesa, up to La Colonia. Some of them tried to follow us, but my father had freed their horses. They had to follow us on foot, and they didn't get very far before they turned back.

My father led the horse with my mother's sister on it. They had tied her hands to the saddle. She was screaming and yelling all the way to the ranch that José would get them and witch them, but nothing happened.

My brother and sister were tied up into neat bundles too, so they couldn't escape. They got her to the ranch and put her in the old cookhouse, the one all blackened with smoke, the one that was no longer used.

She was still screaming most of the night," Jesus said, "but then she finally stopped."

"The next morning they all went over there to see her," he said looking up at his brother, as if Matsiwa was one of the group that went to see her.

"She was dead," *Jesús* said.

"She hung herself from the center post in the cookhouse. The one they hang all the sacks on. She was swaying back and forth from the center pole. Her tongue was hanging out, and her eyes were wide. Her neck was all purple and bruised."

Matsiwa made no comment. He just sat there pensively. He must have seen the whole thing too. He probably helped plan the ill-fated raid, but he said nothing, and Chucho went on with his tale.

"My half brother and half sister were not told what happened. They were tied up in a storeroom, and they didn't see what had happened to their mother. She was taken out of there and buried on the hill, far away from the rancho. Her sandals were crossed so she wouldn't come back. We do this so the dead don't come back.

"My half brother and half sister were still tied up, and they kept them tied up for a week or so. They deserved it. They had been so foul to me that they should have kept them there forever. When father finally let them loose, they wanted to leave and they wanted to see their mother, but no one said anything about her. No one would speak of her. They thought she went home to José's ranch."

This was a vengeful little boy speaking.

"Father told them he wanted them to stay, and he told everyone to keep an eye on them so that they wouldn't leave. I made sure they were always in sight.

We really made those two lazy ones work. If they weren't working hard enough, I would go over and poke them and prod them to do more. My father fed them, though, and gave them clothes. That was more than they did for me. I made sure they kept them there on the ranch. They were never taken to any fiestas, and they never left the ranch without four, or five, of us. They couldn't have found old José's ranch, anyway, even if they tried.

I would talk to them through the walls of the house like peyote talk. The way peyote talks to us, no one else can understand. They didn't know the 'Way.' José had never taught them. But I knew. I could talk the 'Way.' You close your eyes and you go far back, and that's where the Peyote talks to you. But no one else except someone who knows can understand what you are saying. It is not like Peyote Talk on the journey, when we name everything upside down. Old people are nunutsis, babies, and the nunutsi is the eldest grandfather or grandmother. Water is tequila, and to piss is to drink milk. Nothing like that.

The 'Way' is how the Peyote really talks to you. When we want to tell the future to someone who cannot understand it, and cannot see it, then we use it. Matsiwa here cannot understand it. Those awful children had no idea. They were scared!

I told them their future, how they were going to die, but they didn't understand.

I also started seeing my mother, who was out in the desert, and her sister, who was wandering around outside the rancho, so I told them that, too. I told them all about their mother, how she hung herself and how she looked dead and discolored, swaying there in that black hut that was being kept for them to hang themselves in. I told them that they were on the Road of the Dead. They were really scared, and they tried to get away. They tried to run away, but I saw where they went and I told Juan that I had a dream that they were at the *cañada*. My father, my grandfather, and my uncles went after them there and they got them and brought them back.

They kept them there in the old cookhouse again, and they tied them up so that they couldn't get away. They were really scared, and they wept. It was the cookhouse where their mother had died. That was the House of the Dead. They were terrified. They would die.

I would sit outside the cookhouse all day just to let them see that they couldn't get away. I told them that they wouldn't get away next time. The next time would be the last time they would try to escape.

They didn't get out for a long time, and when my father finally let them out, I made sure that they could not leave the rancho. I kept on watching them, but one night they managed to slip out.

When I saw what happened the next morning I told everyone, but father didn't care anymore. They said that they would not go after them again.

That was really dangerous. That was really stupid. They would go to grandfather José and tell him everything, and then he would leave his evil arrows out. Then he would get all of us. I did not want my father to be taken from me.

So I went after them.

I went after them. They were going along the Taimarita Canyon. That's where I saw them.

I went up to the top of the canyon, and I knew that they had to walk along my side of the canyon.

I started singing like old José sang there in the night, and I could hear them talking.

They thought it was José.

'Grandfather! Grandfather!' they both called out.

'Here! Here!' I said with a false voice. A mara'acame learns to use a thousand voices. I could already speak like grandfather and I knew his songs.

They both began to climb the side of the canyon to where I was.

They thought I was old José because of the song.

It was the song that got them.

Then the rocks began to fall, and Hocori, my sister, got it.

She was all broken up there on the bottom of the canyon, but Tutucame just kept on climbing, despite the rocks.

He kept on calling out, 'Grandfather! Help us, my sister has fallen,' and then he called out to his sister, but she didn't answer.

She was already gone.

She was all broken up.

Smashed with the rocks.

She was done for.

Dead!

Tutucame, my brother, tried to keep on climbing and he kept on going up the cliff, but the rocks kept on coming down on him.

Plom! Thwap! Thud-tha-thud! I pushed more rocks down on him.

I thought they were both done for when I left, but Tutucame wasn't quite gone.

They found him and took him back to José.

When he fell, he was all broken up too. That's why they call him El Chueco, the Crooked One, because he is all broken up.

They found him because he was calling out in the canyon.

He thought he had been bewitched.

Later, José told him it must have been old Juan!

But if he had been calling out when I was there, they would have never found him alive.

They would have just found the bones after the bugs and the worms and the buzzards got him. Or, they wouldn't have found him at all. If they did find him, he would have been picked clean to just the bones, he would have.

And that would have been what he deserved," *Jesús* said with finality.

Matsiwa stood there in silence at the table where he had finished the yarn painting a few minutes ago. He was putting the yarn back in the bag.

I was stunned. *Jesús* was obviously finished.

Matsiwa said, "We have to take this over to the German woman to sell it unless you want it. My brother says you can have it for two thousand pieces of silver."

"I do not have 2,000 pesos," I said, "but it is beautiful."

"Do you want it?" Matsiwa asked.

"No," I decided.

"Give us a loan for the taxi, then," Matsiwa said, "so that we can sell it tonight."

I dug into my pockets and handed over a 20-peso bill.

"You can come back tomorrow," Matsiwa said cheerfully over his shoulder, as they hauled the painting out of the refectory and went down to the street to find a taxi.

But I didn't come back the next day.

DRUNKeN DeRVISH XVII

I did not go back to the Plaza de la Veracruz the next day, or the day after. I simply tried to forget about *Jesús* and his brother. I was not about to drop the whole project, but I knew that the brothers would be back. The intensity of dealing with *Jesús* on a daily basis was a bit much. *Jesús* was obsessed with getting the small tape recorder, but it wasn't just the recorder. He was insisting on telling me his tale for more than that. He was somehow compelled to continue his tale. It was some kind of catharsis, and I suspect he was seeking some kind of absolution. He was constantly emphasizing the veracity of his tale. I too had to hear the rest of his tale. We were joined like a pair of twisted wires completing a circuit, a teller of tales and his audience.

Jesús would be back, or I would find him.

The brothers finally appeared at my door about a week later, both wearing bright squares of polyethylene as raincoats. Someone had let them into the compound, probably the *portera*. She knew that all of the *inditos* who came to the door were there for me. It had taken months to convince her to let my indigenous friends into the building, and many of the neighbors were still uneasy about having "Indians" in the building.

Jesús was not about to end his tale. According to Matsiwa, they had been outlining designs for a group of Huichols in the center of the city who worked for *Jesús* producing folk art and trinkets, which was why they hadn't appeared before this.

The brothers returned as if nothing had happened. I got out some beers and offered them cigarettes. They told me to set up the tape recorder. *Jesús* continued talking about his time living on his grandfather Juan's ranch. He told me in a very matter-of-fact way about his father's death.

"Matsiwa went with grandfather Juan that year to Guadalajara, and father went off to Zacatecas. He never came back. The tewali bandits got him there and stole his cattle. Old Juan returned with Matsiwa just before the rains came when the men were clearing the fields. When they heard that father was dead, he and Matsiwa had a huge fight."

"You remember that, Matsiwa?"

"Yes, I do," Matsiwa replied. "That grandfather of ours wasn't going to give me a cent from the cattle we had sold for father."

"He said you spent it all, that you drank it all up. That would have been enough aguardiente for all the Huichols in Kaluitia for a year."

"It sure would. We fought over that for weeks, and I could see that I wasn't going to get anything out of that tight old fool. He wasn't going to part with a cent, not one *centavo*. I was furious. I knew how much we had sold those animals for."

🦌   🦌   🦌

Their father's death seemed somewhat peripheral to both *Jesús* and Matsiwa. They were both much more concerned with Matsiwa's arguments with his grandfather, than with their father's death. Perhaps their father was peripheral. Old Juan, their grandfather, was the paterfamilias on the ranch. From a Huichol point of view he had much more influence on their lives than their father did.

When their grandfather would not accept a man called Pedro's proposal to marry their two sisters because Pedro did not offer a sufficient bride-price in terms of household items and cattle, Matsiwa secretly made a deal with Pedro, arranged for his sisters to "visit" Pedro, and left for Guadalajara with the animals. This left *Jesús* alone in the Sierra.

Jesús must have been about fifteen or sixteen at that time and was not welcome anywhere. He was lost; both of his parents were dead. He wasn't homeless, no Huichol is homeless in the Sierra, but he felt unwanted wherever he went. For all intents and purposes he was a man, could have found a wife and started a family at this age, farming fields of his own or his wife's family. Although he was in reality a man, he was also still a besotted youth. In the Sierra, the young are considered half-crazed until they reach the age of thirty or so and then they become regular participants in the social, political, and religious life of the community.

Jesús continued with the tale: "I went back to Santa Catarina for the harvest fiestas, and José was there again, but Pedro and my sisters never came, so I went with my grandfather José back to his ranch. José taught me to make the arrows and the bowls for the Mothers and Fathers. Each one has His, or Her, own arrows or bowls, you know. And they are all different for different occasions. I spent two months learning all this. It's not easy. Then we offer them those things.

"I went with grandfather to the Kaliwey in Pochotita, and we left things there in the shirikis of each of our Mothers and Fathers."

🦌   🦌   🦌

These shirikis each pertain to a particular family or ranchería group and are for the souls of the ancestors so they too can continue to participate in the religious life of the community. His grandfather was probably trying to give the boy a sense of place and belonging, instructing him in his obligations to the ancestors and integrating him into the community.

Jesús went on, "I sang with the old men there in the Kaliwey. We sang of the Magical Deer and of the Squirrel Sisters and the tlacuache and the armadillo.

"Then I went out 'hunting' with the grandsons, but no one went hunting. They all just went to Mezquitic to get drunk, but I didn't have any money to buy any alcohol, so I just got a little drunk with them. They really got drunk there, though. They showed me how to do it! They were like Taweakame, the Whirlwind, Kieli's father! They staggered and stumbled and vomited and twirled around! What a show! I really wanted to get drunk like that, but I had no money.

I told the cousins that I would sing for them. I would sing myself as drunk as they were if they would give me a bottle of their aguardiente. They had to pay me, I told them, like they paid the judges with aguardiente. I began to sing the songs of the Kuwe Eme, the great green Sea Snakes, even though I had never been there to the sea. I sang of how they writhed and twisted and how they made the clouds come forth from the boiling sea. As I sang, I began to twist about like Kuwe Eme, I began to spin like the Whirlwind. I spun about like my drunken brothers there, and I sang. I sang of the clouds and the Whirlwind. It was great fun, and they gave me the bottle of aguardiente. I drank the whole thing, and I sang once more. I spun and writhed like Kuwe Eme until I vomited and passed out. When I awoke they had left me there on the mesa where we had camped."

🦌   🦌   🦌

To this day many Huichols remember how Chucho would spin and twirl when drunk.

That morning *Jesús's* story rambled on from drunken debauch to drunken fight, as he went from ranch to ranch staying with anyone who could tolerate him. His sexual affairs at this age sounded more like rapes than relationships. He was jailed in Santa Catarina during the Holy Week celebrations. He was drunk most of the time, stealing aguardiente wherever he could and taking it off into the mountains to drink alone, singing and dancing. A few excerpts of the tapes show how truly lost Chucho had become.

"That was about the time that Matsiwa came back with Tutucame, his first wife. He went up to Las Latas with her father Manuel, the 'Long One.' I heard that they were up there and went up to visit. Matsiwa had plenty of money from the cattle and all the time he had been working in Guadalajara and he gave me some cash from the cattle. Matsiwa said there was easy work in Guadalajara with the padre there. I wanted to go, but all I was really interested in doing was getting drunk, then I could sing and dance, then I was happy even when I was alone.

Everyone up there was good to me, and when José came to sing with the old men, I went down to the Kaliwey in Pochotita with them and they showed me many things. Antonino was one of the 'Great Mara'acames.' He knew all of the songs. They sang the history of the world and the other stories of Our Mothers and Our Fathers.

With the money that I had, José said that I should start looking for a wife, but I didn't need one. There were lots of women in Pochotita and they were all looking for something to 'eat,' especially at the fiestas. There was one of the daughters of Tiburcio at the corn fiesta. I was waiting for her when she came out of the Kaliwey, and I took her off in the dark outside the gate. She was really 'hungry' for me. One time I even got Kupiwali, Leocadio's first wife. She was twice as old as me, but they are 'hungrier' when they are older."

The metaphor of a "hungry" woman implies a woman looking for sex, and among the Huichol women are generally considered the sexual aggressors. A woman "eats" a man up with her vagina.

Chucho's tales of drunken debauchery continued. "Finally we all went into Mezquitic, across the Mesa and down towards the plains, to spend some of that money Matsiwa brought back. His wife wanted to buy thread and yarn there, and Matsiwa was to get some supplies for his father-in-law. I was going to get drunk.

In Mezquitic, I borrowed some more money from Matsiwa. Do you remember that?" *Jesús* asked his brother.

Matsiwa nodded. He was grinning. He said, "We were all going to go to Zapopan to make some money. We could make a lot there selling the things we all knew how to make. Things like yarn paintings and beaded bowls. It was easy work, not like working down on the coast in the tobacco fields and at first the padre would even give us a place to stay."

"The first thing that I did there in Mezquitic was to buy more aguardiente," *Jesús* continued, "I was eating *chicharrones* in the street from a big pile of them in front of the butcher shop when Ignacio, the old butcher, came out and asked me for money. By then I didn't have any left, and I was pretty drunk and I told him to just give me a little of his tasty things, but he wouldn't. He called the alguacil, the policeman, with a *sargento* and they took me off to the juzgado! And this brother of mine just left me there!"

"That is not true, Chucho!" Matsiwa said. "You know I thought you were with those who were camped outside of town, the cousins. Everyone was drinking and falling around. I didn't know the police had you. No one knew!"

"Well, maybe. When I got out, it was almost time to clear the fields again, and I went back to Pedro's, but he would not even let me past the gate to his rancho.

"Then I went to my grandfather José's ranch. José and the grand-sons welcomed me back with plenty of *tuche,* which is what we make out of agave. It isn't as strong as aguardiente, but it's stronger than what we call *nawa* or *tesguino,* which is corn beer. It is not like this beer. It is thick and chewy. What I wanted, though, was more aguardiente."

CRAZY KIELI XVIII

"Hoh! More beer!" *Jesús* paused and lit a cigarette. Then he got up by himself and went into the kitchen. He came back with two bottles and was talking as he handed one to his brother.

"That year I did not go on the peyote trip. José said that it might have been dangerous. I had been witched twice. I had to abstain from salt, though, and sexual relations, he said. Just like the pilgrims, I had to bathe in the waters of our Mothers in the springs at Teakata to be sure that all of the evil arrows were gone.

José didn't participate either. He went off to Guadalajara with his wives. I was left alone, and there was no one to make tortillas for me. Finally I bought some from a woman in Pochotita, and then some of José's grandchildren came back. We all went off 'hunting' to Mezquitic.

In Mezquitic, grandfather found me drunk with the others, and he was very angry with all of us. We were all very drunk. He said that we should have been marking and clearing the cornfields. He took us all up to a place where we had camped before on the mesa. We stayed there that night, and he told us about the drunken Kieli, crazy Kieli, Kieli Tewiali, Tutakuli.

That night on the mesa the wind was cold. In front of the fire grandfather began to tell us about the Whirlwind.

Grandfather began: "Kieli was born, but he wasn't born. He was the Wind, the Whirlwind, the drunken one who twists and turns, who falls and stumbles. Kieli is not the Good Wind, the Warm Wind from the

South. He is not the Gentle Wind from the East that brings the clouds. He is not the Wind from the West that comes with the rains. He is the Whirlwind. He is the Wind of the North. He comes from all five directions, but his home is there in the North in Tututsikipa. It is there that he was awaited. It is there that he was expected.

Before he was born he was everywhere. He was the Cold Wind, the Nightwind, the Whirlwind. He was the Wind that came from the Other Side. He was the Wind that came in the Darkness. He was not born of a Mother. He was not born of a Father. He was everywhere. . . .

When Kieli came forth, he was awaited. There were five who kept his vigil there in the North, there in the Place of the Flowers, there in the House of the Flowers, there in the place of the Evil Winds. Those who kept his vigil asked, 'What should we do?'

'Where is he?'

'Where is the One that we await?'

'We sing all night.'

'We sing to the Wind, to the Whirlwind, to the Nightwind.'

'Where is this One whom we await?' They sent one of their number to ask the Mothers and the Fathers where this One was that they awaited.

The Mothers and Fathers replied, 'He is there. He is there with you in the House of Flowers in the North, where you await him. Go seek him out search for him there, and don't bother us. Seek him out in the night. Seek him out in the darkness. Seek him out in the cold northern winds. Seek him out in the whirlwind. He is there. His brother Kauyumali awaits him. His cousins, his brother, his twin, await him too, and he is there.'

That one returned to the other sorcerers there in Tututsikipa and told them what had been said, what he had been told. The five of them gathered together to seek Him, to divine where He was. They peered into the waters, into the mirrors. They cast grains of corn, and they looked to the winds and the stars for signs. They looked in dreams and in the peyote lightning bolts for the One whom they awaited, but they saw nothing. . . .

Finally they sent the last of their number to ask the Mothers and the Fathers where the One they awaited could be found. The Mothers and the Fathers told him that the One whom they awaited was already there, and this is what he told the others. They all began to discuss this and to talk about this. Perhaps with sorcery, perhaps with witchcraft, they could find the One that was awaited, so all five of them turned to sorcery. They sang songs and placed arrows for the One that they awaited, and the winds blew in the night there in that place. They heard something. They saw something. It was the bat, the night bird, the wolf, the coyote, the fox.

That is how he was born. He was born out of sorcery. He moved. He came of the Wind, and there was something inside of Him. He had no father. He had no mother. When he opened his mouth horrible things came out. Snakes came out, bats came out, wolves and foxes came out, the creeping and crawling things came out, the spiders came out, the stinging ants came out. The wasps came out. All of these evil things came out. Every time he opened his mouth, more horrible things came out.

He was just a child but he walked like a drunk, stumbling and falling. When he opened his mouth evil things and darkness came forth. Finally, he knew those were his things and he said, 'I will have them. I will control them. These are my creatures, and I shall have them all.'

All those who awaited him saw this, and they were frightened. They were terrified, but Kieli made them all drunk. He made them all see good things there. Kieli deceived them. He deceived them there in the winds. Kieli was the master of vipers and crawling things, of wolves and bats, and all the evil creatures of this earth." Grandfather's story concluded.

Jesús explained, "This is what grandfather told us there on the Mesa in the night with the winds blowing, and all of the cousins were scared. They were terrified because it was like Kieli was there with us. He was there watching us."

And grandfather went on: "The Mothers and the Fathers were concerned; they were worried about what this One would do. They said to each other, 'We must watch this One. He may deceive the People. He may be no good. We must hope that this turns out well. He has deceived those sorcerers there. He may deceive others too.'

Kieli gathered all of the sorcerers around him. They were dizzy and drunk. He sang to them. He showed them his arrows and his things. He was their leader, their chief. He spun around and around like the Whirlwind, and they all watched him there, crazy, and drunk. He showed them how to become the drunken Whirlwind. . . .

Kieli made them all think that what he taught them was the way things should be done. Kieli was the mirror. When those sorcerers looked at him, they saw themselves, and they said, 'How fine, how good I look.' He taught them to transform people into burros, into snakes and wolves. . . .

The Mothers and the Fathers were concerned. They said, 'Perhaps this One is doing things that are not good. Perhaps he has left the Path. Perhaps we have made a mistake. Perhaps we should not have left this One loose. Perhaps someone must stop him. He is making them all drunk and crazy. He is deceiving all of them.'

The Mothers and the Fathers told Kauyumali to find his evil brother and to seek him out. They told him to see what evil his brother was doing. They told him to spy on his brother's evil ways. They told Kauyumali to find out what evil things his brother was doing.

Kauyumali found his brother spinning around drunk with the sorcerers vomiting when he danced, falling down drunk, telling the sorcerers that he was the Great Mara'acame. Kauyumali watched his brother and learned his ways. He learned his evil tricks; he learned his dances and his songs. He saw his brother's evil ways.

The Mothers and the Fathers said to him, 'What does this crazy brother of yours do? Can you stop him? Can you make him stop these evil things that he is doing? Perhaps we have made a mistake. Perhaps he is not the One who should be going around teaching things to people. Perhaps he is just a crazy drunk who deceives them all.' They sent Kauyumali to find his brother. . . .

He went in search of his brother following this path and then that path, but Kieli was not there. Kauyumali could not find him.

Then he knew what to do. He became drunk and he wandered the paths like a drunk. He came upon Kieli. That is how he found him. That is the way in which he found his brother, falling and drunk. But he could not see his brother. All he saw was the mirror. All he saw was himself there.

'Let me see you,' he said to his brother. 'Let me look upon you,' he said to Kieli, and Kieli lowered his mirror. Kauyumali seized the mirror and turned it on Kieli. He was horrified and fled, and all those others fled when they saw him. He was evil and terrible with crawling things all over him. Yet he continued to walk around drunk, singing and dancing."

Jesús paused, then continued, explaining that his grandfather was looking at him, saying, "There were none who would look at Kieli. When they looked on him, they were revolted. They vomited, but Kieli still went about deceiving people.

The Mothers and Fathers again spoke with Kauyumali.

'This One is certainly evil,' they all said.

'This was a mistake. This was not a good thing to let this brother of yours walk about,' they said to Kauyumali. 'You must stop him from going about,' they told Kauyumali.

And they sent Kauyumali out to seek his brother again.

Teyau told Kauyumali to take his shield. Tatewali told him to take his arrows. 'It is time,' Tatewali said to Kauyumali. 'You must seek that crazy drunk out. You must stop him. He does no good there. You must look for him in the darkness. . . .'

He asked Takutsi Nakawe. Grandmother said that perhaps he was in some deep cave or cavern. Kauyumali went about searching all of those places but he did not find him. He is in a cavern, Takutsi insisted. 'Search harder,' she said. Kauyumali searched all the caverns and caves in the Sierra but did not find Kieli. He went back to his ranch because he thought Kieli was gone. He had disappeared. Then he saw a pot of nawa, of tesguino. 'That is the cavern in which my evil brother hides,' he said and he searched all of the tesguino pots. Kieli had hidden himself in a tesguino pot.

Kauyumali found the pot with stinking tesguino and said, 'Come out my brother. I am going to kill you.'

'Do not kill me,' Kieli cried. 'I have one more thing for you. I have a beautiful woman here in the pot, and she is yours if I can go.'

'Come out!' Kauyumali shouted. 'I will not kill you.' Kieli came out and Kauyumali shot his fifth arrow into him.

'Ay, ay, ay, I am dying,' he shouted and vomited all kinds of evil things, and the Whirlwind came and blew drunken Kieli to the high cliffs where he still lives. The woman came out of the pot and she was as ugly as Kieli and even more evil. Kauyumali shot her, and she was banished to the fields and the coast where she lives to make men drunk." Grandfather had finished his story.

Jesús said, "That was the tale of Kieli that grandfather told on the high mesa that night. The others were afraid, but I liked the tale of the drunken Kieli. Kieli danced and sang in his drunkenness. He was a potent drunk, a strong drunk."

"Now I am tired, professor," he continued, "and I have work to do. Your machine will want to listen tomorrow. We must go to buy some yarn and wood. We have to go, brother? Hah, hah!"

"Yes, yes, Chucho, we have get more wool," Matsiwa said, suddenly standing up and brushing himself off, "That is what we have to do!"

"Professor, give us 50 pesos."

"We will bring it back when we sell a painting, we want to make. Perhaps you will buy it."

"Chucho had a dream about Kieli, the Evil One, last night and he wants to paint it. And he will talk about witchcraft for you, tomorrow," Matsiwa said.

"Huichol witchcraft!"

He said no more. They left.

enchanted music and madness

It was dark, dull, gray, cold, and raining the next morning when I awoke. It was difficult to even get out of bed. There was only a slim chance that the two foppish Huichol brothers would come out in this weather. Nevertheless, I went out to stock the refrigerator with some extra beers on the chance that the brothers would be over.

When I returned the two were crouched under the overhang of the doorway waiting for me. The portera was either not home, or would not let them in. I was pleased to see them and opened the door. The tape recorder was on the table, ready for use. Matsiwa sat down in his usual spot, and Chucho lit a cigarette. He asked for a beer.

"Now you'll really hear about some witchcraft!" Matsiwa said, boasting. "It's what should happen to all witches."

"Tell him what happened to that old witch José. Tell him how you knew grandfather was a witch," Matsiwa prodded his brother.

"Well, it was when we went with grandfather to Teakata that I knew. I knew he was a witch," Chucho said.

Grandfather showed everyone how to make offerings to the Mothers and the Fathers in Teakata, and he sang the songs of Tatewali, the Fire, for three days and nights. He was an old man but he could sing like no one else. Shiraulime was a nunutsi, a *bebé*, compared to him. Grandfather was a 'Great Mara'acame.'

He sang the story of the first Peyote Pilgrims and the First Deer. He cleansed each person there with his movieli, and he gathered the sacred waters of the Spring Mothers that the pilgrims would need to take with them to assure the rains.

While returning from Teakata, before the pilgrims went off to the Kaliwey, grandfather suggested that we all go to visit the Kieli on the cliff near the mesa. The Kieli, he said, could grant any wish, if asked properly, and grandfather knew how to ask the Kieli for anything that he wanted. Grandfather knew all of the Kielis.

He had been to the Ranch of the Flowers where the five Kielis of the Five Flowers, of the Five Colors, and the Five Directions, stretch out their arms. He knew the little Kielis, the Kielisha, the Evil Little Ones, and the Kielitshate, the Dwarfed Little Ones. He knew the Ones that were once Mothers and Fathers, the Kakauyali, and he knew the 'Tree of the Winds,' the Kieli Tewiali. He knew everywhere that Kieli Tewiali had landed. He knew all of the places where Kieli had been blown to the trees, the cliffs, the mountaintops, and the crags. He knew where Kieli lived. He knew Kieli.

On the way to the cliff where Kieli lived, grandfather told a tale of Kieli for the hands: "Kieli played the violin like no other. Kieli played his violin so sweetly that he enchanted all of the animals of the forest: the squirrel, the armadillo, the *tlacuache*, the rabbit and the fox. Kieli was going to lead them all to the cliff, to the precipice with his sweet music, his enchanting violin.

It was the *urashi* bird's scream that foiled Kieli.

The urashi bird's scream is hard and sharp. It could penetrate Kieli's enchanting music. The urashi bird aroused the other animals, and the urashi told them all to beware of Kieli's sweet music. He told them to take cotton, the cotton of the trees and the cotton of the fields. He told them to stuff their ears. He told them not to be deceived by Kieli's sweet music. He told them that Kieli would lead them all to their demise. He told them all that following Kieli meant death and not to listen to Kieli.

"Now Kieli only plays the 'Song of the Dead,'" grandfather said, "The Evil One plays the 'Songs of the Dead' so sweetly that you want to join them."

"When Kieli says it is time to die, it is time to die. Know this, recognize this, understand this! It is true! You will see," Chucho interjected.

Grandfather's story continued: "Kieli's music was so sweet that He could seduce the deer. Kieli did not have to use a net to capture the deer for Grandfather Fire. He simply played his violin. The deer would just stand there when Kieli played his violin. The deer knew it was time to die and submitted. The deer would wander about in a daze when they heard the music of Kieli. They would fall, and they would gasp, the music was so beautiful.

Kauyumali was angered by this for the deer were his. They were his. He challenged Kieli to see who could play the violin the best.

First Kauyumali played, and all of the violins played music with him. Then Kieli played, and all of the birds sang his songs.

Tatewali was pleased by this.

Then Kauyumali played again, and he danced. He danced up big storm clouds. He danced as the deer with the snake of the first rains and all the birds that were singing. Kieli's song took over.

Kieli played again, and all of the snakes came out. They are his creatures. Then there was a huge flood. It washed all of the trees and plants away.

Then Kauyumali played, and the corn grew everywhere.

Tatewali was pleased.

Kieli was angry. He was mad. He played again, and the great black birds, the ones that eat our corn came. The crows—for they are his—ate all of the corn.

Kieli was going to trick Kauyumali. He made him drunk. He made him fall. Kieli had gotten him drunk so that he could not play the violin for our Grandmother and our Grandfather. Kauyumali was so drunk that when he tried to dance to Kieli's sweet music, he made a great storm cloud, and it rained. . . .

Kieli's arms turned to branches and his fingers to twigs.

Kieli can stretch his arms and grow extra fingers to play things that no one else can, but then Kauyumali was so drunk that he fell down in a stupor and slept. The sun came out and dried up everything. Kieli began to wither and die. When Kauyumali woke up, Kieli was shriveled and dead.

Kauyumali played a final time for Grandmother and Grandfather and the trees and plants, the corn and the squashes all grew again, his music was so beautiful, but the 'Tree of the Winds' remained shriveled and dead. Only his hands would sprout each year so that he could play his violin. That is the magic Kieli has for the hands."

Jesús paused, breaking away from his grandfather's story. "By this time," *Jesús* explained, "I was learning how to play the violin. José would let me play sometimes at the festivals. He told about how some people use the yellow dust of the Kieli on their hands to make them play better. I had never done that. He told of how Kieli simply granted the ability to play as he did the sweet and enchanting music of the Huichol violin.

Grandfather told of how Kieli could lure women to his cliffs with his music as he lured the deer. He told of how Kieli lured women to their deaths on the precipices, how He seduced them with his sweet music like the deer. Grandfather told of how you didn't even need to practice the violin once Kieli began to play.

Then he told me about Kieli playing songs off in the mountains that only some musicians can hear. If they follow the sounds up into the mountains, and if they don't get lost and ever come back, they will return playing fantastic melodies. They are amazing songs, and they are so difficult that no one else can play them. Anyone who makes the vow to Kieli can learn to play like Kieli, grandfather told us.

Kieli was a much more difficult master than Kauyumali. He was far more dangerous. He was evil, but he could be helpful too. Kieli haunted the night with his sweet music far in the mountains high on the cliffs, drawing men and women to His places where they fell to their deaths. He hunted them like he hunted the deer. They didn't look for death, but when they found it, they welcomed it. They fell in love with death.

José always said that if you trusted Kieli enough to learn like that, you had to swear to be faithful to Him for ten years, not the five years you must give to Kauyumali and the peyote. Nothing like that! Kieli is a brutal master. He makes us forget all else. Kieli can teach us many things, but He takes that memory from our souls. Kieli leaves us like fools, wandering and lost with no memories, no heart.

You will do worse than die, if you offend Kieli!

Even though He lost when he fought Kauyumali, His brother, He is very powerful. And then José told us about how Kieli didn't lose anyway. Kieli sought to destroy Kauyumali. He sought to deceive all of the people. He sought to make them all follow him and abandon the way of peyote, the way of the deer and the corn. Kauyumali thought that he had finished Kieli off, but Kieli flew up and became the Tree of the Winds, the Song of the Darkness, the seducer and deceiver of men.

As we walked through the forest to the place where Kieli lived, grandfather told me, 'Kieli is one of the Ancient Ones like Takutsi and Tatewali. Kieli will never die. He became the Tree of the Winds with five arms stretching out in five directions, and now he searches everywhere for "Our Brother Deer," seeking to do evil where Kauyumali does good. Kieli seeks to trick us and to teach us that things are not really as they appear to be. Kieli claims to be greater than Kauyumali or Tatewali.'

Grandfather told us, 'You must respect Kieli. You must pay Him great heed. He is powerful, and He is dangerous.'

My uncles Miguel and Ramón brought the tobacco gourds that are sacred for Kieli, the ones with Huichol tobacco that is so strong when it is mixed with the 'yellow flower.'[1] Oh! You fall down when you smoke that! The Mexicans don't know about these things. They think that Huichol tobacco is just like tewali tobacco; just like cigarettes. We sometimes give them a bit in a cornhusk on the trail and they fall all over themselves. That tobacco makes you feel a bit like Kieli, when he takes over your soul.

We finally arrived at the place beneath the cliff where the Kieli lived. We made camp there, and the women went out to gather wood.

Grandfather warned, 'Do not wander far, do not wander off in the bushes with some man, or Kieli might just seduce you.'

My uncles helped grandfather get the ropes and packs off of the animals, and they helped him prepare everything for the climb up to Kieli's rocky crag. It is a long and dangerous climb to the seat of the Whirlwind. Miguel and Ramón would help grandfather.

Their wives brought arrows with miniature *huaraches* for the trip to the desert so that Kieli could help them walk faster. They also made arrows with little pieces of embroidered cloth so that the plant would help them with their weaving and embroidery. Grandfather brought a piece of the horn of the bull that was sacrificed at the Squash Festival. I had made a miniature violin and some others made miniature guitars, so we would play better.

All this was to honor the Kieli. All these things were messages for Kieli. They were tied to arrows for Him. The arrows fly from where we leave them to where They live. We had to climb the cliff to where Kieli lived.

The cliff was very high where this One lived. We were not visiting the wife of Kieli, the friendly little One that goes about at night. This was the One that lives in trees and on cliffs and its long viney feet twirl around and catch you. This was the Kieli Tewiali. This was the Kieli who hunts in the night. This was the Kieli who nearly defeated Kauyumali. This was the sorcerer, I could tell that much. This was the Kieli that seeks us out and embraces us and enchants us into believing what he says is true. This was the Evil Brother. . . .

The women carried small bundles of firewood and laid them out for grandfather there on the ledge. There was just enough room on the ledge for two or three people. The rest of us waited above or below the Kieli.

I could see grandfather taking things out of his bundle there in the darkness. I could see arrows and grandfather's movieli with black and red feathers in the light of Miguel's torch. These were strange things that grandfather had there for Kieli. His movieli was not at all like the ones we use on the peyote pilgrimage with eagle and hawk feathers, or the ones we use on the coast with bright green and yellow parrot feathers. There were other things in grandfather's bundle that I could not see.

Grandfather stayed there with Kieli. He sang to Kieli all night there on the cliff.

Late the next afternoon, grandfather returned to the camp below the cliff where everyone was waiting. He said the Kieli would not bother anyone on the way to Wilikuta and that He would grant them swift passage to the Gate of the Clouds, to Ramusha, to the Great Green Fields, and to the Mountain of the Sun," Jesús paused.

"Matsiwa, go out to get us more beers. I will need them. The tewali here will pay," Jesús was trying to be insulting again.

"Give him some money, professor," Jesús demanded.

"All you tewalis like these stories, don't you?" Jesús asked. "We will wait until Matsiwa gets back and maybe tewali can tell me a story about himself, if he has any."

"Chucho," I said patiently, but bristling at his imperious manner, "there are more beers here." I got up to get the beers and brought them in.

"Good!" *Jesús* said, "That's O.K. Let us drink together, while I talk. Open one for Matsiwa, too."

Matsiwa did not look pleased. He was ready to go out. Perhaps, Chucho wanted to get rid of his brother, I thought.

"Perhaps I can bring us something to eat," Matsiwa said.

"Sit down and listen while I speak!" Chucho commanded his brother. He was not about to have Matsiwa leave. I wasn't quite sure what was going on between the brothers.

a cHaLice of bLooD   XX

"Well, José told me, as we prepared to return to the ranch, that Kieli had told him that I could be shown His ways. Kieli asked for me, grandfather told me. He asked me to come back after the pilgrims had left.

Kieli had many things to teach me, grandfather said. The secrets of Kieli were the most powerful ones in all of the Sierra and only the most powerful mara'acames knew the ways of Kieli. I was pleased. I wanted to learn to play the violin.

Perhaps Kieli could teach me that, and perhaps I could learn his songs, I thought. I did not know how evil Kieli really was at that time, nor did I know what grandfather had planned for me. He had been looking in the waters and casting grain. He knew that I had brought my sister's path to an end and broken up that evil brother of mine. He was a witch, and they know how to divine those things. He was planning something evil there.

'Kieli,' grandfather said, 'is very dangerous and not like his "Good Brother." All of the evil things of this world came forth from Kieli. There are scorpions and snakes, the plants with thorns, and the ones that are noxious, the insects that bite, and the insects that eat our corn. All these things came forth from Kieli. Where his blood fell, evil things sprouted, and it was from him that witches learned their evil ways.'

I decided that I would go with grandfather back to visit the plant after the pilgrims left for Wilikuta. Kieli had asked for me, grandfather said, and I could not refuse, or He might cause some evil to happen. There were things that I wanted to learn from Kieli. There were things that Kieli could help me with, and there were things that Kieli could do that none other could. I did not know what evil Kieli could do.

Kieli is the One who hunts men's souls in the night. Once Kieli has seen a soul he will never let go. He hunts in the night. He hunts the soul in dreams. He sings and he speaks in dreams. Kieli says things that are not true, things, things that are evil, but he makes them seem good, he makes them seem true. Kieli never lets go.

That is why I must have the grabadora. Kieli will hear it, and He will think that I am speaking. He will send his evil arrows and attack the machine. Perhaps then he will leave me; He will leave me forever. I did not know the evil of Kieli then! I was just a boy. I wanted to learn things from Kieli. I did not know that the only things He had to teach were sorcery and evil. I did not know that once he spoke to you he never let go. Grandfather sought me out for Kieli. I was to be his new soul, his new servant, his new *mozo*. This was why Kieli wanted to speak to me. I was grandfather's offering for Kieli.

My father had gone sometimes to visit the Kieli. He didn't play much music, but father told me that Kieli did other things for him. Kieli could help him with his animals, and he helped him on his trips to Guadalajara. He protected father from the arrieros at times, he told me. Kieli could be very useful, that is why I thought that I could learn from Him. That is why I went with grandfather to learn of Him.

José, father had said, was the only one who really knew Kieli. He knew all of the secrets of this Tree of the Winds, this Tree of Music and Song, this Tree of Wisdom. He knew His melodies, and he knew how He could travel as a breeze. Father said José knew where He lived and how He consumed men.

Perhaps if I could learn something of that, I thought, then no one would want to witch me again. I wanted to know the secrets of the Kieli: how to talk to Him, how to sing with Him, how to travel with the winds, how to ask Him to do my bidding, how to make Him work for me. Then I could be protected from all those evil things that people did to my mother and father and to me, and if someone harmed me I could just call Kieli.

That is what I thought, but I didn't know that grandfather was going to let Him consume me.

I didn't know that he would take me there and feed me to that awful thing.

I didn't know that I was being offered to the Evil One. I didn't know that I was to be grandfather's sacrifice. I didn't know that grandfather was going to give me to the Evil One there.

That is what he tried to do.

When we returned to the ranch, the pilgrims all went off and grandfather showed me how to make the arrows and the bowls that we would need to bring to visit Kieli. We gathered all of the materials, some from the canyons and others from the high mesas and cliffs. We killed a crow, and we killed a dove, and we took their feathers. We gathered straight pieces of Brazil wood and the soft wood and the bamboo that we needed to make arrows. We gathered wax and clay that we needed for the bowls. Grandfather got the beads and the candles and the copal incense. He even had a special takwatsi, a special bundle, so that the things of Kieli would not fight with those of the Others.

There were things there in grandfather's takwatsi I had never seen before. There were stones and seeds. There were some pieces of colored eggshells and the skin of a snake that I did not know. Grandfather also had made a new movieli, a feathered arrow, which he said Kieli would make 'live' for us. The arrow was a foul and evil thing, the kind of thing that you bring out when you want someone to die. It had the feathers from the crow, the colors of the night, the dark blue of sorcery. It was like the one that grandfather had there on the cliff.

Grandfather could do no good with that. I did not know what he had it for. Only a witch carries such a thing. It was that kind of thing that caused my mother to die, and my father as well. It is very dangerous.

Finally, we had everything ready. We went back to see the Kieli. We started early in the morning so it would still be daylight when we reached the cliff, but grandfather insisted that we take firewood with us. Grandfather carried the arrows that we had made and the other things that we would need there. He brought the takwatsi, the reed bundle, and in it were his secret things for Kieli.

We climbed the cliff carefully. I had the load of firewood, and grandfather had the heavy burden of things for Kieli. Grandfather was talking all the way up the cliff to Kieli. 'Here,' he was saying to me, 'listen to the wind and the leaves rustling. Kieli was first the Whirlwind before he grew leaves. See, he knows we are here.' Then he was telling Kieli we had come with gifts and that he wanted Him to know me, that I also had things for Him. Finally we arrived back where Kieli lived up there on the cliff.

We set all our things out on the little ledge as the sun was going down. Grandfather showed me where to set the fire, and he began to sing to the Kieli. I answered his songs as best I could. I was learning how to sing to the Kieli.

Grandfather gave Kieli each of the things that we had brought, and then he sang the song of the sorcerer. He gave the arrow to Kieli, then he placed the ulute, the other arrows, among the branches of the Kieli. Grandfather did not direct the evil arrow at anyone, but he sang that it should fly to Kieli.

We sang all night, and grandfather talked to the Kieli. I could not hear what Kieli said, but grandfather told me that I would one day understand. I had to learn the secret of Kieli in order to hear Him, grandfather said. I would learn the secret of Kieli shortly. I would learn how to make Him speak to me. I would learn the secret places where I had to keep Him in order to hear Him. I would take His flower in my hands, and I would take His blood. It would not be long, grandfather said.

Before dawn grandfather sent me off to Teakata to take more gifts to the Kieli. It was almost a full day's walk to Teakata and back. I climbed down the cliff and took the arrows that grandfather had given me for each of the Mothers and Fathers. He also gave me a special arrow. I did not know what it was, but I think that it was an ulusha, a sorcerer's arrow. It was dark and solid with a hard wooden tip. It had the black and red feathers on it that an ulusha would have, but the black feathers were not from the crow we had killed. It was a very special arrow that I was to leave in the cave beyond Aitsalia in Teakata, where the viscous milky water of life enters into Mother Earth every spring when it rains.

I also had five small bottle gourds with me for the waters of the Spring Mothers and I filled them there. Grandfather said that we had to give these waters to Kieli to drink. It was a very long walk to Teakata, but I got everything there that we needed for the Kieli.

When I returned, grandfather was still there singing to Kieli. He had placed several of the evil arrows there in front of the Kieli, the ones with people cut from paper tied on them. These were for those who knew Kieli, grandfather said. There was nothing to fear. Grandfather sent me back down the cliff for more firewood.

He said that I was slow and that I had to hurry up before the sun set so that we could give Kieli all the things that He needed. I left the offerings with grandfather and went for the firewood. It was already dark by the time that I went back up the cliff. Climbing up there was very difficult, but I could hear José singing all the way up the cliff as I climbed.

Grandfather said that I was ready to learn the secret of the Kieli. He had prepared the Kieli for me and he said that the Kieli would then sing to me there on the cliff. He gave me the piece of His flesh and then he showed me how to listen. He showed me the fruit of the chalice of the Kieli, the fruit of the flower, the cup of the Evil One.

He showed me where the secret places were that made me hear the Kieli, but it was sorcery, sorcery, sorcery there.

The Kieli is an evil sorcerer, nothing more. He is the Whirlwind, the Nightwind, the Cold Wind, the Wind of Death. He is not like the Deer, or the Peyote. He makes you crazy!

He makes you drunk, drunk! He makes you whirl about, whirl and whirl.

Foul and evil things, horrible things were all I saw that night. Evil things, venomous things, things that sting and bite, things that eat us and consume us.

Grandfather was trying to poison me!

My tongue swelled up, but there was water, water everywhere, coming from the rocks, coming from the earth.

There were evil things there, foul things. I don't remember them all. I only remember that they were foul things, foul and evil things. I cannot recall the things there, I cannot remember, I cannot recount all of them, all of the horrible, evil things, but I know He was trying to kill me.

It was not like the designs of the Peyote, the Path of the Flowers, or the Heart of the Flower, but evil things, monsters and worms that I saw.

I thought I was dying, dying, I was dying there on the cliff. I was crazy, drunk, mad, whirling, spinning, drunk.

The Kieli made me crazy, and He sang to me there. He sang His evil song to me there on the cliff.

Grandfather grabbed me there and tied me and bound me to Kieli. He bound me. He tied me.

There on the cliff. He sang all night. He sang of evil things. He sang of foul things.

I watched the moon, and it became like the sun, and there was yellow everywhere. The stars burned in the sky. They were great fires consuming the night.

Grandfather told me to open my eyes, so that I would see Kieli in the moon and the stars there in the sky, but I could not. I was afraid I was burning with them too. I could not speak. I could not move.

Once he had shown me the secrets of listening to that Evil One, once he had shown me the secret places that made me hear the Evil One, I knew that José was really a sorcerer.

Grandfather was indeed a witch, as they had all said!

The morning came, and I still could not see. I could not see it was morning. I do not know how long I was there with grandfather. I do not recall. A day, two days; I do not know.

I could not move. I was tied up there on the cliff.

I was crying and weeping for grandfather to let me go and take me down from the cliff.

Finally he led me down. I could not stand up. I fell again and again as we went down the cliff.

José led me down and helped me get to the bottom of the cliff. He tied me to a tree there and then he returned to the place where Kieli lived.

I do not recall how long I was there. I do not know.

He had cast His evil spell over me and I walked in His world, His world of evil there. I could not move. I was left there. Grandfather had tied me up there at the base of the cliff.

I only saw bats and owls and creatures of the night there. I saw foul things that were evil, that were unspeakable. The things you see when you are to die.

All day I saw those things there, and I could hear the wolves and dogs howling and barking. There were snakes and scorpions every-where, and I was just food for them, all tied up there at the bottom of the cliff like a neat bundle.

Grandfather wanted to feed me to those evil things. He was selling me to them for their food.

He had a pact with all the foul creatures that eat us, and he was feed-ing me to them. I knew that.

I tried to break the ropes, but I could not. I was tied there all day and as night came on I was sure that grandfather's sorcery would be the end of me there.

Grandfather kept on singing, and I could hear every word that he said but I could not understand him. He was singing in some strange language to Kieli there on the cliff.

Grandfather was doing sorcery there on the cliff. I knew that. He was doing evil things there on the cliff.

I was going to die there, before Kieli. I knew that grandfather's sor-cery was going to kill me there, but I could not break the bonds that grandfather had made.

I was his offering. I was his sacrifice to the Evil One there. I was the deer, the bull that was to die. I was the bull we sacrifice at fiestas. I was his messenger. I was the deer sacrificed to the Mothers and Fathers. I was to take grandfather's evil message to Them there, the sorcerers.

I would not give up my soul like the deer. I would not give it up that easily. I struggled, but I could not stand up there at the base of the cliff. I had no strength!

It was not my time to die. I was not the messenger that would take his message to Them.

All through the night I struggled to escape, but I could not, and finally, before the stars had gone from the sky, I managed to break loose.

Slowly, I regained some of my strength, and I was going to flee, but I knew that grandfather's sorcery would find me anywhere I went.

I staggered and fell as I tried to walk; I crawled like a baby in the brush. I was cut and bleeding. My clothes were torn to shreds.

Grandfather was still singing there on the cliff, and I was worse and

xx | a chalice of blood

worse, and more and more crazy. I did not know what to do. I had to stop him from singing.

As he sang, I became crazier and crazier. I could not understand what he was singing.

My eyes were weeping and my nose was all full. My tongue was like leather in my mouth. I could barely walk there. I struggled up the cliff, falling and falling on the way up.

I could hear grandfather singing all the way up the cliff. He did not stop. He kept on singing to the Evil One there on the cliff.

Grandfather did not know that I had freed myself. He continued singing the songs of the Evil One there.

Before I reached Kieli, I called out, 'Grandfather, stop! Stop! Stop the evil song!

Stop this evil Kieli!

He will kill us all if he can!

Burn the Evil One!

Chop Him up!

Burn Him down!

Stop the Evil One!'

'Get down from here,' shouted grandfather, but I kept on climbing the cliff, falling more and more with every step.

Grandfather kept on singing with his evil arrows placed there before Him and the movieli tied to the branch of Kieli.

'You do sorcery, witchcraft, there,' I shouted at grandfather as I tried to climb on. I could see he was doing evil things.

'Stay back,' grandfather warned me, 'the Kieli is angry. You took too long in Teakata.'

'Our Brother is not pleased with you. He is angry. This is your fault,' he said.

'There is no sorcery here. You must know the Kieli, and then He will help you too. Listen to His song, but come no closer. You have offended Him.'

Grandfather said, 'Stay right there and listen to Kieli's song. I will tell you what to bring to Our Brother, then you will learn His ways. Kieli can grant you whatever you may desire, but He also can take all that you have. Come no closer!'

Grandfather was a tricky sorcerer. The arrows he had out there were sorcerer's arrows and the movieli he was waving at me was strong enough to make me crazy and kill me.

'Stop this sorcery, grandfather,' I shouted at him. 'You make me crazy. Stop singing to that Evil One. Stop!'

But grandfather would not stop. He just continued with his song to the Evil One and told me to listen.

Grandfather was hurrying through his song. I was sure he was going to sing just long enough to have Kieli take me. I knew that he was going to have Kieli take me and make me crazy forever, and he almost did.

I took a large sharp stone. I was just below grandfather, and I hurled it at him. It caught him in the head, and he fell silent there against the plant.

The arms of the evil sorcerer held on to him. They embraced him.

He knew the secret. He knew how to sing to the Kieli and to do its evil bidding. That was why I had to kill him. He made me crazy, and he was going to kill me with it.

He knew the secret, so I killed him. I finished him off. It was an evil secret that he knew. He was there sprawled out in the arms of the evil sorcerer, Kieli.

I climbed up there and took all of his evil things, all of the arrows, all of the offerings and the movieli, and I threw them all into the fire. I burned his evil tools. I burned them all there in his fire, but the old man still moved, though he was really dead.

His eyes watched me, and I could still hear the songs of Kieli. He was still singing, though his mouth did not move. He was still going to kill me. The Kieli embraced the old man and was out to keep on doing its evil things.

I pulled the old man out of the branches and I began to cut off his head.

If I could separate the head maybe he would stop singing those songs that I was hearing. I cut through his neck to the bone and I could still hear those songs. I twisted his head around and I broke it off.

I took his head and I threw it down the cliff!

It lodged in the rocks there, and I could still hear those evil songs it was singing.

I threw rocks at it until I smashed the thing, and then I burned everything that was there on the cliff, but the Evil One was still singing to me there.

SONG of eviL   XXI

"Singing, singing, and singing, chanting over and over, Kieli, Kielisha, the Evil One, chanting, singing, calling. Down, down, make my way down, tripping falling down, down the rocks, accosted by rocks, stones, plants, earth, and leaves, the branches reached out. His things there, His things, His creatures, the snakes, the scorpions, the spiders, everywhere, on the branches, on the brambles, on the trees, on the vines, on the stones, on the boulders, on the path, on the twisted arms, the twisted roots, through the leaves, the brush, falling and crawling. Water every- where, dry water melted in rocks, leaves with arms and legs, lights I could see that blinded. Roots reached up trying to take me into the earth. Long tendrils, ropes lashed out, long sharp whips cracked on the rocks, striped me, made me stumble, reached for my arms, burned my eyes.

The sharp sparks everywhere burst and made me fall in fire and water tumbling over not knowing where I was, or where I went. Drunk and falling, tumbling, unable to see, light and the darkness. Holding on to the earth and falling into it. Dragged down, pulled into the grass that beat me and made me roll in the leaves, the stones, the dirt.

Teakata, the earth's womb, the waters of our mothers, the stream of life, the place of joy, of satisfaction, the great member that stood erect from the earth. When I could see, I saw it, and when I could not, I still saw it. The organs of the earth, the engendering earth, the home of the Mothers and the Fathers, the invigorating holy waters of life and birth, the seed of man, the Mother's womb. The great tall member, the shaft of life, there stood erect over the womb, the womb of the earth ready to penetrate the moist darkness. I could see it above the canyon, at the edge of the earth. Sometimes it was there. Sometimes it was not. There, erect over the edge of the great deep canyon, the Chapalagana, standing, tall, stiff, engorged, excited, ready to plunge into the moistness, the darkness, Tuapuli showing me where the womb of earth was. The things of the earth, the stones, the dry streams, the gullies, the cliffs, the rocks, the great boulders conspired to keep me from our Mothers and our Fathers, the waters. Dry water everywhere.

Only the waters of Teakata could let me reclaim myself, restore myself, give me life once more. Just to reach Teakata, just to arrive at that place, the Womb of the Earth, perhaps the singing, the chanting, the evil song would end. Grandfather's evil things, the things I had placed there, the evil things, they kept singing, chanting, intoning that song, that evil song of His.

I stumbled and fell to the great erect shaft, the sharp peak, the engendering axis. In a thousand directions I went, in every which way, all around, around, around, and around, everywhere and nowhere trying to keep in sight of the naval of the earth, the sugar-loaf peak, the shaft of our Fathers, Teakata. Through the gorge, up the other side, holding trees that reached out for me, rocks ran from under my feet. I reached the stream, the gorge, the gully before the Gate of Stone. The Gate was crashing open and shut. Giant jaws waiting to smash me, eat me, swallow me up, and take me into the belly of the earth there. At the Gate I fell, rested, waited, for the great jaws to finish their last meal. There was water, water everywhere, but none for me; my mouth was parched. I chewed my tongue until it bled, soft, salty blood, seeping into the throat.

Water of our Mothers on the other side of the Gate. Stones, took stones, tossed them. Did not hit the Gate. Died, stones eaten, did not go through the Gate. Evil things of my grandfather still there where I had placed them, where I had put them.

He kept singing, singing, singing, that was why he kept singing to me. Those evil things! The dark blue arrows, the black arrows, the black and red arrows. The singing was almost constant. The things that came from His mouth were venomous things, the snakes and the scorpions. I waited there at the Gate.

Finally, I could pass, I thought, on all fours like an animal in a hole. I cleansed myself; I fortified myself. I crawled through, found the spring of our Mothers. Fell in it, rolled in it, bathed myself in it.

There I left my clothes, there in the waters, there in the earth. To each of the holes I went, to each of the caves, to each of the tombs, to each of the catacombs, to each of the osuaries, for those things, the things I had left, but the singing, the singing, the songs would not stop. They went on and they went on.

I went back to where our mothers were. The hole of the fire was too hot, the earth oven with Tatewali did not want me there. Tatewali sang, and He sang of the Evil One. It was His Son there He sang of. It was Kieli.

There was still the singing there. It did not stop; it did not end. It went on, on and on.

I gathered all the evil things, the evil things I had brought, the evil things that I had placed there for grandfather, his sorcerer's tools, and I threw them into the Earth's Oven there where the fires would consume them.

I told our Grandfather, Tatewali, to take those things there, and he did, but the singing, the singing, it went on.

I gathered my clothes from the waters and I lay there naked in the cold Womb of our Mothers.

The rest of grandfather's things, I had to get them! The other things, the evil arrows, the things from his shrine, his shiriki, the things from his ranch, I had to get them.

The night in Teakata was cold, it was dark and cold, dead, there in the Waters of Life. I remained in the Waters of our Mothers. I could get around better, but I was still besotted by the Evil One. I was drunk.

Her cloak, her mantle, her entrails held me there in the night behind the entrails of the deer. Takutsi held me there, Takutsi Nakawe, our Grandmother.

Her serpent staff reached out, the staffs were writhing there in the night they moved up and down, in and out there in the night. The fogs and the clouds of the cloak of Takutsi held me there in the night.

The stars sparkled in the cavern of the Waters of First Life. The light attacked the eyes, and the brightness shrunk and moved in the darkness.

My clothes were cold and wet. Scratched, bruised, scraped, and hurt, I rolled about in the Womb of the Earth.

The singing, singing, the singing went on.

His things were still there in the shrine on the ranch; that was where they were singing to me from.

The waters would not cleanse me.

There those evil things were still chanting, still singing.

Stumbling and falling, I dared not go through the Gate of Stone. I climbed around the other side. The earth reached out to hold me there, but I climbed around the other side to the edge, the edge of the Womb of the Earth and made my way up the gorge to the ranch, the shrine, the shiriki where those things must be, grandfather's shrine, his shiriki.

The rocks and boulders gushed with water in the dry stream bed. The leaves, of the oaks, of the poplars, beat down and accosted me there. I climbed through the dry canyon, through torrents of leaves and evil things over the dry stone wash that led to the ranch. Stumbling, falling, twisting, turning in the Whirlwind, I made my way to the ranch.

María was there, the gate was there, the dogs were there, the mules and the burros, the pigs and the chickens. The children were there, the raw ones, the little ones.

The gate held me there. María watched me falling through the gate. I was besotted again, drunk as the wind, a twirling whirlwind.

She called out, but I did not understand her words, and I answered, but no words I knew answered. I called out. I spoke without words.

The storehouse, the shrine, the things there, they were singing. They were what was still singing, singing to me, chanting that evil song, the song of sorcery, the song of the dead, the song of the Nightwind.

I could not speak. María and the women, the children in the cookhouse in front of the patio. The store house, barred, shut, closed.

There were those things, the evil things, the bundles, the arrows, the blood of the Kieli, His blood.

Drunk and twitching against that door I pushed and battered. It gave way, it broke, it smashed. María and the women, the children fled.

There were His things. There grandfather hid His things. They were there. I knew. I heard them.

Throwing things out onto the patio, pots and crates, smashing them, opening them trying to stand, to walk, I threw those things out onto the patio, trunks and clothes, but none of those things were there.

His evil things, they were there. They were there on the ranch. They had to be there. Those things were there! They were there singing, singing, singing His song. All those evil things, the arrows, the movieli, the feathers, the stones, were singing.

They had all fled, they were all gone; the women, the children, the little ones. The cookhouse! The fire! The three stones that guard the hearth. That was where Tatewali, the fire, was seated.

That would destroy them; that would stop the song, the evil song. That fire would destroy them all.

The grass broom, the broom for sweeping the patio, for sweeping the clouds, for sweeping the evil things away. That would sweep away those evil things.

The grass broom into Tatewali's home flaming, the black thatch roof flaming, the house, the cookhouse, the shrine, the shiriki, flaming, burning, smoking, and burning that would stop the singing, singing, singing.

Everything was burning, all of the roofs, the corn cribs, the brush, and the fodder, the broom swept them with flames, singing flames.

The songs did not stop. They did not. The smoke and flames took the thatch, the grass, the tops of all the houses. The singing flames went on singing."

part II

THE GOSPEL
OF MAD JESUS

the other world XXII

In Chucho's bloodshot eyes was the severed head, his grandfather's head, in the rocks speaking, blood all around. His voice held the incoherent behavior of Plaza de la Veracruz. The words that flowed in babbling torrents were mesmerizing.

Images and visions swept past. Chucho's broom, lighting the ranch aflame. The smoke, the walls of the center of the world, the springs and the pools, the waters of life and the flames of Tatewali, the shiriki, all burned.

Jesús went on with his tale in that strange and disconnected way without stopping. His words flowed out in a steady stream with little consciousness of content, or coherence. It seemed almost as if he were still under the influence of Kieli. He had the incoherent madness of a raging river possessed by Kieli, the "Nightwind," the Whirlwind of the mind.

"The burning ranch, and I, up on the mesa: night, cold darkness, stars, and flames.

Besotted, drunk, caught in the center of the whirlwind, stumbling. The rocks reaching out, I fled the smoke and the flames, the tongues, the tails of fire there that smoldered, that smoked.

Up the dry rivers to the mesa, the cold dark mesa. The great oaks reached out for me. They drove me to the ground tumbling on the dry rivers and the dry rocks.

The white wash, the white earth, the white dust, covered me there.

I tried to sleep; the song awakened me. I wandered. I walked. I stalked the mesa. I don't know how many days drunken and dry, besotted, rambling and falling, I was there on the mesa. The songs grew softer and softer, but He still sang.

On the mesa, I don't know how long.

Saw the bus pull in to Tenzompa. Thrump, kerthump, burrrratat tatatatata, atataat; the bus pulled into Tenzompa.

I had the silver, the silver box, the *tomin*, the cash from grandfather's. I would leave, that was how I would leave, the bus, the rattle trap, would go in the morning with the sun, with the dawn, the rattling bone cruncher of a bus would take me away, away from the singing, the singing, that song.

Stumbling and falling to Tenzompa in the dusk. The shadows of the mesa, the long dark shadows hid me there climbing down to Tenzompa.

The bus would go early, with the sun. Along the dry stream, the dry gully, I made my way, not stumbling so, not falling so much, into the town at dusk past the school, the plaza, the church.

It was open there. The church doors were open, unbarred, the bus sat in front, dusty, covered with dust. There was no one there, no one. The singing, singing, singing was softer, softer.

Inside was dark, candles cast shadows. Two old women, old women in shawls, tewali women knelt in front, lighting candles, murmuring.

There were stairs leading up. I held the walls, the dark walls. A few stairs at a time, stair by stair quietly without a sound, not a single sound, I climbed. I rested half way; the singing was soft; it was going. He was not so near. I rested. I slept on the stairs half way up, in the darkness.

The doors closed. They were shut; they were shut from the outside. There was no way out there were only the shadows the dark shadows that the candles made and the cross of Santo Cristo.

The dark red candle. The dark Santo Cristo, the other Santo Cristo.

I am his son. He protected me.

Santo Cristo spoke to me. I heard him singing, singing.

Santo Cristo told me I must leave. Santo Cristo kept me, He protected me; He spoke to me there in the darkness.

Santo Cristo, Santo Salvador, savior, redeemer, bringer of life, bringer of cars and trucks, bringer of airplanes and telephones, bringer of cloth and money; He will save us.

He will bring us all things. That is what He said.

I climbed up the stairs to the loft, part way up and curled up to sleep. There was still the singing in the dark and the dark red shadows the dark Santo Cristo sang quietly. He moved in the shadows, the dark red shadows, and sang to me in the night there.

Santo Cristo had given all those things to the Mexicans. He had cheated us there in the Sierra.

Kauyumali and Kieli, our brothers, were there. They were stronger, they were more powerful, but Santo Cristo gave all of those things to the tewalis first. They did not save us. They did not protect us.

Santo Cristo was singing, singing that He would give us those things.

I wanted to sleep, but they were singing. They could give us everything I heard them singing.

They were Brothers, Brothers there in the darkness. I slept.

The crowing, the braying, morning sounds before the sun, the birds awakening jolted me as I heard the bus.

'Thrrrrruuuum, bagh, bagh, ratatat-tat -tat.'

I had to get to the bus. The door was locked. I was there with Santo Cristo. I had to find a way out to get to the bus. The windows were high. I couldn't reach them.

The Santo Cristo was there singing on His tree, on His cross. I took the tree from Santo Cristo and climbed up to the window.

The latch was broken, and I squeezed through. I fell to the ground and ran, ran to the bus that was just beginning to move. I beat on the door and held on, and the *chofer* opened the door.

'Money! Money,' he asked. 'You have money?'

I had the money, and I gave it to him. He cheated me and didn't give me back the change. There were some other Huichols in the back of the bus, and it stopped on the way out of Tenzompa for more people. There were people getting on and off. I moved to the back to where the others were."

Jesús was again weeping. He was not ritually weeping into the crook of his arm, but profusely weeping, gasping for air. The tears streamed from his bloodshot eyes. A deep sorrow coiled around his heart, squeezing and constricting the grief that flowed from him.

His brother seemed to be paying no attention at all to Chucho's tears. Matsiwa was edgy, perhaps suspecting another outburst from Chucho.

I wanted to put an arm around him, or say something, but I just watched, wary of what that might provoke, as he gasped for air. I had no idea why he was sobbing so.

"It was the last time, ahhh!," he gasped, "The last time I saw; I saw the mesa. The last time I saw the road, the path to the Sierra. The last time I saw the land, the earth that is of our Mothers and our Fathers. The last time! Ahhh! Ahhh!"

He could not continue, but wept more and more, gasping for air.

"*Jesús*! Chucho, Chucho! Stop, Stop! Drink this. Stop!" Matsiwa said, begging him to take something to drink. He began to shake his brother.

I said nothing.

"*Jesús, Jesús*, stop!" Matsiwa continued as Chucho gasped for air between his sobs. Finally he took the beer and drank deeply.

The sobbing subsided. Matsiwa said, "Let's go my brother, let us leave. You have said enough."

"No, NO! I will not go! I will tell him, I will tell him the one true story! Leave me! I will say to him those things that he wants to know."

Chucho finished his beer and went on, still gasping for air.

INTO THE WORLD XXIII

"It was the last time, the last time I saw the mountains, the trees, the mesa, the paths to the Sierra. Ahhh!" he went on weeping in a more subdued ritual fashion.

He was gasping for air and weeping. "We went on through clouds of dust, past dry riverbeds, stone houses.

The others there in the bus were talking. They were speaking of the fire on the mesa. The man, I think it was Hacame's brother, tried to speak to me, but I could not speak.

'*Borracho!*' he said. He thought I was drunk. He did not know about the fire, or grandfather, the evil old witch. I could not speak. I could not tell him. The bus stopped in Huejuquilla and others, other Huichols, got on. They knew nothing. I heard them. They were going to Guadalajara. I would follow them and they would lead me to you," *Jesús* said, speaking to Matsiwa.

"The bus rattled on to Fresnillo and the others got out there with all of their cargo, all of their things. I followed them, still falling and stumbling like a drunk. They all thought that I was drunk. My clothes were tattered, and I was covered with dirt. The driver on the next bus asked me for money, and I gave him what the others gave him. It was night by the time we reached the big open yard where the buses went in Zacatecas, and I was asleep.

The driver was shaking me. '*Eh! Indio! Pinche borracho. Vete pendejo!*'

There was no one else on the bus. He took me by the shoulder and threw me out of the back door of the bus onto the ground in the dirt and the dust. They were all tewalis there. I did not know how to ask them. I did not know how to speak much Castillano. I thought that this was perhaps Guadalajara. I stumbled into the great room with bright lights where there were many people, sitting, standing, waiting. There were no other Huichols there. I sat in a corner on the floor and tried to sleep. The men with brooms poked me and pushed me, and I walked outside. There was another Huichol there with his wives and their children and many things they were taking back to the Sierra, cloth and shovels, axes and brightly colored wool.

I could barely speak. 'Guadalajara?' I asked him. I did not know him. 'Guadalajara. My brother?' I tried to ask again, but he would not speak to me. 'Borracho!' was all he said. I walked on in front of the station. There were cars and taxis, fumes and dust, little *puestos* with *chicharones* and *carnitas;* I was hungry.

I took one more silver peso and pointed to the carnitas frying in heavy *manteca.* It was a good women there who gave me a big taco with carnitas dripping with fat, chili and onion and *cilantro.* I ate it and pointed to another. She gave me another. I ate it and turned away.

'*Ay, Indio, que tonto. Tienes vuelto,*' she called out to me. 'Eh, dumb Indian. You've got change!' and one of the men made me turn around. I was going to belt him, but the woman reached out with money for me.

'*Adónde vas, joven?*' 'Where are you going, young man?' she asked me in Castillano, but I could not understand her Spanish.

'*Ay, pobre!*' she said.

'Where go you?' she asked in Huichol.

'Gua— Guadalajara,' I said.

'*Pues vete indito! El camión sale a las ocho,*' 'Get moving, Indian! The bus leaves at eight.' I did not understand her, and she said, 'Bus, bus. Three star, three star, Guadalajara. Go! Now!' in Huichol.

'*Ay, este tonto no habla,*' 'Ay, this fool can't speak,' she said. '*Oyes chamaco, llévate éste a tres estrellas a Guadalajara! Su camión se va!*' 'Eh, kid, take this guy to the three star bus to Guadalajara. His bus is leaving.'

Her boy took me into the station and helped me. I gave him the money and he told the man behind the bars that I wanted a third-class ticket to Guadalajara. The boy took me to the bus, but there were no seats, and I climbed on the top with all of the cargo, but they would not let me stay there. I showed them my ticket, and I went inside the bus. It was full, and no one more could fit in. The *cobrador* opened the back door and shoved me in on top of the cargo that was piled up there. The horn sounded and the bus pulled out to Guadalajara.

All night we stopped and started people got on and off the bus. They took their bundles and their livestock. I never got a seat. At dawn we got to the terminal and the bus stopped. The cobrador yelled at me to get out, and I was there. I walked past all of the people in the terminal. They were all looking at me there, and I went through the bright lights past all of the taxis.

I didn't know how to find my brother here, and I walked along the streets full of cars and fumes; I was all alone. I didn't know where Matsiwa was. All I knew was that he was with the padre and I didn't know which padre.

I looked for a church. It was not hard to find. There are many. They were not like the church in Tenzompa. There were many people going in and out, but there was no one I could speak to. I could not speak much Castillano. I went into the church. It was all gold and white. The men were on one side and the women were on the other. The priest was talking in Castillano.

I crouched in a corner. He finished and everyone left, then an old man came and kicked me out. I tried to sleep in the plaza in front of the church. There was no one I could speak to. I thought I would see Matsiwa. I wanted to find the padre, but he didn't come out."

Matsiwa said to *Jesús* in Huichol, "Chucho, you didn't even know where that church was. It was just near the bus station. We were all the way in Zapopan." Then he turned to me and said in Spanish, "This brother of mine thought that all churches were the same. He did not know that there were many, many of them there. He had never been to Guadalajara with our father, or grandfather."

"The afternoon sun was hot and dusty in the plaza in front of the church," Chucho said, "and I was hungry. I got up to look for something. I walked by the stores, but they had nothing to eat. There was a woman selling *gorditas*, and I pointed and tried to buy one. She would not look at me. I was not there. I walked on to a place with swinging doors. It was a little cantina.

I went in and there were three men standing at the bar; others were sitting at tables with beers playing with squares. There were big pots of things on the stove behind the bar, and I pointed and made signs. I said I wanted to eat, but the mozo at the table came up to me.

'*Eso es un lugar para gente de razón. Vete Indio!*' and he pushed me to the door and threw me down on the street.

'*Pinche Indio!*' he yelled. 'Go back with the savages. This is a place for real people, not Indians,' and he went back in.

One of the men standing at the bar came out. He looked down at me and said, 'Wishalica, eh?'

'You are going to get thrown out everywhere looking like that. This is Mexico, not the mountains. You have to look like a Mexican, brother,' he said in Huichol. He didn't look Huichol though, and he spoke strangely.

'Get up! You have any money?' he asked.

'Yes,' I told him.

'Good, then come with me,' he said, and I followed him to the market.

He showed me where to buy pants, a cheap shirt, a belt, and a hat, a real cowboy hat.

'Now put them on,' he told me in the last stall. I didn't even know how to put on tewali clothes, I said, and he asked the man if we could go in back of the stand. He took my belt and my pants and pulled my shirt off. He gave me the pants and told me to put my legs in, then he unfolded the shirt and gave it to me. I did not know about buttons, and he showed me how to button the buttons. The belt had a big bull on it, and he showed me how to thread it and buckle it. Then he showed me a big mirror, the biggest mirror I had ever seen. I was really surprised; I had never seen myself like that. I was a tewali.

He took my Huichol clothes and said, 'This is garbage,' but I took my belt and bag and the shopkeeper gave me a plastic bag to carry them in.

'You have any more money left?' he asked.

'Yes, plenty,' I said and showed him my bag of silver coins.

'Good, then we have to get you boots. You can't wear those huaraches, those Huichol sandals. They are for Indians. Real Mexicans wear boots.' I had never worn boots, or shoes for that matter. He took me to a place to buy boots and, whew! were they expensive. I couldn't walk with them. I had to buy socks too.

The new clothes hurt. They bound and they scratched, but the boots were terrible. It was like walking on the stones of the river the first time. I could not balance on them.

'Now we can go and get liquored up,' he said. The man's name was Pedro, he was a San Andreseño and had just returned from working in the tobacco fields in Nayarit. I asked him if he knew my brother, or the padre he stayed with. Pedro did not know the padre and he had never met Matsiwa. He may have known father, or grandfather because his father sold cattle here too, he said, but he was not sure. He didn't know anyone from Santa Catarina.

We had to walk very slowly because I couldn't balance in the boots very well. When we finally got to a cantina he said to me, 'Now you just shut up when we go in here. We cannot speak Huichol, or they won't serve us. If they ask you anything just say *Carajo*! Or *Pinche*!, or, *Chingao*! and stick to *sí* or *no*. I'll do all of the talking.'

Pedro led the way in and ordered us beers. The beers were expensive, 3 pesos each.

'But I want aguardiente,' I whispered to Pedro in Huichol.

'*Dos tequilas*,' he said, '*de lo mejor para mi amigo*.' He called out to the mozo, and we got two tequilas in little glasses. They were 5 pesos. I paid him with pure silver. He bit the coin and gave me back some other coins that weren't silver.

Pedro whispered to me to put them in my pocket in the pants. I couldn't get my hand in, so I just put them in the pants. When I got up everything fell out and I could not find all of the coins. Pedro showed me how to put my hands into the pockets, which were very strange. Every time I paid with a piece of silver the mozo gave more of those worthless coins back and some pieces of paper that Pedro said were money too.

We drank more beers and tequila, and I got very drunk and then we went out and bought a bottle of real aguardiente. We sat in the plaza and drank it as the sun set. The birds were screeching all around to find places for the night. We talked about work on the coast, and I got really drunk. I slept.

When I awoke it was cold and my boots and bag were gone. All I had was what was left in my pockets and the plastic bag the man at the market had given me with my belt.

I did not know what to do. Pedro had told me of a place on the coast where he had worked and he had said there was a Don Manuel Alvarez who would give me work. He said that Don Manuel even spoke some Huichol. I would go there.

I had to get some sandals. I had only the socks and I took them off. My feet were sore from the boots. I got some huaraches for 5 pesos at the market and went to where the bus had left me. There were buses to everywhere there."

THe coast

XXIV

Chucho continued his story without taking a break. "There was another Huichol there, Miguel Santos, from the coast and I told him I wanted to go to Santiago to work. He said it was a very bad place, but he helped me to find a bus and pay for it. I only had 5 pesos left then, and the bus was all night stopping and starting through Tierra Caliente, the hot tropical lowlands.

'Santiago!' the cobrador yelled, and I got off there in the plaza. There were no other Huichols around, and I began to ask for Don Manuel. In a store a woman pointed down a road and said Don Manuel was that way. She showed me with her hands, and I began walking out there. I walked, and I walked, and there was no one, just the birds in the trees.

It was late in the afternoon when I heard a Huichol violin. There was a big shed near the road. The shed was very tall and there were only rough boards covering it. It was filled with racks and racks of drying leaves, tobacco leaves, and there were many, many people there, Wishalica people. I listened and then I went in.

'Ke'aku,' I said to another young man about my age there and he answered. He was from San Andrés too, I could tell by his clothes.

'I want to see Don Manuel,' I said. 'He has work. I want to work.'

'He is gone,' a big fat Huichol told me. His name was Pablo. He wore a blue Huichol shirt and white calzones with a flower belt

'Don Manuel is gone, but he will be here tomorrow.'

The young man told me, 'This is a very bad place to work and there is no money until the end of the season. All they give us are tortillas, and everyone gets only a kilo a day. There is not much food. We grow some chilies and things, but you will have to work like a man, not a boy, here, cowboy.' He called me a cowboy because I had on tewali clothes.

I said that I would work like a man, and Pablo said I could stay with his family until tomorrow.

In the morning Don Manuel came and everyone got into the trucks that took us out to the fields. Pablo went with me to see Manuel, and he said that I could work there. I had to come to him in the afternoon to give him my name and to let him write it in his book and then I had to promise to stay until the end of the season when the rains came. I would only get three-quarters pay, 700 pesos and 1 kilo of tortillas a day.

I shot little birds and caught lizards to eat with the tortillas, and they were all very pleased when I brought them some birds. The women gathered greens and other things to eat. Every day when we finished with work, we lined up for our kilo of tortillas. Pablo only got 2 kilos because only one of his wives worked in the fields. I let them have some of my tortillas each day. His children spoke Spanish. I began to learn Castillano from them.

I could still hear the singing sometimes, and when I heard it I went off hunting little birds and things.

Pablo heard me singing there in the jungle and asked me if I could cure his son. I sang for Pablo and the sickness in his son went away. Then I began to sing for the others. I was their mara'acame.

Pablo was the most important man there with two wives, and I was his mara'acame. I made a movieli and a takwatsi there with Pablo and the other Huichols from the next ranch came too. They would pay a peso, or two, for me to sing and sometimes bring things to eat that I would share with Pablo's family. I was the mara'acame, and Pablo was the tatoani, the gobernador of the Huichols there.

I was with Don Manuel there until the end of the season, and then he asked me if I would work on the irrigation ditches through the rains. Pablo and his family went back to the mountains to plant their corn. I stayed on. The others left and Manuel gave me a bunk in the house with the rest of the tewalis who worked there because I wore tewali clothes. The men there all called me Indio, but I worked with them through the rains, and when the season came, Pablo and his family returned.

The tewalis told me that Manuel was cheating the Huichols there, that each one should receive 1,500 pesos not the 1,000 pesos that we were being paid for the season; that was what they got. The patrón there was a very good man and paid everyone the same, they said, tewalis and Wishalica.

I told Pablo this when he arrived, and he became very angry. We spoke to each of the Huichols as they arrived and as their names were put in Don Manuel's book. Finally everyone agreed we had to talk to Don Manuel. I went with Pablo, and there was a terrible fight. Manuel said 1,000 pesos was all we could get.

Pablo and I talked about this and we went to the *dueño,* the patrón who lived in the big house one weekend when he was at the ranch. He did not come each weekend, but we waited until he was there, and we went to the house and told them that we wanted to see the owner. We waited almost all day, and finally, in the early evening, he sent for us. We were escorted into the house, and he stood in front of a large table.

'What is it you want,' he asked, and Pablo said that we could not live on only 1,000 pesos for the season.

'But you are getting almost 2,000 pesos a season,' the patrón said. Pablo told him that we were not, that Don Manuel only paid 1,000.

He sent the man in white who escorted us into the house out for Don Manuel. Finally he came back with Don Manuel.

'Manuel,' said the patrón, "how much are each of these *indígenas* to get for the season?'

Manuel replied, '2,000 pesos.'

'But that is not what we are paid,' said Pablo.

'*Pinche indios mentirosos,*' shouted Manuel.

'They must be beaten and whipped,' he said. 'They lie!'

'Manuel bring me the book,' the patrón said, and Manuel, with the man in white left.

He came back with a big black book and the patrón looked it over. He signaled to Pablo to come forward.

'See, it says right here before each of your names that you are to get

2,000 pesos at the end of the season.' But Pablo could not read the letters, and I could not either.

'But, sir,' Pablo said, 'that is not what we get, and that is not what we were told. We are just poor Indians, and not one of us can read what it says in that book. All that I know is that we were told 1,000 pesos, and 1,000 pesos is what we got last year.'

'Only 1,000 pesos! I paid 2,000, did I not?' the patrón said.

'These are nothing but lying Indians,' Don Manuel told the patrón. 'I should beat each of them, and then we will see what they say!'

'Are these the same Indians working here who worked here last year?' the patrón asked.

'I have no idea,' said Manuel. 'Indians are Indians.'

'I am going to send Eduardo here to ask them each their name and if they worked here last year, and we will see.'

'Maybe they are some of the same ones. What do I care?' said Don Manuel.

'Eduardo, will you also ask each one who worked here last season how much was received at the end of the season,' the patrón said.

'They are nothing but lying Indians who won't work!' Don Manuel shouted out. 'If one of them lies to you, then all of them lie to you!'

'Eduardo, go to see the Huicholitos and take the book see what they say and come back here immediately. Let us see what they say. You will all wait here meanwhile.'

Don Manuel was furious, '*Pinche Indios mentirosos.* You'll suffer for this!' he said in Huichol.

We were told to sit down, but we stood. Manuel was furious, and he had a seat brought. He was talking to the patrón in Spanish, but I could not understand most of what he said.

Finally the man in white came back and he said that the inditos were mostly the same ones who worked last year and they all had said they received only 1,000 pesos.

'*Mentirosos,* Liars! Lying Indians!' shouted Manuel.

'Manuel, shut up!' the patrón said. 'Someone is lying and I don't care who it is. I will pay the *raya* this year and everyone will get 2,000 pesos. Now go! All of you!'

'Now you'll get nothing, *pinche indios,*' Manuel said on the way out.

That night two men came to the shed. They grabbed Pablo and started fighting. I fled, and almost everyone else did too, but they got one of his wives, Marta, as well. They tried to grab me, but I escaped and ran all night. I think one of the men was Diego and the other was Raúl. They were real *matones*. Don Manuel sent them. I am sure. They killed Pedro, his wife, and one of their children. All "the people" there fled.

I walked all night and all day the next day, but I did not want them to find me, so I kept on walking, but mostly at night. I was stumbling and falling in the darkness and I dove into the brush when there were cars coming. I did not want Manuel, or his men to find me. I was sure that they would kill me too."

a teacher

XXV

"Finally I came to a place with a big wire fence all around it and a concrete white sign in front. I did not know what it said, but it was the Agricultural Station. I slept in front of the sign that night and when I awoke in the morning I could see two Huichol men working inside the fence; I called out to them. We talked through the fence, but they would not let me in. I went to the gate and waited until someone went in, and then I went in to see them. They said that there was no work, but one of them said that I could help him. I was there for almost a week, and no one knew it, I helped them in the fields and in the gardens. They always had plenty of food for everyone there, not just tortillas, and whatever we could find to go with them. Then one of the professors asked me if I could stay. I did. They were all very good to me there.

There was one of the professors there, Juan Melendez, who was always in his classroom writing things on the big green boards until very late. When I was finished, I would watch him, rather than sit with the other Huichols. There they were all San Andreseños, or *costeños*.

One evening, Professor Juan asked me to come to his classroom. I watched him writing things on the big green board with a piece of white stone. While he was writing things I took another piece of the white stone and made designs on the other big green board. I drew the haiku, the water Snake, and some other things. Then I began to copy the things that he was drawing, the words he was putting on the board.

'So you can write,' he said.

'Can you write your name?' he asked me.

'No,' I said.

'Well, what is your name?' he asked, and I told him.

Professor Juan wrote my name on the board and I copied it. I copied it again and again.

'See,' he said, 'you can write.' And he wrote the letters of the alphabet on the board. He told me the name of each one and I copied it. I copied the letters that he had written. It was a tough job, but I copied them well. Professor Juan wrote words with the letters and I copied those. Then he asked me if I could read what I had written, and I could not.

He had a book for me with letters and words, he said, and the next day he would bring it. Every evening I wrote letters and words on the board. I read them to him and I copied them from his book. It took a long time, but I learned all of the letters and numbers. I learned to read and to do ciphers. Juan had me write things on the board for his classes and he gave me books to read. At first I would read the books to the professor, and it was very difficult. Then I began to read the books he gave me. I read them again and again until I knew every word.

I worked there until the rains came and all of the other Huichols left. Professor Juan asked me to stay and continue my lessons. I worked there through the rains and spent every night with Professor Juan.

He asked me to come with his students to help in the fields. I liked his students. They were good young men. They didn't call me a 'little Indian' like the others. I went out with the students to the town and one of them, Miguel, taught me to drive his pickup. When he saw that I could drive, Professor Juan told the director, and then they sent me to town quite often to get things.

In the town there were two cantinas and there was plenty of aguardiente, but there were only the tewalis there. I was still afraid to get drunk with the tewalis. They might beat me and steal my money if they knew I was an Indian. They all got drunk there in the town, really drunk. Even some of the students got drunk there, but I was afraid that the students would tell everyone I was just an indito. I was still afraid that Manuel and his men would find me. Once I thought I saw Raúl there in the town with some of the others from the tobacco plantation. That was when I knew it was time to leave. I liked the students, but it was lonely there without any other Huichols. Before the rains ended I asked to leave. And then I went off. I wanted to see the ocean, the place of Our Mothers.

Professor Juan went with me into the town. He said if I went to the normal school with the Instituto Indigenista I could get a *certificado,* then I could come back as a student at the school. I told him that I was going to the sea first, but that then I would find the *Indigenistas.* He told me where to go and wrote down the name of a professor there. I took the bus to San Blas. Then I went to Guadalajara, but that is another story and I am tired."

I was tired too, I said, and the Huichols left. It was already late in the evening. The Huichols had been there since early morning. I was still in a state of shock. I was tired, but I couldn't sleep. I went into the kitchen and poured myself a stiff drink. Then went back to the tape recorder and started to replay Chucho's tale of that day. For some strange reason he was as compelled to tell his tale as I felt compelled to listen.

I, too, was in a way possessed. I wanted to hear more. Was I now his accomplice, listening to his words again and again, his disciple? I tried to distance myself from his words. The reels kept turning; *Jesús's* words dissipated in the air. I no longer even heard them. I dozed in front of the tape recorder.

It was nearly three by the time the twirling reels of tape drummed their way into my consciousness. I shut off the recorder and went to bed.

I needed help to understand *Jesús.* The only person I could think of who might be able to help me was my friend and colleague José Amparo. José had been one of Erich Fromm's students. I called him in the morning and spoke to his wife. I made an appointment to see him that evening.

It was raining by late afternoon when I left for José's with a sheaf of notes and a tape of excerpts from the tale of Mad Jesus. Along a street of high walls that hid elegant homes, about two blocks off Avenida Las Palmas, was his home and office. The bell at the second door, which was the entry for clients, was the one I rang. He buzzed me in, and I went up to his study.

"Well, let's see what you brought," José said as I walked in with my sheaf of papers.

He read my sketches of what was on the tapes and then started straight off asking rapid-fire questions about Chucho, his family, his background, what he looked like, my impressions of him, what I thought of him, what I felt about what he had told me thus far, and on and on. We spent almost two hours talking about Chucho before José even asked to hear the tape I had brought. I translated for José. All the time he was scribbling notes and asking me about Chucho.

Jesús was too strange, too unusual to categorize even as a Huichol, I told José.

"That is not true," he said flatly, "*Jesús* is just the same as any of us. It is his experience of life that is different."

"He is a man with no affectionate relationships and is probably incapable of forming these basic kinds of relationships. He obviously never had such relationships as a child, at least since his mother's death and the little girl's death—what was her name, Tuturica?" José said. "From what you have told me, he is very much isolated from not only his own culture but meaningful human relationships. His relationships with women sound more like rape, than anything else. If what you say is correct, he is not even close to his brother. He seems to be reinventing Huicholness from his own perspective. There is a lot of power in all of the magic and myth he lives with. The myths are prototypical events that he is acting out. He may be in a way acting out that Huichol version of the Christian myth. I can't tell from the tapes whether he sees himself as the Santo Cristo, or as an emissary of Santo Cristo."

"I don't know either," I told José.

"The miraculous birth sure makes it sound like he does consider himself to be the new Huichol Christ," I told José. "And the way he insisted on telling Luís the Huichol Christian myth in the first person makes me think that he considers himself the new Huichol Christ. But I just don't know."

"What about his relationship with Crazy Kieli?" I asked, "Could he be acting out parts of that myth too, sort of in contrast to the Santo Cristo figure. After all, Santo Cristo is in reality Kauyumali, a culture hero in Huichol myths, and Kieli is the evil counterpart of Kauyumali."

"It could be that *Jesús* is modeling his own self-image, his notion of ego, on these myths," José said.

"Luís was right. You should be very careful with this *Jesús,*" José warned me.

"Now to the more important question, my friend," he said.

"What do you see in this man, this *Jesús*? You have told me you are trying to distance yourself from the Huichol. This *Jesús* is not typical of all of your other Huichols. Why do you insist on continuing these interviews with someone who is potentially dangerous, a possible murderer?" José asked.

I started to answer José with social science explanations, but they didn't ring true. There was more: I didn't want to admit that I found *Jesús* fascinating. The potential danger got my adrenaline going; the myths were captivating. *Jesús* was charismatic in his madness, tragic in his loss, very successful professionally as an artisan, and driven by demons I didn't know. He was in a way like the self-styled gurus and radicals of the communes and "families" of the Haight, Big Sur, Woodstock, and the Lower East Side in the 1960s.

Perhaps I was using *Jesús* and his tale for pretexts even I didn't understand. But *Jesús* was using me too. It wasn't just the tape recorder that he wanted. For some reason he was compelled to tell this tale. Maybe it was some kind of self-vindication, or justification. I didn't know then, and I don't know now, why he chose to tell me his tale.

José and I talked about extended families, the imperious nature of the Huichol, their cultural superiority complex, their contentiousness, their constant arguments, but there was more, so much more.

I wondered just how much José could really tell me about *Jesús*, whether an analyst like José could extrapolate from Freud's Victorian Vienna, or Fromm's deep humanism, to a world like that of the Huichol. José felt that there were universals in human emotions that made it possible to understand, or attempt to understand, the mind across culture. His insight into *Jesús*'s lack of personal relationships was brilliant. We talked until quite late, and then I took a taxi back to the Colonia Napoles.

THE MOTHERS' LAND

XXVI

Several days later the brothers returned, and *Jesús* began his story with the tale of his ride in a broken-down old bus to San Blas. The tale was long and uneventful, but when he arrived on the coast he recounted what happened there.

"There were other Huichols there in San Blas. I met them near the market when I got off the bus. Pedro Hernandez was a San Andreseño who lived there with his young wife. He had on his best brightly embroidered clothes, four necklaces made of huge coils of expensive little beads, the kind imported from Japan, a new hat and four finely embroidered bags. He was not in San Blas as a pilgrim to leave offerings for the Mothers at the Sea. He didn't have the old worn clothes of a Huichol on pilgrimage.

'Ke'aku,' I spoke to him, 'What's a Wishalica doing here who's not on a pilgrimage?' He sold things he bought from other Huichols to the tourists here, he said. He asked me what I had brought from the Sierra, and I told him that I had nothing and that I had been on the coast for almost two years.

'Well, it looks like it,' he said. 'You don't even look Huichol. You look like a tewali.'

He told me I would have to look like a Huichol in San Blas if I was going to make any money. The *turistas* there would buy things for plenty of cash that could be bought from other Huichols for a few pesos, he explained, if you really looked like a Huichol.

'You got any money,' he asked me.

'Yea, I've got a bit of tomin,' I told him. 'I've been working at the agricultural station.' I didn't want to tell him about the tobacco plantation.

'Well, you see those Wishalica over there,' he said, pointing to some other Huichols who had come in with me on the bus. I hadn't even spoken to them. They looked very poor.

'They all have belts and bags in those bundles they are carrying. I don't have enough *plata* to buy them, but if you can buy them, I will show you how to sell them.'

We both went over to the Huichols who were sitting on the steps of the market.

'Eh, Brothers,' Pedro said. 'You look like you need some cash for some food, or maybe a beer. If you've got some bags, or some belts, I would buy them. The women down here on the coast don't know how to weave and they don't do pretty embroidery like at home in the mountains. The tewalis stole my Brother's clothes. He needs some new ones so that he can look like a Huichol again. Maybe you have a whole outfit you could sell us, no?'

We bought all of the things that they had for a few pesos. Pedro told me I should keep those things to sell, and his wife would make me some Huichol clothes.

He asked me what I had brought for the five Mothers of the sea. I had nothing, I told him. I had never been to Haramaratsia before, I told him. I did not know what things They needed. He said the Mothers would not be happy if I came without things. He said that I would have to buy things for them. There was a mara'acame coming who would sing the songs of Our Mothers for three days. This man, he said, could show me what I needed for the Mothers, and maybe I could even learn a song or two from him.

Pedro's wife made me clothes in the San Andreseño style. They were very expensive and they had little embroidery, but in them everyone thought I was a San Andreseño. I even tried to speak like Pedro. We sold all of the things I had bought from the other Huichols for plenty, and Pedro told me all the things we would need to buy for the Mothers. I bought the things and finally the mara'acame arrived.

Old Juan had long white hair. It was not braided but hung everywhere. He had no woman to braid it for him. He had the stubbly beard of an old man and deep dark skin furrowed like rivers flowing from his eyes. He was nearly blind. He did not wear fancy clothes, but plain white cotton with red piping. He had just one belt and one bag where he kept his takwatsi.

When old Juan had everything ready for the Mothers, all of the people gathered on the beach in front of the great white rocks. Old Juan sang, and he cleaned each one with his movieli. He sang for three days on the shore. He was not a very good singer, but I listened to his songs and learned the stories of the Mothers there in San Blas. I had to pay the old man for his songs. He wanted a lot of money too. I sang with him and I learned all of the stories.

If I wanted to be a mara'acame, old Juan said, I would have to find all of the places where the Mothers had emerged. I would have to find all of the places where the haiku, the coiled water Snake, was pecked into the stone. The songs would tell me how to find those places. He could describe some of them, but it had been many many years since he had visited those places. I would have to sing the songs each morning and each evening when the Mothers welcomed Teayau, the Sun. When I thought I could find those places I would have to go to them and sing to the Mothers there. The Snakes, the Serpents of the sea, would help me he explained.

Each morning after Juan left, I went to the sea and sang the songs of Kuwe Eme and the songs of our Mothers. I threw offerings into the sea, corn and chocolate. I prayed as the Sun Father, Teayau, entered the sea and prayed as he emerged from the Eastern Mountain in Wilikuta. Pedro saw this, and he knew that I was a mara'acame. I built a little house from palms there on the shore so that I could sing each morning and each evening. The flies and the mosquitoes ate me, and I was very ill, but I persisted. I began to try to find the five places along the streams and rivers where the haiku was carved in the stone. It took a long time before I found the first place above San Blas.

Meanwhile I bought and sold things to the turistas with Pedro. When his daughter became ill, he asked me to cure her. I cured her and he told all of the other Huichols there. He told the tewalis too. He began to bring people for me to cure and when we were selling things to the turistas he told them all that I was a mara'acame. I even cured a couple of rich turistas, and, for sure, did that pay!

I spent almost a year searching for the places where the Mothers had emerged. The whole time I was living in that palm house on the beach. There were many Huichols who came in the dry season and there were plenty of turistas. Pedro and I bought and sold things, and I split the money I made curing with him.

I went to Tepic twice to see old Juan, but there were other mara'a-cames who knew more about Haramaratsia and the places where our mothers had emerged. Many of them brought peyote from Wilikuta and the sacred waters from the Sierra. I bought those things from them too, along with their clothes and belts and bags.

When the Kuwe Eme did speak to me, it was almost the end of that year, when the sun is farthest from the great white rocks. As the sun set, the winds began to blow very sharply and the rains followed quickly.

I was standing in the waters when they began to boil up in the winds. The Serpents twisted and turned. The waters were white. I swam toward the white boiling sea, the white mist.

All things, all things were for the Wishalica. All things were Huichol at the first emergence. They were for the people, the Mothers, the Fathers, the Brothers, and the Sisters, our mothers and fathers, brothers and sisters.

Santo Cristo had misled the people.

He had given too much to the tewalis. It was not good; it was not right; it was not just.

The Kuwe Eme had been at the first emergence and that first emergence was for the Huichol. I could see the Kuwe Eme writhing and making the sea boil as they had in the first emergence of our Mothers. They knew!

The Kuwe Eme would restore the Huichol, the Wishalica, the people. Once more the sea would boil, and the tewali would be gone. Then all things would be once more as they should be.

The Snakes, the great green venomous Serpents of the sea, prom-ised me this. There would be a new emergence for the people, for the Wishalica. There would be a new Huichol Santo Cristo who would help the people and give them the things that the tewalis had taken.

The waters had taken me far out to sea while I listened to Kuwe Eme. I was strong, and I had learned to swim well, but I did not think that I would make it back to shore. I swam as hard as I could, but I could not get to the shore.

The water was pulling me to the rocks, so I followed the waters and swam to the rocks. Kieli, the Whirlwind, was laughing. The Whirlwind followed me and was sucking me out to sea.

I swam for the rocks. The waves would dash me on the rocks if I was not careful. That was what Kieli intended to do. He allowed me to see the Kuwe Eme, and then He would dash me on the rocks.

If I took the waves just right, I could grab on to the rocks and climb up away from the waters. My leg was gashed on the rocks, and my feet as well were cut. I held to the rocks and managed to climb out of the waters.

I was drunk and besotted by Kieli. He was singing to me again. I held there on the rocks all night not knowing how to get back to the shore and heard Kieli mocking me, laughing at me. I was trapped on the rocks just as the whirlwind had been. He laughed at me.

The sun turned the great white rocks where Kuwe Eme slept a dark maroon then red then pink. I sang to the Mothers there but I could still hear Kieli singing softly and laughing, mocking me. I could not climb the rocks, and there was no other way off of the ledge where I was perched. The Mothers called out to me.

Kieli teased me. I was stuck on that ledge of rocks just as he was, just as the 'Tree of the Winds' was. I leaped into the waters. Kuwe Eme would protect me there. I saw the Snakes there in the waters swimming and I swam for the shore.

The Snakes guided me. The current was flowing into San Blas. I knew what the Red Snakes had said was true, that they would give the world to the people once more. I saw the way it would be when the tewalis were gone. I saw the Kuwe Eme rise up and the sea boil again as in the first emergence. Santo Cristo would bring all that was forgotten and all that had been stolen. I would bring all things back to our People.

The Snakes and the Mothers would help us and protect us. They would make the Wishalica what they were once!

I reached the shore and I was exhausted. I had seen what would be. I slept, but I still heard Kieli's song. He would not let me sleep. It was as if I were drunk again. I walked and staggered and fell on the shore. I found my way to the house of palm leaves there on the beach, and I slept there. I would tell no one about my vision and I told no one about the Snakes, the Mothers, Their promise. I slept.

'Eh, Indio,' a voice said.

There was a foot kicking my shoulder. I reached over for the knife I had there in the hut.

'Eh, Indio,' it said again and kicked my shoulder. I rolled over with the knife and slashed at the foot kicking me.

'*Ay, Pinche!*' said the voice. I just missed the foot with my knife and the voice said in Huichol, 'Eh, we have work to do, *cabrón.*' It was Pedro. In my sleep I had remembered Juan and Raúl in the tobacco shed when they killed Pablo and his wife. I knew that they had been killed by those two whom Manuel had sent. I was still afraid that they were looking for me. I thought that they were after me again.

'It has been two days. Where have you been, brother?' Pedro asked. 'I have some curings for you to do and these people have been waiting for you. There is a tewali woman here at my house with pain in her legs and maybe I've even got us a turista girl, a little *güera.* Get your things on and come over to my house. Stick that knife back where it belongs in its hole. You almost got me, you *pendejo.*'

I put on my clothes and went over to Pedro's. The woman waiting there was María. I sang, and I cleaned her with my movieli, and I rubbed her legs where the pain was. She said she was cured.

When I finished I asked Pedro about the turista.

'You've got a little gringita to cure, eh?' asked María. She understood Huichol. Her father had had many Huichol friends among those who fled the Cristeros, she explained. She spoke only a few words of Huichol, but she understood a lot.

This woman, María, was very strange. She looked like any other tewali. She came alone and she had no man. Pedro told me that she lived in San Isidro, and that she knew many of 'the people.' She had long black hair braided but with no ribbons, a long silver streak through her hair like a lightening bolt. . . .

After I had cured her she said, 'Take some things with you to sell and make sure that all of the gringos come around when you cure the little one.'

'You'll take home plenty of cash with you then.'

María went with us and helped us talk to the turistas. She told us what kind of things to take along to sell them. She told those turistas all kinds of things and she made us wait until almost sunset when all of the other gringos were there to begin to cure the little one. . . .

María came with me down to the shore, but she did not stay there. She left with the first bus in the morning. She came back many times and helped us sell things to the turistas.

She lived in San Isidro by herself, she said, and there was a big house there. There were two Huichol houses in the back of the compound. She said that I could have one of them there, but I wanted to stay on the shore to speak to our Mothers there at the sea.

I sang to the Mothers each morning and again when they received our Father, the sun, each evening. I told no one of the Kuwe Eme. Finally old Juan returned. He would purify all of the people and he would sing to our Mothers there. Everyone brought offerings for the Sea Mothers, and María came too. I sang with old Juan, and he told me many things about our Mothers. I told him that I had found the place where the Mothers had emerged and that I sang to them each day.

He asked if they sang back to me. I hesitated to tell him of the Kuwe Eme, but then I told him of the Sea Snakes and how they had taken me out to the sea, how Kieli had laughed at me and mocked me. He asked me if I could remember their song. I could, I thought.

Old Juan was very pleased and asked me to sing the song before he sang of the emergence of the Mothers. After he had sung, he told me I should sing the emergence of the Virgin of Guadalupe for she was one of the Mothers too. After that he said I could sing of what the Kuwe Eme had told me and what they wanted. It was good. He asked the people to bring more things to offer to the Mothers of the sea. Perhaps if the Kuwe Eme spoke again, They would tell me other things, he said. . . .

María stayed and listened to me, but I don't think that she understood any of my songs, for later she asked me what the Virgin had to do with the Sea Serpents. I told her of my vision. She was the first I told of what the Serpents had said to me. Some of the others understood what I was singing about. I think that Pedro understood. . . .

We sold all of the things that we had, and some of the turistas asked for more things. They wanted beaded bowls and arrows; they wanted more bags and belts. We could have sold them plenty. Pedro's wife could weave, and María asked her to start on some more bags. I knew how to make the arrows and I knew what designs to put in the bowls.

Pedro went to Tepic with María for all of the things that we needed. She convinced Pedro that we should all come to her house in San Isidro. When they returned, Pedro and his wife and two other Huichol families went with María to her house to make the things the turistas wanted. At first I stayed in my house on the shore so that I could sing to the Mothers there. I was hoping that the Kuwe Eme would speak to me again."

saLve maRía

"Without Pedro and his wife there I had no one to cook for me. I would buy some tortillas and some chilies, but there was no one there and there were few other Huichols. I bought things every time I found some other Huichols in town, and I sold them to the turistas. Often I did not find the other Huichols until after they had sold their things because I was living out on the shore and did not come into the town often. Pedro had been right there waiting for each bus as it came into San Blas.

María came with Pedro, and I went with them to María's. There were really six houses there. María lived in a big block house, and each family had its own house. There was even a house for me. . . . Pedro stayed there in San Blas. He would send more people to us in San Isidro to help with the work.

At María's we each had a house. I showed each one there how to make the arrows, and María showed them the types of bags and belts the turistas liked. . . .

María and I went to Guadalajara to buy the wool and the beads that we needed.

There were twelve of us living at María's, and everyone was making things. While we were in Guadalajara I bought a radio so that we could play music for everyone. María bought brightly colored cloth and plenty of beads. We bought good sewing needles and mirrors. María bought red face paint. I bought rubber shoes for the women and tewali boots for myself. We did not dress Huichol in Guadalajara.

XXVII | salve maría

When we returned from Guadalajara I sang over all of the bundles that we brought back and gave them all Huichol names. I made them all Huichol things there. We would be more Wishalica than they were in the Sierras. I decided to build a shiriki, maybe we would even build a tuki we thought. I was the mara'acame there and we organized our own festivals."

Perhaps it was at this point that *Jesús* began to constitute his little cult. He obviously dominated the group and was weaving his vision into their everyday lives. His little band of artisans gave him a purpose and direction. It also gave his vision a direction. He needed those people. They gave him what he was looking for: a way of completing his vision.

"Pedro sent us more people from San Blas to help us make things. Often Pedro did not get much money for what he sold. María could always get more than anyone else.

We had over twenty people living in the compound at María's and everyone was making things to sell. When our shiriki was built, I wanted to bring the Mothers of the Sea there so that they could watch over us, but we needed three mara'acames to sing for that, and we would have to hold a great *mitote,* a dance feast there.

I went to San Blas to find Pedro and then we both went to find old Juan in Tepic. Old Juan told us that we would have to obtain the waters of emergence of each of the five Mothers, feathers from the five birds of the dawn and the darkness for arrows and for our movieli. We would have to buy hikuli and plenty of aguardiente for the fiesta in San Isidro.

After the fiesta he told us he would go with everyone to Haramaratsia, to San Blas, to pray with the last light. I wanted to ask him about the Kuwe Eme and to tell him more about my vision, but I did not. I went to gather the waters of our Mothers, and Pedro with the other men from the compound went to find the birds whose feathers we would need and the other things that we would have to have, we would have to gather. We had to make many things that we needed for the fiesta.

Once we had all of the things that old Juan told us we needed, I went to Tepic to bring him down to San Isidro. Pedro brought several other Huichols from San Blas. The women all made food and we bought a bull to sacrifice. Old Juan, Pedro, and I sang all night the first night.

We assembled all of the things at the shiriki for the Mothers. I had carved a stone with the haiku to cover the hole where our Mothers would live there in the shiriki. Juan brought the crystals and the seeds that were their hearts. He had brought Takutsi Nakawe along with him. We had all of the others assembled there in the shiriki. There was plenty of hikuli. Pedro tried, but he did not sing well.

In the morning old Juan asked me to sing for our Father, the Sun. I told him I would sing of the first emergence and the first light of day. I sang the song of my vision, I sang the song of the Kuwe Eme there on the rocks in San Blas. I sang of what they had told me.

I sang that there was another Santo Cristo. I sang that there was a Huichol Santo Cristo coming. I sang that the Kuwe Eme would make the waters boil, that only the Huichol would emerge. The clouds and the Serpents would strike all others down. The time of the tewalis would be ended when the new Wishalica Santo Cristo spoke to the sea properly.

Old Juan understood my song and he told the others the tale of the new Santo Cristo as the sun rose. I was still singing and I sang until it was time for the bull to be sacrificed. Old Juan had me speak to the bull. I told him what to say to the Mothers and Fathers. The women made soup from the bull, and we sang all night. About midnight I left Juan and Pedro.

I had arranged for a truck to take everyone to San Blas. María's friend Pancho was a *camionero*. I paid him for the truck and drove back to María's. When I returned Juan and Pedro had finished singing and almost everyone was asleep. I woke them all and told them to get into the truck.

Then I drove to San Blas. Everyone was very impressed that I could drive. We got to San Blas before the sun rose and everyone walked out to the beach where we could see the Great White Rocks.

Old Juan asked me to sing again and he told everyone that I was their mara'acame. Pedro was not pleased by this. He did not sing at all. He left us there. María sat behind me as I sang. Old Juan took each one of the people with us into the waters and asked our Mothers to clean their souls. When he was finished everyone went back to the truck. Pedro had disappeared. His wife and child, though, came with us back to San Isidro along with everyone else.

When we arrived everyone danced from the truck to our shiriki. Old Juan led the way. At the shiriki he sat in his uweni. He had me sit with him. He told me that this was my shiriki now, and he told me what I would have to do for the Mothers and Fathers there as everyone danced around us. Old Juan told me that I was now the father-mother of all of these people, the mara'acame. I had to care for them as I cared for the Mothers and Fathers in the shiriki.

Everyone danced well into the night, and there was plenty of food, hot soup, fat beans, thick atole, and hot tortillas. There was plenty of aguardiente too. Old Juan and I got very drunk. He told everyone there I was their new mara'acame.

The next day old Juan left on the bus for Tepic.

María told me that we had no more money left. We had spent it all on the fiesta and the shiriki. We had all been making things for the fiesta rather than making things to sell. We had enough for tortillas for a few days. María gathered up all of the things that we had to sell and tied them in a big bundle for me. I had to go to San Blas to sell all of those things. She took the clothes that I had. They were stained with the blood of the bull. That was good, I told her, I was a mara'acame, but she insisted that I have the best new clothes to go to San Blas.

I went to San Blas and I went to the turistas whom I knew there. Pedro had already been to many of them. There were two gringos there who wanted bags, lots of bags, to take back with them. They didn't have much money. They were the ones who told me about their friends in Mazatlan. Their friends had a store there that sold things to the turistas. Raúl, who owned the store, was Mexican, but his wife was a gringa, they said.

I went back to San Isidro with the money for María. She told me I had to go to Mazatlan right away. María went to Guadalajara to buy the wool and the beads that we would need.

Mazatlan was a big city with lots of tourists. I did not know where to go there. I had written down the address and asked people at the bus station where to go. They said the place was far away where the hotels were on the beach. There were cars and buses everywhere there. The man at the bus station said to take a taxi but the taxis were very expensive. I finally found a bus going out to the *playa*. The bus took me near the address, but then I walked and walked until I found the shop of the friends of San Blas.

Don Raúl was very brusque with me at first. He called me an Indio. '*Ay Indio, no toques nada,*' he said when I came into the shop.

'I have things for you, sir,' I told him in my best Spanish. 'I have Huichol things that your friends from San Blas said that you might like to buy. I have very fine Huichol things. I have the things of the singers, the priests, the mara'acames that you might be able to sell here. I have very fine things.'

Raúl told me to show him what I had, but that he only sold *arte muy fino* not *artisanías,* folk art. His wife came in just as I was showing him those things. She liked all of those things. She spoke very good Spanish. She told Don Raúl to buy everything, but he said that these were not the kind of things that he could sell. Finally, I showed him the stone I had made for our Mothers with the figures of Takutsi and the Kuwe Eme carved on them and colored.

This Don Raúl liked. He said that they were very *primitivo* and that he could sell these things. I showed him how we place arrows and bowls around an altar, and I made a little altar for him there in the back of the shop. I brought out my takwatsi and I began to sing. I waved my movieli over the stone and told Don Raúl that the stones were hungry. He had to bring them some corn and some aguardiente. Some customers came into the shop, and they watched too. I sold the turistas one of the bags for 500 pesos, and Don Raúl wanted to buy the stones and the arrows, if I would set them up in his window like I did in the back of the shop.

Don Raúl agreed to pay me 1,000 pesos for each of the stones I brought him. I also sold him the arrows and the bowls for the altar and the next day I set up a small altar in his window. There were many people who came by to watch and they came to buy things from Don Raúl too. His wife took me to other shops. I sold some of the bags and belts, and they all gave me money to bring more things in two weeks.

I stayed with Don Raúl there in Mazatlan for five days and I sold everything that I had. I also got four shops that wanted more things. When I left I had over 15,000 pesos. I tucked it all into a special belt that María had made for me and took the bus back to San Isidro."

the cult of santo cristo XXVIII

"María was back and I told her about Don Raúl and Mazatlan and all of the money I made there. She told me not to tell any of the others and she hid the money away. The next day María went to Guadalajara to buy more things and I went to San Blas to see if I could find some more of our brothers and sisters who would help us make things for all the people in Mazatlan.

I waited around the market for the buses, but there were no other Huichols who came so I walked out of the town to the beach. Before the great white rocks there was a small group of Huichols. The mara'a-came was seated in his uweni before a fire there, the rest were standing around listening, waiting for the sun to be received by our Mothers. They were San Sebastianos. I walked toward them and I could see Pedro there. He was talking and they were passing around a bottle of aguardiente. Pedro was drunk.

'Ay, Jesús,' he called out to me, 'What brings you here? You are not happy with my wife?' He told the others that I had taken his wife and child away to San Isidro.

'Your wife awaits you,' I told him, but he was drunk and in a very bad humor, so were a couple of the San Sebastianos with him.

They came over to me. Pedro put his arm around me like a friend and said to the others, 'This is Jesús, our new Santo Cristo, the mara'a-came, the singer. He's going to save us all from the pinche tewalis, isn't that so, brother.'

Then he grabbed me around the neck and yelled in Spanish '*Pinche ladrón! Donde está mi mujer?*' You damned thief! Where is my woman?

He was choking me. Some more of the San Sebastianos came and they pulled him off of me. The mara'acame stopped singing and told Pedro and the two others to leave. They took the bottle of aguardiente and staggered down the beach.

'*Pinche ladrón!*' Pedro yelled, '*Te mato!*' Damned thief, I'll kill you!

'Borrachos!' the mara'acame yelled after him, 'our Mothers will take you.' And he went back to his uweni and began to sing. . . .

I began talking to the other San Sebastianos there.

'Do your wives weave?' I asked the San Sebastiano who helped the mara'acame sing.

'Of course they do. They weave the finest belts and bags in the entire Sierra. Look at this!' he said, pointing to the bag he had with him which was very well made with an intricate design of the Wealica, the two-headed bird.

'We need help weaving,' I explained to him. I told him he could come to San Isidro with his wives. There was plenty of food there, and we would pay 5 pesos for each bag his wives could weave.'

This was an incredibly low price even at that time, especially considering the days it took a woman to weave a bag, but *Jesús* later paid his followers nothing for all the trinkets they produced for him. He provided food and shelter for his followers, but paid them nothing. Everything that they produced went for offerings.

"Some of the San Sebastianos came back with me to San Isidro that night and the others followed the next day when the mara'acame had finished. We had almost thirty people there, and they needed plenty of food. There was still dried meat from the bull, and some of the women cooked while the others wove. The men made arrows, but I couldn't sell that many arrows. The arrows that couldn't be sold were for the Mothers and Fathers.

I told them it was time to visit the Mothers there on the coast. The old mara'acame agreed and I led them to the five places of emergence of the Mothers. . . .

María returned the next day from Guadalajara. I went back to Mazatlan.

Don Raúl and his wife were very pleased to see me there. Raúl asked if I would replace the things on the altar I had erected to Tatei Nieli in his window. The food for our Mothers had all dried and was moldy. The shrine was looking sad. Didn't this man know that the Mothers and Fathers only ate fresh food? . . .

I spent a whole day preparing the arrows and the bowls. I bought the things for offerings, and the night that I was going to construct the shrine Don Raúl had many people in his shop. He called it a *galería.* There were all kinds of people: some were Norteamericanos, others were French, and there were Germans, and others from other places like Suiza and Italia. There were Ingleses and Japoneses and all kinds of people. The ones who spoke Castillano asked many questions, but often I could not understand them.

They spoke worse Spanish than most Huichols. They wanted to know about the hikuli and the deer and the journey to Wilikuta. Don Raúl told them that I was a *curandero,* too, a mara'acame, and there were several of them that asked me if I could cure this or that malady.

They asked what medicines I used, and I told them that peyote was the only real medicine that was used among the Huichol. Some were very interested in this and asked me if I could find them some hikuli. I told them that we would have to go to Wilikuta to find the peyote, and many of them wanted to visit the Magic Peyoteland. I told them that this would cost them a lot of money, 10 or 20,000 pesos and they were still interested. Everyone stayed very late that night, and there was plenty of aguardiente in the *ponche* that Don Raúl prepared.

I sold all of the things that we had made from beads there. Doña Hudit, Raúl's wife, said that some of her friends had shops in other places like Manzanillo, Puerto Vallarta, Guadalajara, Acapulco, and even in the City of Mexico. . . .

When I came back to San Isidro I had almost 20,000 pesos and plenty more orders. María put all of the money away and she organized the women making the belts and bags. With everyone there and with the bags that María's friends in Tepic bought we had everything ready in two more weeks and I went back to Mazatlan with all of the things that people had ordered. I did a few more curings and found another person who wanted a shrine in his house. . . .

The German woman in Manzanillo was very good to me and she showed me other Huichol things that she sold. The things that she said sold best were the cuadros that she got from a Padre Cerillo in Guadalajara. They were made of wool pressed into wax and were like the nealikas that we made for the Mothers and Fathers, but they had no mirrors so that They could see us and we could see Them. I didn't know how to make those wewia then, but I knew that they would be very easy to sell. I asked the German woman how to find Padre Cerillo and she said just to go to the fathers at the Zapopan mission outside of Guadalajara. Perhaps I would find this brother of mine there, I thought.

When I returned to San Isidro things were not yet ready to take to Mazatlan. María suggested that I take the men to visit all of the places of our Mothers while the women wove the bags and belts that had been ordered. We chose the arrows that were for our Mothers, and the women wove special pieces of cloth to tie to them to ask our Mothers to help them with their weaving. I sang for two nights before we were off to visit the places of our Mothers. Some of the women wanted to accompany us, but I convinced them to stay. They were to weave for us.

With the men and some of the boys—the little ones stayed with the women—we visited the shrines of our Mothers. I insisted that everyone bring plenty of offerings to each place the haiku danced with the waters of our Mothers. It took us almost two weeks and everyone had to abstain for the entire period.

I began to tell them all of the new Santo Cristo, the savior, the one who would return to us all things, the one who would create for the people, the Wishalica, all of the things of the tewali world, all of the things that had been forgotten, left undone, ungranted. Santo Cristo would emerge from the boiling sea; the Sea Snakes would dance, I told them; the sea would boil, the tewalis would be gone!

The old mara'acame, Andrés, the San Sebastiano, was very pleased with my songs. He told the others that I could bring things for the Wishalica. He told them that I was the one who could bring the new Santo Cristo forth, perhaps I was the new Santo Cristo, or would become the new Santo Cristo. Old Andrés told them I would lead them to the new Santo Cristo and the new age where 'the people,' the Wishalika, would have all things.

It was then that I began to hear Kieli again. It was the first time that I had heard Him singing to me for a long time. He sang to me in the night at the place of Tatei Nieli.

He was singing softly but he was singing to me there. He was singing, singing, singing, softly singing. When we got to San Blas for the offerings at Haramaratsia Kieli was singing more loudly and I included Him in my songs there.

I sang to Him.

He may have scared them there. I sang to that one, 'The Deceiver,' 'The Evil One.'

Old Andrés warned me to be careful of the Whirlwind. He could tear things apart and scatter them everywhere. He knew that I was singing to Kieli, even if the others did not. He warned me to be very careful of the 'Evil One' and not to listen to Him.

Pedro came to the shore while we were at San Blas. Old Andrés said he would be trouble. His wife preferred to stay in San Isidro. Pedro began to tell the others that we were selling their things for hundreds of pesos. He told them that María and I were thieves stealing their things from them and selling them for thousands of pesos to the tewalis. I don't know how he knew that, but that was what he told everyone. I told him to come with us back to San Isidro to see his wife, but he refused. He said that he was going to find another wife in San Blas. . . .

Once we returned, María told me that almost all of our orders were ready. When they were completed, I went first to Guadalajara and Puerto Vallarta, then to Manzanillo and Mazatlan. They were all very pleased with the things that we had made and I came back with plenty of cash.

When I got back, old Andrés said that we would have to make offerings to the Mothers at our shiriki. We began to make preparations for a great fiesta for the Mothers. Andrés helped us arrange things and told all of the others who were from San Blas. Slowly everyone began to arrive.

We made arrows and bowls, and María gave me money for some things for offerings for our mothers. She helped the women to make the tortillas for everyone. Many people came.

Pedro came too, but he was there to do evil things. He fought with his wife, and María told me that he had beaten her, he had maligned her, and he had hurt the children. He kept telling the others that María and I were thieves.

We did everything to care for the people there. We provided food, and they all slept there in María's courtyard, in our houses, around our shiriki.

Pedro was there to cause trouble. Old Andrés came to me with the other San Sebastianos. They too agreed that Pedro must leave.

I told him that he would have to leave, and we had a huge fight, but all of the others joined with me and he left.

Pedro was furious. His wife would not go with him.

His heart burned. He called me a thief.

His iyari spun and twisted tight with revenge.

He stayed in San Isidro getting drunk.

He stayed there watching us and talking to everyone, telling them about us, about his stolen wife, about how the mara'acames were going to take everything from the tewalis in the town.

He told them all that we were thieves, that we would take their women.

He wanted revenge.

We began to sing that same evening. Andrés and Raúl and I sang all night in front of the shiriki.

The next morning we gathered all of the offerings together and one by one placed them in front of the shiriki. We mixed the magic waters of our Mothers in the morning when the sun rose.

We didn't have much hikuli and the blood of the deer was hard and dried. This was not good.

The maize of five colors was ground and mixed together. They were not well ground and toasted, so the waters were not very good.

They remained there under the face of the sun. They remained there all day. The Sun was not pleased.

We sang and made offerings all through the day.

Some of the women prepared food for that evening. Some of the men danced and others played music.

When the sun began to set and the women had finished their

weaving everyone began to dance. We all danced back and forth around the shiriki. We sang in front of the shrine and made the magic peyote water with the waters of the five Mothers.

Old Andrés placed the haiku, the coiled Snake, the great spiral, the heart of the flowers, in front of the shiriki.

He drew it on the ground there; he drew the great spiral design of the haiku, and we began to sing the tales of all of our Mothers.

That is when I began to hear Kieli singing stronger and stronger. Evil things, evil things, he was singing. The Whirlwind was about, the Whirlwind."

I looked at Matsiwa. Jesús's eyes were darting about the room so fast his head did not even have time to follow.

His thick black hair only followed his movements reluctantly. Jesús was like a dog trying to shake the water out of its coat.

Matsiwa was concerned and watched his brother carefully.

Without a word we both knew that Jesús could become completely unhinged at this point, but we were frozen, two birds looking into the jaws of the serpent about to strike.

"Pedro came in. He was there.

He was really drunk. He was weaving; ranting and raving.

He was screaming at everyone. He called me a thief and we fought.

He came after me. He attacked me there in front of the shrine.

He pushed old Andrés aside and shoved Raúl to the ground.

I fell and he was on top of me.

Kieli was there. He was singing. He was making me boil and twist and turn.

The Whirlwind tossed Pedro off, and I fled to María's house of stone, but he broke down the door and came after me there.

He smashed things. Pedro called María a tewali whore. He smashed many things.

The others tried to hold him; they tried to throw Pedro out.

It was Him, Kieli, the Evil One, the Whirlwind, that was singing to me there. The Whirlwind, the Nightwind, He had me. I was the Whirlwind who would take Pedro, who would finish with Pedro.

I chased Pedro out, out into the swamp, the lagoon, out into the mangrove.

Dark black mud, cold night, our Mother Moon, arms, branches, legs; the Whirlwind.

Kieli told me what to do with him in the swamp. I killed him in the black mud, the stench.

With stones I weighted him, the arms, the legs, the body, beneath the water, the black water, the night waters.

All night Kieli sang to me there. He would not stop. My clothes were torn and black. The night reached out for me in the fowl black waters.

Our Mother shot lightening bolts into the waters and they burned.

The waters burned with every move I made. They glistened in the darkness and burned bright blue and green.

I could not find my way out. Kieli was speaking to me.

Our Mothers were speaking to me. Santo Cristo chanted to me.

Our Mother Moon left me. I found my way out and back into San Isidro.

I told María what had happened. She told me I had to flee.

The tewalis, the neighbors, would be furious. They would be after me. They would send the Police.

We agreed that I should go to Guadalajara. We told everyone that Pedro had fled back to San Blas, but they would know when he was not there.

I fled.

I took a car to Tepic and then a bus to Guadalajara.

That was when I left the coast," *Jesús* said with finality. His rapid searching movements ceased and he stared directly at me.

He was focused, a viper about to strike.

He was upset, angry.

He turned and looked at his brother.

His movements were studied and deliberate now.

The beast behind his eyes that fueled his fury for the last few minutes was suddenly gone.

He rose and told his brother that they were going and walked to the door.

Matsiwa seemed as shocked as I was at the sudden departure, and he followed *Jesús* out the door.

Their departure was so abrupt that I didn't even turn the tape recorder off.

I put a voice label on the tape before turning the machine off. "*Jesús*, Chucho Loco, Mad Jesus, Mexico City, August 12, 1970." That was the last tape I made of the story of Mad Jesus.

the apostles

I had a feeling that I would never see *Jesús* again. The way he left my apartment that night, the curt clipped words as he pivoted on his heel and walked out seemed final.

I still wondered what had happened after he left for Guadalajara. I wanted to know more about *Jesús*. There was something about him, some feeling that he drew from me. I justified it as anthropology. Maybe I could get a couple of academic papers out of his story, maybe a book, but that was not really why I wanted to know more about *Jesús*.

Jesús did not mix with other Huichols living in Mexico City. He had a small group of followers living somewhere in the downtown area. He apparently did not live with his followers. He directed their work, told them what to make and what designs he could best sell. Then he peddled what they made to collectors, shops, and galleries all over Mexico City.

Jesús's little band of artisans constituted a lucrative urban Huichol cottage industry. They all kept pretty much to themselves, and I knew very little about them. I did know that they sold plenty of cheap Huichol folk art to shops in Mexico City, because their work was everywhere. *Jesús* must have been a very effective salesman.

About a week after *Jesús* had stormed out of my apartment, I went down to the Plaza de la Veracruz to see if I could find his brother. I wanted to know where *Jesús* had gone. I wanted to find him, speak to him. I wanted the rest of his story. Matsiwa was very apologetic when

I saw him, but he had not seen *Jesús* either. I asked him about *Jesús* in Guadalajara. He just parried my questions with vague generalities and finally said that if I really wanted to know about his brother he would come over to the apartment sometime.

With a motion of his head he made it clear that he didn't want to talk about *Jesús* in front of all of the other Huichols. There was something ominous in this. Something he didn't want anyone else to hear about, perhaps another murder, I thought.

"If you are really that interested," Matsiwa said, "why don't you go over to see 'them,' those he keeps down there."

He motioned with his head and lips toward the downtown area, the Zócalo, the center of Mexico City.

"Perhaps some of 'those' would know where to find *Jesús*," Matsiwa intimated.

"Neyaucame, the young one, your friend," he explained might be able to help me find *Jesús*'s little band of followers.

"Yes, Neyaucame knows how to find those people," Matsiwa stated with a knowing nod. "He should be back shortly. He just went to get us some wool."

I knew that this short foray could mean an all-day trip admiring the wonders of the city. Neyaucame, especially, had a habit of just wandering in the city looking in shops until he was kicked out and watching the Mexicans go about their daily business. These kinds of things fascinated him.

Finally he returned. Matsiwa spoke to him and he asked me, "You want to go see *los santos apóstoles*, eh? Well, I know where they are but you'll have to pay the taxi."

Neyaucame seemed to think that taxis were the appropriate mode of transportation for Huichols in the city and he took taxis whenever he could afford them. He took taxis far more often than I did.

Tutuwari immediately chimed in, "I want to see the apóstoles too!"

"Do they live in a church like all the other santos?"

"No," Neyaucame explained. "These are the people who work for your uncle *Jesús*."

"May I go, mother, father?" he pleaded.

I looked at his parents and then to Neyaucame.

"He can come with us, but I will probably not come back here, so he will have to return with Neyaucame," I told them and we left.

Only a few blocks behind the cathedral, the National Palace, and city hall in the heart of the old city Neyaucame signaled the cab to stop.

"Here we are," he said. We piled out of the taxi. I paid the driver. It was actually no more than ten or twelve blocks from the Plaza de la Veracruz. We could have walked, but Neyaucame preferred taxis when someone else was paying, and Tuturica had had so much fun that the ride was worth the small amount I paid.

Neyaucame lifted the latch to a sheet metal door in front of us. This was a typical *vecindad* where the urban poor reside. There was just one spigot for water near the entrance for the hundreds of people that lived in this pile of colonial rubble, yet everyone seemed contented going about the business of daily life.

Tuturica and I followed Neyaucame down the passageway almost to the end where we saw two Huichol women sitting on straw mats, petates, weaving. Their backstrap looms were both tied to a stone ring that had served as a hitching post in the not-too-distant past. There was something unusual about them but I couldn't tell what it was immediately. Neyaucame looked around and went into one of the rooms through a large sheet metal door covered with the same aluminum paint as the main gate. Tuturica and I stayed outside watching the women weave.

There was a large altar at the end of the passageway that was apparently kept up by all of the residents of the vecindad with a tile image of the Virgin of Guadalupe. The altar was festooned with faded red, white, and green crepe paper, more cut paper banners, red, white, and green Christmas lights, dozens of votive candles and urns of dead flowers. In the center of the altar was a pumice Huichol altar stone, a *tepali*, with dozens of arrows stuck in it. The arrows all had bits of cloth and little amulets tied on them. They were real offerings, not arrows made for the tourists.

The Huichols here had made their own contribution to the community altar. I wasn't sure what the other residents thought of the Huichol addition to their altar, but with the incredible synthesis that has made religion work in Mexico for at least a thousand years, the arrows did not seem at all out of place. Traditional peoples in Mexico have just kept adding new gods to altars as conquerors and cults came and went.

Neyaucame came out of the building with two young Huichols who greeted us.

"Ke'aku, 'Watermountain,'" the taller of the two greeted me—they knew my Huichol nickname—"My brother here tells me that our Jesus has sent you."

Neyaucame gave me a quick nod and told me in Spanish, "They don't know where *Jesús* is, but they think that he will be here this afternoon. He usually comes before two or three with tortillas for everyone. Just say that he sent us."

Neyaucame spoke freely in Spanish and no one understood. None of them apparently spoke Spanish. I was amazed.

"Yes," I told them, "I have a grabadora, one with the snake that eats itself and speaks"—this is a fairly common Huichol term for a tape recorder—"for him. I want to give it to him. It is a payment for many things he has done."

There was something strange about the men too and finally it struck me. Though they wore typical Huichol costumes, there were no adornments on them at all. Standing next to Neyaucame with his baroque costume the two men looked very plain. They wore no earrings, bracelets, or necklaces. Their clothes were of plain white cotton *manta* with red piping around the edges. There was no fancy embroidery. They wore no capes or hats and even their belts were nothing but unpatterned light and dark wool bands.

Among the Huichol even the clothing of children like Tutuwari was elaborately embroidered. Their mothers, grandmothers, and aunts would not dream of letting even children go unadorned. Children are precious things that need adornment from the Huichol point of view.

I turned to look at the women weaving. Their clothes likewise had no adornments. They wore multiple skirts of white cotton manta with piping of different colors; plain white blouses, white cotton cloth *quechquemitls* and red printed bandanas folded over their hair. The white costumes, unadorned, made them look like nuns and priests of some missionary sect. The purity of their outfits, the white sameness, the shining colorlessness, set them off from everyone else in the compound with brightly colored cotton shifts, white shirts, deep-blue pants, checkered aprons, and patterned shawls. There was color everywhere in this backwater of urban squalor. It was alive with color, but these plain-looking apostles *Jesús* had gathered did not participate in the urban kaleidoscope.

There were no necklaces, bracelets, or earrings on these people. There was no makeup either. Huichol men and women will often put two-inch circles of bright red lipstick on their cheeks, something typical of circus clowns, but considered very becoming by most Huichols. In the Sierra sometimes my Huichol friends would glue brightly colored flowers to their cheeks. But none of the Huichols in this group had on any kind of adornment. This was very strange indeed. Elaborate costumes are almost a part of being Huichol.

A woman came out of the building and brought us two uwenis.

"Be seated," the little rounded woman told us. She was probably in her mid thirties, although I was often wrong when trying to guess age among the Huichol. Her smile was a crescent moon beneath the two dark eyes that sparkled with sincerity.

"Our brother, our Jesus has sent you and you are welcome here. Our Jesus sends few here to see us," she explained. Here in the heart of Mexico City it seemed unusual that they did not have regular visitors. All of the Huichols in my house on the edge of Mexico City had a constant stream of friends, relatives, and guests visiting. It was much more difficult for the Huichols to get to a place like my house in Leones than this vecindad in the heart of the city, but there were no visitors.

The short round woman was followed by another woman who was working on an elaborate embroidery. Neyaucame and I sat down while Tuturica sat on one of the mats watching the women weave.

The woman who was embroidering brought out a stool, an upali, and sat down in the sun.

The short, rounded woman explained that she had nothing to offer us, since *Jesús* brought their food when he came in the afternoon.

"I do have some *canela*," she said, "and that might make a good tea."

"Would you like some?" she asked.

"We would," I told her and something else struck me. Canela, which is cinnamon in Spanish, was the first word of Spanish I had heard from any of these people. I wondered if they were monolingual. Most Huichol speech is laced with Spanish borrowings, yet these people seemed to make a great effort to avoid even Spanish words common in Huichol speech.

When Neyaucame agreed that cinnamon tea would be good, the plump woman with the crescent moon smile asked one of the others to bring some tea.

Neyaucame introduced me to his "brother" who was actually a distant cousin by our reckoning. His "brother," he explained, was his father's mother's sister's son's son, which made him a brother by Neyaucame's standards. I asked if any of them were related to Pedro, whom I called "my father," and we managed to find a couple of distant family relations, which also made me a "brother" to the older woman embroidering. We had established kinship and now the conversation could go on.

Once relationships had been established everyone started gossiping. We were brought tea, which in the usual Huichol manner was almost a syrup. Sugar is, for some reason, always used to excess. While we were talking, I noticed that whenever anyone referred to *Jesús* he was always called "our Jesus." The women and even the two young men seemed to hang on every bit of gossip that Neyaucame or I had about the Sierra. The older woman embroidering seemed especially interested in gossip about anyone with whom she could establish even the most remote kinship relation.

For reasons I could not understand at first, every tidbit of gossip seemed new and interesting to these people, even things that had happened years ago. When I mentioned that Uluwari, a well-known mara'acame, had died two years ago it brought about a shocked reaction from the old woman embroidering. Then I realized that unlike most Huichols these people had been out of touch with events in their homeland for quite some time.

"How long," I asked the little round woman, "has it been since you have been to Kaluitia?" which was the region where she was born.

"Oh, a long time, a very long time," she said wistfully, looking off into space at some unseen object. "It was when we went to Haramaratsia that I left the mountains. We went to the sea with Motoapoa and Kucame to greet the Mothers. That is where our Jesus helped us to find our lives there in San Isidro. He showed us the way to make offerings, proper offerings to the Mothers there. He told us about Santo Cristo and all of his new works. How He would give us all of those things that he had given the tewalis.

Our Jesus has shown us all the path. Our Mothers will give us another Santo Cristo, who will give us all that was not given. Santo Cristo was too tired to return to the Mountains before the Virgin captured him, before she took him to live there with the women who sing him across the sky, to the place of our Mothers. He is their captive. Our Jesus sings to the Mothers to free Him so that he may return to us, so that all will be given again as it was in the beginning."

Her certain explanation made me feel uneasy. As a devout agnostic with a penchant for questioning all things, I was stunned by her sincere faith. I was sure that *Jesús* had concocted this scenario. Somehow *Jesús* offered her something, something that made her want to believe. *Jesús* was the Huichol redeemer; that was apparently how he saw himself. *Jesús* was the father and mother of this group. He was their high priest, chairman, shamanic leader, and caretaker, so they believed him.

I asked how long everyone had been in Mexico City and what kinds of things they sold to the tourists. This was typical idle conversation with my Huichol friends.

"We sell nothing," one of the young men blurted out. "We make the things that our Jesus wants. Our Jesus needs these things for the Mothers there at Haramaratsia. He brings us what we need, our food and the supplies for the things we make."

"We make all these things for the Mothers," the rounded woman interjected "and our Jesus is going to lead us singing and dancing to Haramaratsia.

"There we will give the Mothers what They want and what They need. They will release Santo Cristo among us so that He may finish His work among the people, the Wishalica."

"You are going to Haramaratsia, not to Wilikuta?" I asked. It was the time of year when most Huichols began planning their annual journey to the deserts of San Luís Potosí to hunt the peyote. Most of the

Huichols I knew did not go to the sea until after the peyote pilgrimage was over, if they went at all.

"We do not go to Wilikuta; that is not how Santo Cristo will be freed," the older woman stated flatly. "The Mothers must release him first so that he may complete his path among us. Our Jesus will take us to Guadalajara. He will drive the truck and then we will go to the sea." This seemed rather strange, as the peyote journey was such an important part of Huichol ritual activities. For some reason this was more important to them than the peyote pilgrimage.

"Those in the mountains," one of the men told me, "are those who do not know yet that Santo Cristo, if He is released by the Mothers, will come back to us with all of the things that were not given before.

"Santo Cristo was captured. He was taken by María Santísima to the place of the Mothers. It is there that he is held. It is there that he is kept. Santo Cristo is not dead. The Santo Entierro is there in the depths of the sea; that is where the Mothers hold Him. The Mothers keep Him there. They release Him each day from the Hill of the Dawn in Wilikuta and they take Him back each night into the sea, so that He cannot return to us, so that He cannot complete his creation. They do this because the tewalis pay Them. The tewalis make altars of silver and gold. They build churches everywhere for Them, for Guadalupe, El Rosario, Los Remedios, and all the other Virgins.

"If we give Them things, things that please Them, things that They like, They will release Him. We must give Them things. We must pay Them. We must do this in San Blas. We must do this at Haramaratsia. We must do this before the white rocks where They reside.

"We must ransom the Santo Cristo so that He may return to us, so that He may give us all those things that haven't been given, so that He will give us all those things that He gave the tewalis. Santo Cristo made the last creation, the most important creation, our creation, but He has not finished.

"He must bring us all the things, all of the cars, all of the airplanes, all of the moneys, all of the buses, all of the trucks that He has made for the tewalis. If we pay the Mothers properly, They will release him.

"The Kuwe Eme, the two great green venomous Sea Serpents, will dance together there in Haramaratsia and create the clouds, the fog that will envelop the world. They will obscure the Sun. There will be a new Sun. Santo Cristo will be released."

At this point the man stood up to illustrate his determination, speaking with evangelical fervor and gesticulating at the sun. He was not telling a tale but a prophecy that he passionately believed he would be a part of. The rest of this little band sat in awe of him.

Only Neyaucame, Tutuwari, and I looked at each other, not quite comprehending the significance of what the young man was telling us. The tale was so strange and so bizarre, yet it was the truth for these people. It was their Gospel, the Gospel according to *Jesús,* Mad Jesus.

"The tewalis will all be gone, the Chinos and the Negritos, Americanos, the Alemanes, the Gachupines, and the Franceses. Maybe there will be some of the Mexicans, the tewi. Santo Cristo will return and dispel the clouds, the fog. The Mothers will release Him. Then we will dance with Him. Santo Cristo will play his magic violin, and we will dance with Him into the Sierra where He will finish His creation. He will bring us all those things that he did not give to the people before. Those in the mountains do not know this. Our Jesus tells us we must not return there to the Sierra. We must not return until we return with Him, with Santo Cristo. Those in the mountains are ignorant; they do not know that we must sing and make offerings for the Mothers so that He will be released."

This was what held them together. This was what, I was sure, *Jesús* had told them. They could not return to the philistines of the Sierra, or even apparently associate with them. This was probably why this little band of Huichols clung to every bit of gossip we had about the Sierra. None of them had seen their homeland for a long time, and they apparently had little contact with the Huichol who came and went regularly to the mountains.

Now I could see the part *Jesús's* tale of his own miraculous birth on Easter Sunday played in the scheme of things. It made him an obvious prophet and messiah. He was not Jesus, in his vision, but John the Baptist in the desert, the herald of a New Age for the Huichol. *Jesús* would bring forth the new Santo Cristo. Perhaps he saw himself as the avatar of Santo Cristo. He would lead his little band back to their homeland triumphant. Perhaps he would become Santo Cristo transformed into a man-god. He would lead them to a new world in which there would be no outsiders, no tewalis, no foreigners, and only a few Mexicans.

I was beginning to feel quite uneasy. I wondered how much these people actually knew about *Jesús*. What about their Prophet's dark past? Did they know Kieli, who haunted him?

We talked and gossiped until late afternoon. These people were starved for word of their homeland. We talked about insignificant things, things that meant nothing at all. I doubt that anyone other than *Jesús* ever visited very often. They were all extremely pleasant. Tutuwari played with one of the children who was about his age.

As in the Sierras everyone went about their business while idly chattering away. The Mexicans in the rest of the compound seemed to avoid the Huichols. I don't know if it was disdain for them, or embarrassment at having to live with Indians. Though they all lived one on top of another in the vecindad, the Huichols were almost living in a separate world.

It was nearly four o'clock and *Jesús* had not appeared. *Jesús* was to bring tortillas and chilies for everyone's midday meal. I asked Neyaucame if we should perhaps go out and get something to eat. He immediately agreed; a midday meal was long overdue. I didn't feel right about just walking out for lunch, though. I suggested that Neyaucame could go with one of the women to get tortillas, maybe some chilies and some eggs, or carnitas for tacos.

It was rather strange, but none of the women wanted to go with Neyaucame. I don't know if it was due to modesty. They all seemed afraid to venture out of the compound. Both Neyaucame and I asked them where we should go for tortillas, and no one seemed to know. They obviously almost never went out. It was as if they were prisoners by choice, walled off from the rest of the world in their own little corner of the vecindad.

We asked the portera, who was in charge, so to speak, of the complex, where there was a *tortilladora*. She directed us to one about two blocks away, which, though it was probably closed for the day, would most likely still have some tortillas. She mentioned that there was a grocery store on the corner across from the tortilladora.

"*Ay, pobrecitos!* They never leave and that royal turkey, that peacock, who brings them their *taquitos* every day, has forgotten about them. Sometimes when he forgets I go out for them, or Marta over there goes out for them. Those poor little Indians don't even know how to speak properly. They are so dumb, but that's the way those little Indians are."

I gave Neyaucame and Tutuwari some money for tortillas and things. With a few pesos we could feed the entire band. While we waited for them to come back with lunch, everyone continued embroidering, weaving, and gossiping.

They all did superb work. I walked around and looked at each item that was being made. The wool paintings had already been out-lined by Chucho. His style was unmistakable. The bags all depicted flowers or birds. These were the designs that perhaps he thought were most saleable. The bead work was fine indeed, and some of the designs were unique.

As I was watching him string beads three at a time on a wire needle, one of the young men said to me almost in a whisper, "Don Timoteo, tell me where your house is and I will visit you"—this was a Huichol euphemism to ask for a place to stay. He seemed nervous and rather desperate. He was not much younger than I was at the time, but all of the Huichols, because of my beard and glasses assumed me to be far older than twenty-three. His face pleaded with me; his smooth dark skin and long black hair contrasted with his gleaming white outfit as he dipped his needle into bowls of brightly colored iridescent beads.

He was no longer a boy, but not yet a man. I felt an immediate empathy for him, caught in a bizarre world not of his own making. I remembered the communes and crash pads I frequented when hitchhiking between the Lower East Side and the Haight-Ashberry District in the late 1960s.

"Write it down for me on a piece of paper for a taxi driver," he whispered. He was scared. His eyes darted about to see that no one was watching.

This young man, whose name I didn't even know, was perhaps not a true believer in *Jesús*'s message. He was a prisoner in the world of Mad Jesus.

I didn't hesitate to give him the address as I might have with other Huichols who were just looking for a free place to stay and a new patrón to colonize. His eyes told me he was risking himself. I wondered if he would really come up to the Casa Huichol.

I walked around to the other side of the alleyway so that no one would see me. I wrote my address on the back of a card with specific directions in Spanish. I took it over to the young man stringing beads and slipped it to him so that no one would see. He put it into the coils of his belt.

I then explained how to get to my house on the edge of Mexico City with peseros from the Metro Observatorio. I doubted he knew how to use the subway. I wondered whether I should slip him some money for a taxi. Did he speak enough Spanish to tell the taxi driver what he wanted, I wondered.

I hoped this callow young man could find his way to my house on the edge of the city.

There was little I could fathom about this strange group that seemed so typically Huichol, yet so very different. None of them spoke any Spanish in my presence. I wondered whether they were all monolingual, but was sure that at least some of the men had been to the National Institute for Indigenous Peoples' schools in the Sierra and must speak at least minimal Spanish. Neyaucame and Tutuwari finally returned.

The women heated the tortillas that Neyaucame and Tutuwari brought back. They made a salsa from the chilies and chopped the hard-boiled eggs with cheese and onions for tacos. Finally after everyone had finished, I suggested to Neyaucame that we return. He agreed that it was time to go, and even Tutuwari was bored enough to leave. The young man with no name barely noticed us as we left.

Outside the great silver-painted gate of the compound I gave Neyaucame enough money for a taxi back to the plaza. I told Neyaucame that I wanted to speak to Matsiwa. As they were leaving Tutuwari asked me, "Don Timoteo, is that true what they said about Santo Cristo? Will he return to our people with all of the things that were not given?"

Neyaucame answered the boy, "It may be true, but it may not be true. What tales say will happen may be true but things may not happen in just that way. Your uncle tells them this is all true, but I am not so sure about it."

He and Tutuwari walked to the corner and caught a ride. I wondered what they would talk about in the taxi.

I just wanted to wander around the old city. I needed time to think
about that strange group of people. I started walking vaguely toward
the Zócalo. These people were believers, followers of *Jesús*'s strange ways.
Walled off in their little compound, they were both physically and
socially isolated from other Huichols. They seemed to live in a world
of their own, economically and socially controlled by *Jesús*. They
believed that *Jesús* had some kind of a solution for all of their problems.
They believed in *Jesús*'s strange message. What was his message really?
What kind of redemption did he offer them? I was troubled and thinking about the young man without a name. Would he come up to the
house on the edge of Mexico City? Did he have the money for a taxi?
Where would he go? Probably to *Jesús*'s brother if he could find him.
I wondered if Neyaucame had told him where Matsiwa was in the Plaza
de la Veracruz. Though the plaza was only ten or twelve blocks away,
for a Huichol lost in the city it might as well be on another planet.

I was so lost in my own thoughts in the crumbling backwaters of
the old city that I barely noticed a Huichol walking toward me. The
traffic and belching buses obscured him as he walked toward me then
darted through traffic to my side of the street. It was *Jesús* in all of his
finery, walking straight toward me as if he owned the street. What would
I say to him. He had obviously seen me. I wanted to hide behind the
woman with a *rebozo* walking in front of me, but I couldn't. *Jesús* bore
down on me like a hawk. I waved and greeted him in Huichol.

"Ke'aku, I have been looking for you. I have your tape recorder," I
told him.

"Where is it? Give it to me!" He demanded right there on the street.

I did not have it with me, I explained, and of course he would have
to finish his story, I told him.

"Well it is finished. I am going to the sea and I want my tape
recorder!" he demanded.

I could leave it with his brother, I told him, or I could leave it with
the Huichols at my house on the edge of Mexico City, though I really
didn't want him going up there. I didn't want him coming over to my
apartment alone to pick it up either. I was very cognizant of Luís's

warning now. I was going to Puebla for a few days anyway, so that was out of the question.

"Do not give it to my brother," he said. "He will keep it. I need it now! Bring it to Don Enrique, Enrique Croft." He reached into his bag and gave me a card from Enrique Croft with a telephone and address.

I vaguely knew Croft. He was a dilettante Englishman, second-generation Mexican who lived just off Avenida Reforma. He was a some-time artist who was more interested in being seen at all of the openings than producing anything himself. He bought quite a bit of Huichol folk art and paid top dollar. He apparently had family money. He was never engaged in any type of gainful employment that I could remember. He must be one of *Jesús*'s patrons, I thought.

Jesús's eyes stared through me, through the beaded pendants that hung from his broad-brimmed hat. The red-felt cross on its crown and the red piping around the brim blazed in the late-afternoon light. I could barely see his shaded face through the brightly colored beads, but I felt his gaze like the sharp sun beating down on me. His eyes glared and he looked away. He never looked at anyone thing too long.

"Where are you coming from?" he demanded. His words were accusations spat at me.

He would know shortly that I had been to the vecindad to see his little band of followers, but I decided to be vague. There were too many people out and about on the streets for him to create any kind of problem. After all I could simply walk away.

"I have been looking for you," I told him. He was carrying a large shopping bag of tortillas, which I was sure was for his followers. I didn't know whether to mention that I had seen the people who worked for him.

"Good, then get me that tape machine. I will be at Don Enrique's tonight," he said.

"I want it now! Go get it!" he demanded, hissing like a serpent.

He frightened me. I turned and left to look for a taxi back to my apartment.

I would get him his bloody tape recorder, drop it off with Enrique Croft, and be finished with this lunatic.

a brother's tale

As I got into the taxi I thought once more about the young man stringing beads, the man with no name, and I told the taxi to take me to the Plaza de la Veracruz. I would give Matsiwa some extra money for a taxi for the young man just in case he managed to find his way to the plaza.

Matsiwa was there with Tutuwari and his wives. They were diligently trying to finish their things for the day before it got too dark to work anymore. There were no lights to speak of in the refectory hall. Matsiwa looked up from his work and said, "They're going to the coast and *Jesús* wants his tape recorder. He went to your apartment, but you were not there. He was really simmering mad when he got down here. I told him that you were looking for him but that didn't seem to cool him down much. I didn't tell him that you had gone with Neyaucame and my son to see his people. How could you spend all afternoon with those apostles of his? I thought you were just going down there to find out if *Jesús* was there. *Jesús* doesn't like anyone hanging around with his people. I hope he doesn't get crazy on you."

"Well," I hedged, "we just shared tortillas down there with them."

"And," in a low voice I told him, "there is one of them who I think wants to leave. I gave him my address and told him how to get up to the Casa Huichol. That is what I came here to talk to you about, I don't know if the boy has cab fare to get up there. I would like to give you some money in case he shows up here."

"I'm not taking that," he said sharply. "Those are his people.

He will come after them like he did in Guadalajara. He will come after you too, if you help them.

You had best be very careful and get him that tape recorder fast. He is not going to leave without it. Just hope he leaves soon, or he is going to get crazy again. Then you really will have to be careful."

"You were going to tell me about Guadalajara," I said. "How about telling me on the way to my apartment to pick up the tape recorder." I figured this would be as good a time as any to hear what happened to *Jesús* in Guadalajara.

Given Matsiwa's warning I wanted to know what happened in Guadalajara. I also wanted him along in case *Jesús* was there waiting for me. This whole situation was becoming too ominous for my taste.

I didn't understand why he would refuse to help the young man with no name.

Once I got the tape recorder to him I would be rid of *Jesús*, I thought; or rather, I hoped, at that point. I had had enough of this crazy character and his demands. If it took a tape recorder to get rid of him then that was what I would invest to absolve myself of Mad Jesus. I planned to leave for Puebla the next day.

Before we even got out of the refectory Matsiwa began hurriedly telling me about Guadalajara: "When *Jesús* arrived we did not know what had happened in San Isidro. I wasn't really sure about what happened until the other night at your apartment. All we heard was that Pedro had disappeared. Some of the people said that my brother had 'taken care' of him, but I never believed them.

José's death is a different matter. José was a witch and whatever *Jesús* did to him, he deserved," Matsiwa observed with cold determination.

"The old man was a wretched witch," he added spitting the words out with disdain.

"The two children I never knew about, but the one that is still alive, the crooked one, still says it was José's witchcraft that killed his sister and made his mother hang herself. And that is the truth.

Even if what my brother says is true it was still José who must have placed the evil arrows," Matsiwa told me as we walked through the courtyard of the monastery.

"We didn't know about Pedro's disappearance until months after *Jesús* arrived in Guadalajara, but my brother sure finished him off there in the swamps around San Isidro. *Jesús* was really crazy when we first saw him. But even then he had already been at the mission for a couple of months. He was going to be a priest.

When he got to Guadalajara he went straight to Zapopan to that crazy priest there, Padre Cerillo. The padre knew where to find me, but he told my brother he didn't know where I was. He bought all of our work for the mission store and he gave us all our supplies, so he knew where to find us all right. The old padre just liked my brother. He let *Jesús* stay with him in the mission. He thought *Jesús* was quite a handsome young bird. That is what he called him, his *perico guapo*.

That fat priest never offered me a place to stay there with my wife. I was with my first wife there, Shuricame. Our son, Nicolás, was not a year yet. We had to find our own rooms near the mission." He told me all of this as we crossed the Alameda.

We hailed a taxi in front of the Alameda Park on Avenida Juarez.

"What was this priest like?" I asked Matsiwa once we were in the taxi in order to keep him going on the story.

"I have never met him, but all of you talk about him. Can you describe him for me?" I asked.

"Well, he was a *barbón,* he had a big beard like you do, Don Timoteo, but his beard was thick and black with two streaks of white on the cheeks. Though balding in front his hair was a rough black. His face was dark and weathered, set off by a shiny pate that was usually sunburned. He was fat, a *gordón*"—Huichols called anyone who was not totally emaciated fat. It seemed to be almost a term of respect rather than an indication of someone's weight, more like calling someone a big man, or great man. "He was a strong, powerful man who spoke a funny kind of Castillano. He always wore black, but he carried Huichol bags, brightly colored bags. He was almost as tall as I am, " which meant that Padre Cerillo was just about 5 feet tall, "and he walked with a slight limp, but he rode a horse like a cowboy, and when he was outside of the mission he usually carried a gun, or had his *pistoleros* with him.

He could be a mean character, but he liked my brother.

This old padre was a tough one.

He bought *Jesús* all kinds of things. He bought my brother all of the materials that he needed.

Like he did with all of his boys, he made *Jesús* study the *Evangelios* with him. They each had to study individually with the padre an hour a day and they all had to go to Mass everyday. *Jesús* learned the Evangelios. My brother learned to recite the Gospels from memory. He liked San Juan and San Marcos the best. He learned the prayers of the Mass too. *Jesús* was already a *cantador*, so the padre had him sing in the choir. *Jesús* can still say the whole mass just like the padres do and he can still sing all the songs.

He had been with the padre for a couple of months before I even knew he was there. Why, when I saw him my brother was almost a padre. *Jesús* even got to wear a long black skirt like the padre.

Sometimes the padre punished him by taking away all of his Huichol clothes and locking him in a dark little room. I suppose that was when my brother got crazy.

He heard Kieli there, *Jesús* said, when he was locked away, at night, when he was in his room—he had his own room there. The Whirlwind sang to him, even when he was in the church. He must have been crazy then. He was always crazy when the 'Evil One' sang to him. The Sorcerer told him to flee, but he resisted.

He did everything a padre would do, he prayed, he sang, he recited the Gospels, but Kieli kept singing to him. He kept telling him things; that the padre was evil, and the church belonged to the Huichols; that Santo Cristo had cheated the Huichols; that the gachupines and tewalis had bought Him off. If the People could give Santo Cristo all of the things that the tewalis gave him, then Santo Cristo would give the Huichols all that was created by the Mothers and Fathers. That was what *Jesús* said.

Jesús was working in the shop next to the church when I first saw him. We went up to his room there in the mission. It was the first time that I had ever been inside the mission. He was a little crazy and he wanted to talk.

He told me something about San Isidro and the woman María. I thought she may have been his wife, but he said she was not. She was more like his *patróna*. *Jesús* said nothing about that one named Pedro.

He liked it there with the padre. He said there was plenty of food and he didn't need a wife so long as he was there.

When that priest found out that *Jesús* was my brother he became much easier to deal with. He gave us things too and let my wife bring Nicolás to the shop with her. Cerillo would baptize him for us, he said, but we told him Nicolás had been baptized in Tenzompa. Antonino and his wife were my *compadres* at the baptism, and I thought because of that Nicolás would become a mara'acame like Antonino.

Jesús stayed with the padre almost half a year. The Evil One kept telling him to leave, but he resisted.

It was when my wife became ill that he left the mission. That was when all the trouble started. Shuricame was weak and she kept on bleeding. *Jesús* came to care for her.

He was a mara'acame. He had become a mara'acame there on the coast. Everyone knew he would someday be a great mara'acame. He tried to cure her, but nothing worked. She kept on bleeding. *Jesús* chanted and used his movieli. He said she needed the blood of a deer and the waters of our Mothers to fortify her. I bought the blood of a deer from other Huichols and waters of the five directions. Nothing helped. *Jesús* kept on singing.

My brother was a mara'acame, a good mara'acame, but he could not cure my wife. She died. We should have sacrificed a bull. I know that would have made her better." Matsiwa's words hid a whimper in his voice.

"Nicolás, our little one, was too small to be without a woman. I could not care for him. *Jesús* said that we should go to see that woman of his, María. We took little 'Colás to San Isidro and there were his people there, his apostles. They received 'Colás well there, but he died a year later.

It was that María woman of his who took him. She gave him to another." Matsiwa was choked with emotion, but he continued. He was beginning to weep in the taxi.

"Colás, 'Colás, 'Colás," he muttered, softly shaking his head. "That María was not his mother and those apóstoles did not care for my son. I should have never have left 'Colás with them. But my brother said they were good; they were his family and they would care for him. I could not care for him. I had no one there. 'Colás would never have survived the trip back to the mountains.

When we took 'Colás up to San Isidro some of those people of his came back with us, a woman, her husband, and that woman of his, María. She was his woman, but not his wife. That brother of mine found lots of other women, but for just one time. He never kept a woman. The only one who would stay with him was that María and she was a tewali. Sure, she dressed Huichol and she was even learning to talk like 'the people,' but she was not a Huichol. I told *Jesús* he ought to go back to the mountains and find a wife, but he never did.

Some of those people from San Isidro came back to Guadalajara with us. They were my brother's family, his charges, he said. *Jesús* told them of Santo Cristo. He told them of the Gospels, the prayers, the chants he had learned. He wore the black shirt of the priest. Kieli and Santo Cristo spoke to him. He was a priest and a mara'acame, they said.

Jesús brought those apóstoles to Guadalajara to make things for him to sell. At first we tried to sell everything to the padre, but he was furious with *Jesús*. He wanted *Jesús* to come back to the mission. *Jesús* had told no one we were leaving.

Padre Cerillo wanted to make my brother a priest, but he was already more than a priest. He was a mara'acame. Those people of his knew that.

Jesús and that woman of his took our things to Puerto Vallarta, Tepic, Manzanillo, and Mazatlan when the padre would not buy our work. That priest told him he would starve if he didn't come back to the mission.

Jesús and that woman of his, María, were very smart though, they sold all of our things.

While *Jesús* was gone, the padre kept coming to visit to see if he had returned. He told us that *Jesús* had stolen all of our things and that he would not return. He said my brother was a wicked young man and a thief. We had no money then, so the padre bought a few of our things and he told the apóstoles to come to the mission. He fed them there and he gave them a place to stay. They started working for him and making things at the mission.

When my brother returned he had plenty of money, but he was furious that the padre had stolen his apóstoles. Kieli was speaking to him.

The padre was evil. He was a thief. They were his people, those apóstoles, and the padre had stolen them.

He spoke all night to the Whirlwind. He was crazed when he went
to the mission. I don't know what happened there, but he was beaten
and thrown out. He made his way back to our place bruised, bleeding,
and staggering. They said he smashed things and attacked the padre.

That night the gunmen came to me looking for *Jesús*. I told them I
had not seen him and then we fled. He was on the roof laid out from
the beating. We went to a ranch on the edge of Guadalajara with some
other Huichols so that the padre's pistoleros would not find us. My
brother was so badly beaten that we had to make a litter to carry him
out to that ranch on the edge of the city. He was getting crazy singing
of Santo Cristo and Kieli. We had to tie him down.

Jesús finally calmed down, and we released him. He was still crazy
though. He disappeared again. None of us knew what had happened
to him.

There was trouble over at the mission again, and two of his people
who were there disappeared. Maybe they fled after he went there, but
I don't know what happened to them.

Jesús went to San Isidro. When he came back he told me, "'Colás
died.'" He had the boy's soul with him, his ulucame."

We had arrived at my apartment. I paid the taxi and got out onto
Calle Nueva York. Matsiwa's warning was well taken. Great gray and
purple clouds tinged with pink were illuminated by the sun's last rays.
The grackles and starlings flocked to every tree up and down the street.
They were vying for position, staking out roosts for the night. There
was a potential for real trouble.

I never saw the callow young man with no name again. I don't know
to this day whether he ever left Mad Jesus.

çuapaLajara mapness XXXI

We entered the compound and went up the stairs to my first-floor apartment. There was obviously more to the Guadalajara story. Matsiwa sat down in one of my big colonial chairs with shocking Mexican-pink cushions. I rummaged through the closet for the recorder I was going to give *Jesús*. It was beginning to get dark so I switched on some lights. The lamp *Jesús* had broken was still in the corner.

I had three cassette tape recorders. I would give *Jesús* the largest one with a radio in it. I asked Matsiwa if he wanted a beer and went into the kitchen to get one for myself.

"Well, what else happened in Guadalajara?" I asked Matsiwa while handing him a beer.

"There were a lot of things that happened in Guadalajara. I didn't stay long with my brother though, he was just too crazy. *Jesús* had real money when he came back. He arranged for a bull sacrifice for the Mothers. He brought the souls of my wife and my son together. We tied them to arrows and we put then in a shiriki there on the ranch on the edge of Guadalajara.

Jesús sold all of the things that we made, but he was afraid to take them to the stores in Guadalajara. He was constantly going back and forth to the coast; that was where he sold things. He was afraid that the padre's pistoleros were still after him. He sold plenty of things. But it wasn't until he met the Germans that everything changed.

The Germans bought everything that we made, and we could not make enough for them. *Jesús* got all of the young men that belonged to the padre to help us. He paid them more, and the padre became very angry!" Matsiwa said.

"You tell me the story while I put the last of these tapes on cassette for *Jesús*, then we will both go down to Enrique's and drop this stuff off for your brother."

"I'll tell you about the Germans, but I am not going down to Don Enrique's. Why, if that brother of mine even thought that I knew Don Enrique, he would say that I had stolen his patrón."

"But you already know Enrique, don't you?" I asked. "I have seen him at the plaza several times buying things."

"Yes, of course I know who he is, but I don't go to his house to sell things, at least not very often, and never when *Jesús* is in town. It is like with the Germans in Guadalajara. They bought things from me even after I left *Jesús* there, but those people were his patrones. They were his people. *Jesús* would have been furious if I had brought them things and made things for them.

The Germans found out about *Jesús* from Don Raúl in Mazatlan and they came to San Isidro to look for him, but he was in Guadalajara. María came with them from San Isidro. She brought them to us there on the ranch.

They were a very strange pair, both yellow blond. They looked sick. They were pink and burned by the sun. Don Hans was very tall, taller than you are, and he was a little bit bearded, just around his mouth. It was a funny little beard almost white and not too long. His woman, Katarina, was tall and round with long yellow hair. She spoke better Spanish than Don Hans.

María said that those two wanted to buy everything that we could make, everything that we had, and they bought everything. They bought it all!

They asked *Jesús* to make more things for them. Every month they went back and forth to Europa. They bought all kinds of things, and we could not make enough for them.

María went back to San Isidro and had the others there making things for the Germans. They wanted bags and earrings and bowls, belts, arrows, and wool paintings. They bought us materials and they paid us very well too.

I went with *Jesús* several times to their hotel in the center of Guadalajara. Don Hans bought us aguardiente, the good stuff, real tequila, when we brought him things. Sometimes we got really drunk with Don Hans. That woman of his got really drunk too. Katarina liked my brother. They were always together. They went to the market together. They bought wool and beads together. *Jesús* was spending more time at their hotel than he was on the ranch. The Germans are very strange, very strange indeed.

Each month Hans and Katarina would return for all of the things that we made. María and the others bought things in Tepic and San Blas, but we still did not have enough to give the Germans everything they wanted.

Some of the others came down from San Isidro and stayed with us on the ranch outside of Guadalajara. That was when I knew that I could not live there any more. My brother kept all of the money and he spent it on offerings and ceremonies. That was all that he spent it on. We barely had enough to eat. There were just tortillas. I still made some things for my brother after I went back to Zapopan. Finally *Jesús* agreed to let me have half of what I made like he does now. Whenever he makes the designs he takes half of the paintings.

Jesús dreams the designs for his paintings. He is a real mara'acame and he makes the designs the way the Mothers and Fathers show him. He sees things in dreams and he makes the designs. His paintings are the way things should be they are much better than the ones that I make."

For some reason Matsiwa had always deferred to his brother as an artist even though his own style was a vibrant mix of symbol and story. His designs were more elaborate and more highly patterned than his brother's. What *Jesús* did was in some ways more primitive. *Jesús* seemed to prefer figures, where Matsiwa covered his paintings with stylized objects and symbols. I, in fact, had always preferred Matsiwa's style. And I had purchased a number of his works. I only had one painting that *Jesús* had made. It was of Kieli. *Jesús's* work was often more sinister, somber, and threatening than his brother's. Matsiwa's work always sold better than his brother's.

"The people who worked for him then were not like his apóstoles.

He didn't really have his apóstoles yet. The ones in San Isidro were the most like his apóstoles, but he still paid them something. He pays those apóstoles of his nothing. They don't work for my brother; they work for the Mothers. They are trying to pay them off to bring back Santo Cristo. That is what *Jesús* tells them, but he takes all of the cash and he sells everything. My brother just pays them with tortillas."

I still didn't understand how *Jesús's* little band worked, so I asked Matsiwa, "You mean your brother gives those people of his nothing?"

I was nearly finished copying the tapes and began putting things away. Matsiwa got up and went to the window. He looked out into the dark courtyard and turned to me.

"*Jesús* gives his people nothing. He brings them food and finds a place for them to stay. He buys all of their materials and takes all of their work. He sings for them," Matsiwa said cynically.

"*Jesús* sings of Santo Cristo. He tells them Santo Cristo will return and there will be no more tewalis, so they all work for him. They think that they are paying off the Mothers to release Santo Cristo, but they are just paying my brother and that woman of his in San Isidro. Those two are really making it. They are rich," he declared sarcastically with more than a twinge of jealousy.

I had finished making the tapes. I asked Matsiwa if he would like to come with me at least as far as the Reforma. It would be much easier for him to get back to the plaza from there and I wanted to hear the rest of the Guadalajara story.

I took the recorder and put the tapes into a Huichol bag. I threw in some blank tapes for *Jesús* and a few tapes of Huichol music, to boot. We walked out onto Calle Nueva York and started hunting for a taxi.

"What else happened in Guadalajara?" I asked Matsiwa. "You said something about the padre and pistoleros, no?"

"Well, that Padre Cerillo came after us a second time and he went after my brother again, too. *Jesús* stole his boys, he said."

We got a taxi just before arriving at Avenida Insurgentes.

"I would wait out in front of the shop at the cathedral and when I saw them bringing things to sell I told them, 'Bring those things here, brother, sister. I can pay you more than the padres.' Some of the other padres there at the mission kicked me out, but I went back almost every day. Some days I would sit in the plaza across from the church. There were always hundreds of people visiting that church.

Maybe *Jesús* was right, the tewalis just paid Santo Cristo more so they got everything from him. The tewalis went to visit Santo Cristo all of the time, every day, not just during Holy Week.

Every time I saw some of our people I went up to them, and some of them came to stay with us. *Jesús* came into Zapopan about once a week and he started to tell all of those people who were staying with me about Santo Cristo and the Mothers. He told them that if they went to the sea with him and made offerings they would be blessed, they would have more cattle and more children and their corn would grow, and they would be helping Santo Cristo to return. Every time *Jesús* went to the sea he would take some of the people with him, and some of them would go to San Isidro with him too. My brother taught them all how to make things. They all worked for him every day.

The ones he didn't pay, though, were jealous. Some of them left. Some went back to the mountains, but others went to the padres. Some of the boys went back to Padre Cerillo. They said they didn't have to work as hard for the padre if they studied with him every day.

People came and went. They all learned to make things and some of them went off on their own to sell what they made to the turistas. This made *Jesús* furious. He threatened and beat them when they returned. Some of them left and told the padres all about this.

I was out in the plaza one morning waiting to see if there would be any of our brothers and sisters going to the mission when Padre Cerillo himself walked out of the church and straight over to me. He looked mean, all dressed in his black robes, and he came straight at me.

Cerillo was angry. He told me to get out of there and not to come back.

He said, 'You tell that brother of yours that he had better be careful. He's not *Jesús,* our Savior, and he had better not tell those poor Indians that he is the Santo Salvador. Our Lord is here in the church and nowhere else! The people who come here are my people, our people. They make things for God, not your pagan gods and goddesses, mothers and fathers, grandmothers and grandfathers.'

'What we sell here is for God. God helps you poor Indians. Jesus Christ is their salvation, not those gods and goddesses; and not your brother! If he keeps taking these people away from God, we will take care of him. Our Lord is Jesus Christ, not your brother *Jesús!*'

'He's going to get it, if he says he is our Lord!' and he made the fingers on both hands into guns that he started shooting with in a fury. Bang! Bang! Bang!

Cerillo turned and walked back to the great iron gates of the cathedral. Just before the gates he turned and shouted at me, 'You be careful! And tell that German couple to be careful too. If they know what's good for them they had better come to see me.'

I went back to our place there in Zapopan and told the others about the padre, then I went out to find my brother.

Jesús was not at the ranch on the edge of the city, and I was told he had picked up everything that everyone had made. He must have been going to see the Germans.

I went to the center of town to the hotel where the Germans stayed. My brother was there with them. He was singing and dancing with the German woman, and Don Hans had a fresh bottle of tequila. I told my brother about the padre, but he and Don Hans both said that the padre was just trying to scare them. He was jealous, they said, and could do nothing.

'We've got a good business here, a good *negocio.* That padre just wants the money,' Don Hans said and poured tequila for all of us.

Then the two men came to the door. Hans thought they were from the hotel so he told us to go into the other room. Perhaps we were making too much noise, we thought.

Katarina came back and told us to get out of there, that these were the cops. But my brother was sure they were the pistoleros from the padre. We climbed out of the window and onto the roof and escaped.

'Damned priest!' my brother said. He was sure it was the padre that sent the mordilones, the cops, to the room. We saw them taking Hans and Katarina out of the hotel. They had all the things that we had made with them and probably all of the money, too, because Hans had not paid my brother yet. We were ruined.

I went back to the mountains. I think that *Jesús* went to San Isidro.'

We were just turning onto the Reforma to Enrique's as Matsiwa told me this. I wasn't sure if all of this was actually the padre's doing, but it sounded like someone had denounced the Germans and had them deported. *Jesús* was definitely out of business there.

Matsiwa got out of the taxi, and I continued on to Enrique's.

enGLISH enRIQUE

Enrique Croft, born and raised in Mexico, was a thoroughbred Brit. An aesthete and sometime artist, he rode with the Mexico City Hunt Club, which was where I first met him. Enrique was a product of the British schools and social life in Mexico with an anglophile family.

Gaunt with sandy hair and dark eyes, Enrique seemed the quintessential Englishman. His family had a ranch in Tlaxcala, a couple of hours outside of Mexico City where they bred and trained horses. Enrique's grandfather had originally come to Mexico to build railroads to the rich mines of northern Mexico, and his father had textile mills in Tlaxcala, but so far as I knew, Enrique had no interests except being seen at the proper openings and receptions. He had no political or religious convictions and seemed about as bland as his sandy hair.

I told the cab to let me off on the Reforma and found a pay phone in the Sanborn's in front of the Angel, the great column of Mexican Independence. I called Enrique to let him know I wanted to drop off some things for Chucho. He was pleased, but told me that he didn't think that Chucho was in at the moment. He invited me over for a short drink anyway.

I walked down the Paseo de la Reforma a few blocks to Enrique's apartment, wondering what Chucho was up to. Few of the great *ahue-huete* trees planted at the time of Emperor Maximilian remained along the Reforma and the trees that had taken their place were all showing signs of stress from Mexico City's constant traffic and pollution. The great stone benches and tiled walkways of the Reforma were still alive though with people coming and going, or just taking an evening walk. I wondered just how much Enrique really did know about Chucho as I walked down the Reforma.

Enrique's apartment was on the ground floor of a twelve-story building. The only lights in the whole building were in Enrique's apartment. The darkened edifice was a looming grey building of no discernible architectural style. It appeared that Enrique was the only tenant. His was the only name on the buzzers at the front door. It seemed rather strange, but I rang, and he buzzed me in. Through the darkness the only light in the building came from under Enrique's door. Twelve stories of darkness hovered above Enrique.

When Enrique came to the door I realized that I was seriously underdressed in my usual jeans and a shirt. I thought that he probably had guests. Enrique was wearing an Oxford tie and a tweedy sport coat that was obviously British. I told him I just wanted to drop off the tapes and recorder for *Jesús*, but he insisted that I come in. There were no guests; we were the only ones there. This was apparently Enrique's casual wear around the house. Enrique was drinking whiskey, he said, but since I was not a Scotch drinker, I asked if he had any sherry.

We sat in the large living room, which was furnished with great overstuffed chairs, a long sofa, and English antiques. The staid English furniture was in contrast with the multicolored scintillating Huichol wool paintings, arrows, votive bowls, rough altar stones, and embroideries that hung everywhere. Enrique had quite a collection of Huichol art, some, but not all of it, from Chucho.

Enrique showed me some framed embroideries and a deer skin quiver with finely made arrows that his grandfather had acquired. Around the turn of the century his grandfather helped build the railroad through El Catorce in the heart of the Huichol Magic Peyoteland, Wilikuta. That was where the arrows and embroideries had come from, Enrique told me.

We talked for some time, but there is little that I remember of the conversation. It was mostly about other expatriates living in Mexico, about the riding clubs and the perennial problem of finding good servants.

Enrique told me little about Chucho, but there were two things that stuck in my mind concerning him: first, that Enrique helped Chucho sell most of his artwork; and second, that he actually knew very little about Chucho. Enrique didn't know anything about Padre Cerillo, or much of anything else in Chucho's life. I was not about to tell him what I had learned of Chucho's story. Enrique would have probably booted the poor man out right there.

The building, which was owned by his family, was undergoing renovations. This was why there were no other tenants. Enrique and his maid were the only ones there besides Chucho, who had a room on the roof. Twelve stories of dark vacant empty space separated him from Chucho. If he had known much about Chucho, twelve stories of darkness would not have been enough to keep him safe from *Jesús*. Enrique did not strike me as a particularly brave, or foolhardy soul.

It was nearly ten when I told Enrique that I would leave him with the tape recorder and tapes. He said that he had heard something while we were talking and thought that Chucho had returned. He suggested that I go up to the roof before leaving to see if Chucho was there.

Dark City Lights

I made my way through the darkened hallway and took the elevator up to the top floor. I began to climb up the rickety steel staircase to the roof. There were no lights. I heard someone distinctly chanting in Huichol.

Chucho was there. I would tell him that Enrique had the tape recorder and be finished with the matter.

As I reached the roof the wind caught me and I held tightly onto the staircase in the darkness. There was a long row of rooms. It was completely dark except for a brightly burning fire at the far end of the passageway. All the rooms had at one time been painted, but the weather and sun had left nothing but rough concrete and stucco covering them.

It was definitely Chucho singing somewhere at the end of the row of rooms, probably in front of the fire. I listened to the song. The language of a Huichol shaman's song is extremely difficult to understand, even without the noise of Mexico City.

The songs of a shaman are long, drawn out, repetitious, and very strange. I caught a word here and there. The flames flashed along the little passageway. They did a sinister little dance against the walls and on the weathered doors. It would have been better if I had gone back down the steel staircase and never seen Chucho again, but I didn't, and he awaited me. His song drew me on.

It was a song about Santo Cristo and the creation, or it sounded like the Huichol version of the creation. It was a strange creation indeed. The ontology of a different world: Chucho's world.

As I walked down the crumbling concrete passageway in the darkness past the rickety doors—thirteen doors total, one for each of the twelve floors and one for the portera—I listened carefully to Chucho's low chant. Flames were leaping out of a large bucket at the end of the passageway, but I could not see *Jesús* in the darkness even as I approached the twelfth door.

Chucho must have been right around the corner chanting in the repetitious drone of a mara'acame. It grew louder as I approached the final door. I could imagine he had before him his wands of power, his movieli, his medicine bundle, his takwatsi with crystal souls, hair and bones of animals he had seen in dreams, and other strange things. I could imagine him sitting there in an uweni, wearing his most baroque costume and staring off into blank space with peyote visions swirling through his head.

I came out of the dark narrow passageway to the blaze of Mexico City all around me, on one side the golden angel atop the floodlit monument to independence, on the other, Chapultepec Castle where Maximilian and Carlota had lived. Below the castle the gleaming white marble monument to the Niños Heroes, the cadets of the military academy who leapt to their deaths from the castle rather than be captured by invading U.S. Marines, and Diana the huntress leaping from a fountain of light. Tall buildings above and below gleamed in the darkness, dwarfing Chucho's fire in an old paint bucket.

Chucho was seated just as I had imagined him with his movieli and takwatsi laid out before him. He had the glazed look of someone in a trance.

I walked over to where he was seated, ducking below laundry lines held aloft by flimsy sticks strung all across the back half of the building's roof. He was about 3 feet from the fire, chanting, looking into the flames as if he didn't even see me. I walked to within about 4 feet of the blazing bucket. The entire back half of the roof was open. There were laundry sinks on one side and a low wall, less than 3 feet around the rest of the roof. Chucho just kept on droning out his song among the glittering lights high atop his precipice in these urban canyons. I was trying very hard to catch as much of his song as I could. I crouched down to listen.

He paused, looked up at me, and asked, "You like my song, Don Timoteo? Do you understand it? I am singing of the Mothers and of Santo Cristo. It is a tale that I am sure you have never heard."

He was right. I had never heard anything like his song.

"You are almost a mara'acame, would you like to help me sing it?" he asked. His voice was soft, sly, and almost patronizing, otherworldly and enticing.

I could not refuse. I agreed to help him sing the song, to answer the final two lines of each section. He put some more wood on the fire, and I began feebly to help him sing that song.

It was not just a song, but a mythic tale told in a precise and very repetitious way. At first it made no sense at all, but after answering section after section it became a myth, a subliminal tale, a picture, that moved through my mind. What I really remember of it is a set of whirling images, not the constant repetition.

The song told a tale that went on like this: "The two great Sea Snakes of creation, the Kuwe Eme, writhed in the rocks off San Blas at Haramaratsia until the sea boiled and the rocks were shrouded in fog. The four primordial Mothers of the Huichol convened and began to discuss what must be done about this Mother Guadalupe, the one who brought forth Santo Cristo, the fifth Mother who would not heed their command to attend this discussion. 'This Santo Cristo had not finished his work. He had cheated the Huichol and yet she kept him from returning to the people and completing his destiny. Why was this?' they asked.

"The Mothers called on Their Grandmother, Takutsi Nakawe, to send forth Kauyumali to search for Guadalupe. Kauyumali searched the four sides of the world to no avail, and the Mothers sent him back a fifth time to search all the waters of the world. He found her at a spring in Tepeyac on the edge of Mexico City, but she refused to leave her home, claiming that the Mexicans gave her all that she needed and she had no desire to see her poor Sisters, the other Mothers. The Mexicans were now her people. Kauyumali brought this message to the Mothers, and they conferred with each other once more. 'Perhaps it is not Kauyumali but his evil brother who will bring her forth,' they said. They called forth Kieli."

As I became tired and began to miss my lines answering Chucho, he handed me some peyote to ward off the drowsiness. I peeled off the rough outer bark of the root, took off the little white tufts of fur, broke it apart, and began to chew the foul little cactus. The acrid, bitter taste alone woke me and slowly my mind began to follow Chucho's song in a thousand different directions. I was no longer tired; my mind danced with every word that Mad Jesus sang.

The tale in his song continued: "The Mothers sent forth Kieli to search for Guadalupe and trick her into attending their discussion. He searched the four sides of the world and tried to trick the Mothers with images of Guadalupe. Finally they sent him into the sea and told him not to return without Guadalupe. He returned with Santo Cristo instead, but it was really the Santo Entiero, the dead Santo Cristo, who could do nothing. Kauyumali appeared and told them they had been tricked again and they banished Kieli back to the cliffs that he had come from. 'Mothers,' Kauyumali said, 'This one, this Guadalupe, will not let Santo Cristo walk this earth again. Send another *Jesús*.' The Mothers conferred with each other. This was a good idea, they determined, but this new Santo Cristo must be of both our Sons, Kieli and Kauyumali, they decided."

The song was much more than the second coming of a Huichol Christ. It was the end to repression; a new Huichol world where men, women, Fathers, and Mothers shared the earth. It was a hope for the world as it ought to be.

"The Mothers sent forth both Kieli and Kauyumali to search in each of the five directions. After a great search and many trials they found the one who was to be the new Santo Cristo."

At this point *Jesús* stopped his song and shouted into the burning darkness.

"I am He!"

Jesús picked up his Huichol violin in front of him and began to play. He leapt from his seat and began to dance the up and down, bouncing peyote dance and called to me to join him.

We were both bouncing up and down, dancing around the bucket of flames as *Jesús* threw all of the remaining wood into the fire. Dawn was not far off. The lights of the city had dimmed. The effects of the peyote were beginning to wane.

Jesús quit playing and picked up a piece of fatwood. Shoving it into the fire he turned to me with a glinting grin and said, "Come, you must see what is for our Mothers here." We danced thrice more around the blazing bucket, bouncing up and down, Chucho carrying his flaming fatwood torch. And then we danced toward the passage way. The exuberance of the peyote dance was hard to stop once the jumping motion had begun.

Just around the corner, inside the passage way, *Jesús* stopped. He handed me the flaming ocote, the fatwood torch. Fumbling through one of his shoulder bags he found a set of keys and removed a tiny padlock from the door.

"Loooooook!" he told me, drawing his word out with a singsongy intonation and a diabolical grin.

I thrust the torch into the little room, which was filled floor to ceiling with boxes of different sized and shapes, bolts of cloth, plastic bags of brightly colored yarns, gunny sacks of beans and chilies. It looked like he was starting a general store.

"What is all this for, Chucho," I asked him "Your store?"

"No, no, no, it is for Them. It is for the Mothers. It is for the Virgin. It is for Him to return. It is for the vows I made to Them."

"Tomorrow I have a truck and we will take all of this to Them, to the Mothers at San Blas. Kieli and Kauyumali have asked me for these things. I am the one, the one whom they sought, the one whom they commanded, who they spoke to. All this is part of my promise, part of my vow. It is what They have ordered. It is what They have commanded. I am their new Santo Cristo."

In the chanting voice he said, "Take offerings and gifts to the Mothers of the West, so He will be released, He will walk this earth." And then he continued.

"It is so that He will return. It is so that the other Santo Cristo will grant us what is rightfully ours. He will return with the Whirlwind, the Tempest, the Hurricane that will flood the land of the tewalis, that will cover their ranches with water and will inundate all of them. Kieli will bring Him to us with the winds that will rip their ranches and houses apart. Then Santo Cristo will live among us and grant us all of those things that were promised. We will build him a great shrine a great church there in Santa Catarina with all of the tewali gold and silver.

Santo Cristo will live among us and protect us as a father and mother to all of the people. He will come! You will see!"

Jesús was truly mad, but his insane scheme made sense to him and to his followers as well. *Jesús* had gathered together more miscellaneous goods than any store in the Sierra.

"Why don't you start a store with all of this," I naively suggested.

"No, no, no," he cried out pulling the door shut and fixing the lock, "This is for them; this is what the Whirlwind has told me to bring them. He will not stop singing. He sings to me all the time. He finds me wherever I go and he begins singing his evil songs again. I try not to listen but he has been sent by the Mothers and I must do this, or he will never stop. Perhaps if he hears that tape recorder of yours speaking, speaking with my voice, he will mistake it for me and leave me alone.

Come, we must dance before the dawn, before the sun shows his face here, before the Whirlwind must depart," he said as he danced back to the fire.

Jesús picked up his violin again and began to play as we danced. Up and down, back and forth, around the fire bucket we danced. The flames were slowly dying as the first birds began to cry out for the dawn's light. Cocks began to crow; someone on a nearby building obviously kept chickens, or perhaps some prize-fighting cocks.

The peyote was still affecting me. I could see trails as Chucho danced up and down. We bounced across the rooftop in the dark city lights as dawn approached with the undulating patterns of flowers, colors, and lights all blending together.

Then he shouted out, "Tatewali," the name of the old fire god, "Our Grandfather," and took a giant leap over the fire. I followed him, jumping over the bucket, but then he jumped up onto the low wall around the roof with the same up and down peyote dance and danced on the crumbling bricks twelve stories in the air with nothing between him and the ground. I danced next to him hazarding just a glance over the edge. Little lights illuminated the garden of the home below. From our perch it looked like a doll's house.

Chucho twirled around and jumped back on the roof.

"Yes, a mara'acame," he shouted, and we danced around the fire again.

As we neared the wall again he shouted at me "Dance like a mara'a-came," and he pushed me toward the wall. I was terrified. I didn't know what he was going to do. Chucho shoved me roughly to the wall. I turned and fell on the roof. He grabbed my shoulder.

He was a powerful man for his size. He pulled me up and shoved me toward the wall. Half way over the edge I could feel myself begin-ning to fall. I swung around and grabbed Chucho's arm ripping the sleeve of his shirt and pulling myself back on the roof. Chucho was shouting incoherently something about dancing between light and darkness, life and death, earth and sky.

My blood ran cold as my heart pumped out adrenaline. I ran toward the passageway, the low clotheslines caught my throat and flung me to the roof. I got up and began to flee in a low crouch, but Chucho tack-led me and again began pulling me back to the edge of the roof. I was easily twice his size and threw him off of me. I got to my feet and kept on toward the passageway. Just as I got to the first door he shoved me again. I fell to my back, ripping a deep gash in my arm.

He was coming after me again. With both feet I caught him, lifted him into the air, and threw him against one of the rickety wooden doors. His body shattered the rotten door.

I pulled myself up and ran to the steel stairway. Tumbling and trip-ping down it.

I heard *Jesús* on the staircase. He was shouting something at me. "Damned tewali!" or something like that. I was shaking. He was going to kill me. I couldn't wait for the elevator. I began running down all twelve flights of stairs in the darkness, tripping and stumbling. When I got out of the building, I couldn't think of where to go.

Chucho knew where my apartment was and that would be the first place he would look for me. I didn't think that he knew the Casa Huichol, but I didn't want to explain what had happened to the other Huichols. I just didn't want to see any more Huichols.

I couldn't stay in Mexico City. I was too afraid of what Mad Jesus might do. I ran all the way out to the Reforma. By the time I got there I had managed to stop the bleeding on my arm. I flagged down a taxi and told him to take me to the bus station to Puebla.

I took the first available bus to Puebla. As the bus roared out of Mexico City the sun was beginning to rise and as we reached Rio Frio I could see the pink rays illuminating the snowcapped volcanoes. I was free of Mad Jesus, I thought.

But it was impossible to escape from Mad Jesus. His story kept coming back to me. It came in bits and pieces, his tears, his apostles, the man with no name, the women in white.

I dutifully transcribed and summarized the tapes, but could not really make sense out of his story.

What I wrote was a dark tale about a man driven mad, stalked by the sorcerer Kieli, a murderer, a drunk, a thief; not a prophet for his people, a charismatic leader, a cultural broker. The book was never published. It was not *Jesús* anyway that I was writing about in 1974. It was my own fear of him that bred the black tale of murder and sorcery, the man hunted and haunted by Kieli.

There were bits and pieces of his tale in an article about urban Huichol artisans, in an article about *Solandra*, the botanical form of the sorcerer Kieli. There was a piece I never finished about drug-induced schizophrenia for a psychoanalytical journal.

Several times I started to work the Mad Jesus story into an academic treatise, but each time I got little beyond the outline stage and an incoherent first chapter. I never could make sense out of Mad Jesus, yet he still haunted me.

Gradually I put the tale in the back of my mind and filed the notes and tapes away. I could never quite forget the roof in Mexico City. Mad Jesus was always there lurking in the back of my mind, haunting dark twilight thoughts wherever I was.

part III

RESURRECTING

JESUS

tHe DeatH of Jesus

INDIOS NARCOSATANICOS screamed the headline from a yellow-bordered clipping sent by a colleague with Mexico's National Indian Institute. It had to be about Mad Jesus!

A glance at the clipping from one of Mexico's most notorious scandal sheets brought on a feeling I hadn't had for years. Mad Jesus rarely entered my mind these days.

Miguel's hand-written note simply asked if this could have possibly been the same Huichol I had interviewed years before.

It was! Just the by-line told me that: Francisco Mendoza y Tello, San Isidro Tepetitla, Nayarit.

According to the article a cult of drug-crazed Indians led by a Huichol messiah calling himself Jesus Christ had terrorized the small town of San Isidro for many years. "Upon hearing of murders and even possible human sacrifices in the cult's compound, police surrounded the area. For days there had been rumors of licentious debauchery, drunkenness and sacrifices. Officers said that the leader of the cult and his wife, one María Ibañez, were carrying arms when accosted by police and were shot on the spot by trained sharpshooters. Other armed members of the cult put up serious resistance to investigating officers. The fight lasted several hours, but eventually surviving cult members fled. Six men, five women, two children and one infant were killed, including the cult leader and his wife." The body count was quite authoritative.

The article went on to say that considerable quantities of narcotics were found in the compound and two recent graves of what were obviously sacrificial infants were also discovered. Officers speculated that other graves found in the compound were also of the cult's victims over the years. For all the details, the sensationalistic journalism of the scandal sheet provided little real information and almost no names; not even the name of *Jesús*. Only María had a name.

A cult with a nameless messiah, a narcosatanic cult, an Indian cult: the words strung together the collective fears of the unknown. But what was a cult? Tim Leary and the Millbrooke estate? I had hung with Tim's ill-fated daughter there. The communes and "families" of the 1960s with their gurus and dealers, the drug-laced agglomerations of lost seekers: the Bear Commune, the Family Dog, the Hog Farm. Were these cults? There was something far more menacing about the idea of a cult post Manson, Jim Jones, and David Corresh, more menacing than the impish lunacy of Tim Leary or Richard Alpert, who become Baba Ram Das. Over the years I had counted Jesuits, Zen masters, and high Tibetan reincarnations among my close friends and mentors, charismatic and inspiring souls, but none of them cult leaders. Mystery cults and cargo cults, satanic cults and saint's cults, secret cults and covens, ashrams and monasteries were all a part of that specialized knowledge of the initiated. I had delved into this realm too.

In the 1970s, a kindly old sorceress in the remote Sierra de Puebla in Mexico had initiated me into the tradition of her ancestors. It was the tradition of small groups of trained practitioners, dreamers, who owed allegiance to a *tlamatini* few had ever met. The cells of this tradition spread to Texas and California and as far south as Nicaragua. I still bear a burden of service to this tradition, and I practice it to this day. In a way it is a cult like the communes and ashrams of the Haight or the East Village, but so different. And *Jesús,* had he become a messianic cult leader, or was it just his name that implied his messianic status? The messiahs who proliferated under Roman occupied Judea were a reaction to cultural tensions. Perhaps there was an analogy to the Huichol in the twentieth century. There was more, so much more, I had to find out about *Jesús* to make sense of his tale, especially after seeing that yellowed clipping. What was he for his followers, and what did he represent for the others who eliminated him?

It was then that I began to dig through my files and tapes for the story of Mad Jesus. Much of my professional library had been destroyed in 1989 when a cold snap burst the pipes in my office behind the kitchens in the Auberge des 4 Saisons. Fortunately, I was able to find most of the original material, and the pieces all began to fit together. But what had happened in the ensuing eighteen years between the time I last saw Mad Jesus on that rooftop in Mexico City and his assassination by Mexican police? Was there any way to reconstruct, or resurrect, the story of Mad Jesus?

I looked over the material and tried to listen to the tapes again, but they were garbled with hiss and print through from years of not having been regularly rewound, and from heat and humidity. My notes, transcriptions, and summaries represented a nearly incoherent mass of jumbled information with differing interests and points of view. The manuscript of *Mad Juan* that I had written in 1974 was dark and sinister tale of a schizoid deviant. It was not Mad Jesus. What came through constantly was the memory of *Jesús* as a person, weeping, shouting, furious, mad, chanting, dancing, and caring for his flock.

He was no longer the nightmare for me that he had once been. There was a man here, troubled, haunted, and, yes, more than a bit mad. He was violent, fearful, possessive, and harried by the spirits and memories of his homeland. He had forged a vision of a new world from the troubled history of both himself and his people.

The *Jesús* I had known was a far more complicated person than the "narcosatanic" leader portrayed in Mexican scandal sheets. It was then that I sat down for the first time to really try to piece the story of Mad Jesus together, to determine what I knew of him and what I didn't know. How could all those pieces make a coherent story?

It was almost a year before I finally had an opportunity to visit Mexico for an academic conference. Meanwhile, I kept the Mad Jesus files in the bottom drawer of my desk, puzzling over them, piecing together what I could of his life history, trying to make sense out of the man. I began to write the tale of Mad Jesus chapter by chapter, draft after draft.

When I got to Mexico I started asking colleagues if there was any solid information about the assassinations on the coast of Nayarit. A few had vague recollections of having seen something in the *Excelsior,* or in *Proceso,* but there was no exact information. I would have to start digging through newspaper morgues.

But before I did that, I wanted to see what the notorious Huichol gossip network could tell me about *Jesús.* The Huichols were not difficult to find, even among the twenty million souls inhabiting Mexico City. A few questions in the *artesanía,* folk art, markets that cater to tourists led me to a small group of Huichols from Santa Catarina at the Ciuadela market.

Walking through the stalls draped with clothing, serapes, belts, and leather bags decorated with Aztec calendars and lined with tables of silver from Taxco, copper from Michoacan, and talavera ceramics from Puebla and Guanajuato, I finally saw masks covered with intricate Huichol designs of beads pressed into wax, bracelets and earrings in the Huichol style. The Huichols were there, all right.

I asked where the Huichols lived and was directed to the workshops on the far side of the market. Two women in full Huichol costume were sitting in front of the workshop, so it was not hard to find them in the labyrinth.

"Ke'aku," I greeted the two women.

I introduced myself and asked to see some of their work, but there was no recognition.

I told them that I had spent much time in the Sierra and even mentioned a few of my friends from the Sierra, but there was still no recognition.

Finally I said, "In the Sierra they called me the 'Watermountain.'"

And before I could finish the sentence the woman called out to the rest of the little band, "Miguel, Tutori, Tomás! Come out here! The Watermountain is here!"

Even after more than twenty years I was recognized by my Huichol nickname. That was not unusual, though, for in the Sierra people talk of Lumholtz, Diguet, and Zingg as if they had visited the remote region only a short while ago.

"You may not remember, but when I was just a girl you were lost in the mountains in a terrible rain storm and you came to my aunt's ranch. She wasn't going to let you in. She thought you might be a witch or something, but as soon as we saw you drink all that water we knew you were the 'Watermountain,'" the woman told me.

"You are the son of Pablo, which makes you a grandfather for me and I think a brother for Neyucame here," she said, introducing me to the young man who turned out to be her husband. His name was Miguel Tello in Spanish, but Neyucame in Huichol. He was a "brother," which actually meant a not-too-distant cousin in our terms, of my friend Neyucame in the Sierra also.

I heard all the gossip from the Sierra. We talked through morning.

Miguel and I went out for tortillas. His wives, he explained, didn't have time to make tortillas. They were too busy making things to sell. I heard all about the ups and downs of the folk art market over the last twenty years; the comings and goings of dozens of families from the Sierra; the latest gossip about drunken brawls at Huichol religious festivals in the Sierra and a friend's wife who had run away to Ciudad Juarez and became a very successful artisan. I had asked several times about *Jesús* but got no response. No one apparently knew him.

While we were out, I asked about *Jesús* again.

All Miguel said was, "If you want to know what happened to that one, you should ask that brother of his." And that was the end of the conversation about *Jesús*.

I suspected they simply didn't know anything about *Jesús*. I thought I had hit a dead end with the Huichols in Mexico City. It was time to start combing the newspaper morgues.

In Mexico City the newspaper morgues proved almost useless. What information there was on the assassinations in Nayarit was buried on back pages, fragmentary and often highly inaccurate. Oftentimes the incident was not reported until almost a week after it occurred. There was little specific information in the newspaper reports and a lot of sensational filler concerning the strange practices of this "cult."

Narcosatanic cults were quite popular at that time, probably creations of police, media, and popular culture; all of it preying on people's fears. Depending on the political slant of the newspaper the police were either saviors of a town terrorized by drug-crazed Indians, or brutal murderers of poor, oppressed natives.

In order to arouse the interest of police there must have been actas, documented complaints, denunciations, some kind of official records. Especially in Mexico this kind of incident always leaves a paper trail. The big problem, though, is getting at the documents. Documentation can usually be found through friends in high places, or a few well-placed bribes to clerks and secretaries.

I knew that there had to be a police report on the incident, but how to get hold of it was the problem. The police involved in this incident were under the direct control of Procuraduría General, the Mexican Attorney General's Office in Mexico City.

Uniformed Mexican officials produce in me a visceral fear; a trip to the Procuraduría was like a visit to the dentist for a root canal. I prepared myself for the ordeal by getting out my old identification from the National University and getting a letter of introduction in case I needed it. I put on a rather dumpy-looking academic suit I had brought and I was ready, I thought.

Entering the offices of the Procuraduría I could immediately see that the only kinds of people there were police, lawyers, and their *coyotes,* the low-paid assistants who wait in interminable lines for official documents to actually be produced.

All of these types chill my bones. They're like jackals waiting for someone else to kill, so that they can gobble up all the tasty remains. At the reception I explained that I was there to look up specific details of a case that had happened several years ago. Logically, I was directed to the Archivo Historico, the archives in another building.

The public office of the archives was in the basement of a great gray concrete building. Under sharp florescent lights, the chaos was total in that basement room. I tried for what seemed like an hour to get the attention of one of the clerks. Lawyers, coyotes, police, and clerical workers came and went, some getting immediate service, others waiting interminably like myself.

I finally asked a clerk who seemed to have nothing better to do than file her nails what I would need to get a particular file. My stupidity and utter ignorance of proper procedures within the bureaucratic maze disgusted her. She looked at me like I had just asked her to lick up the trash on the floor. She warmed a bit when I showed her my university identification card—a professor, it seems, was an oddity here. She explained that I would have to fill out a *solicitud,* a specific request with the location of the incident, date, crimes involved, and names of those involved and then come back in two or three weeks to see if anything had been located.

"I don't have two or three weeks," I tried to explain.

But the woman with a 1950s-style beehive hair and makeup so thick it seemed to flake off when she spoke replied indignantly that it would be two or three weeks minimum once I had filed a formal request just to find out if the documents were available and whether I could be authorized to see them. She handed me a form, and I went over to one of the long desks to fill it out with every detail imaginable, including my mother's maiden name.

There was a young man with a large bundle of files making notes on them and checking them off against a list on the letterhead of a Mexico City law firm. He was obviously their coyote.

"How does this place work?" I asked him. "I need some papers today and the lady at the desk is telling me that I can't have them for two to three weeks."

"The one to see is Rosa, the fat one over in the corner. She usually gets me anything I want, but it takes a little cash," he said rubbing his fingers together.

"If it is not something real important, half a C note in a file folder like this with your solicitud," he said showing me how to fold the bill to make it just barely visible, "if it is a lot of stuff, or it is really important, you'll need a whole C note." A "C note" was only 100 pesos, as little as 10 dollars.

I finished filling out my request, put 100 pesos into the file folder, and went over to see Rosa, who seemed to be overflowing from every piece of clothing she had on. I told her that her friend had suggested I see her.

"Oh, which one?" she asked.

"The handsome one over at the desk," I told her.

"Ay, Raúl, he makes so many promises for me," she said as she looked over at the young man and waved, batting her long artificial lashes and smiling.

"What can I help you with, professor?" I had my I.D. card on top of the file folder figuring it wouldn't hurt. "We don't get many profes-sors here."

I explained to her what I needed, the dates and location of the inci-dent, and told her that I would really appreciate if she could arrange for me to get the files today.

She looked at my request rather quizzically—noted the 100-peso bill—made a few annotations on the form, and said she thought she knew someone who could find it, if I came back after lunch when there weren't so many people around.

I thanked her profusely and asked what time I should come to see her. About four was fine, she said.

I went out to a local cantina for a long lunch and returned exactly at four. About quarter of five Rosa walked in, rifled through some papers and signaled me to come with her as she walked out of the building.

"Ay, you picked a hot one," she said. "No one is authorized to see this kind of stuff."

"I could get it, though," she told me coquettishly, "but it would cost you."

"How much?" I asked.

"At least a grand," she said. "I would have to pay someone else to get it and then you would have to pay for the copies too."

That was more than 100 dollars, and I explained to her that I just didn't have that much, that I was just a poor university professor, not some big-time lawyer.

"Well, then, maybe you can get it from someone else; there were lots of copies made." She rambled off a half-dozen government offices that had copies of the report and finally she mentioned an institution where I at least knew some people.

That was it! Rosa had earned her 100 pesos. The name of that one office was all she had to say. I had enough friends, colleagues, and former students there that I was sure I could get a copy.

I thanked her profusely and apologized that I couldn't afford a copy of the file for my research.

"Well, anytime you need anything else here, you know who to come to," she told me fluttering her gaudy overly made-up eyes like some kind of coquettish whale.

fiLe of tHe DeaD

I decided to stop at the offices of the government institute Rosa had mentioned on my way back out to the south of the city where I was staying. Those files were essential, and I had to figure out a way to get a look at them. It was impossible to know what happened without them. In my mind I was already turning over different ways to get a look at the police reports. Having been out of Mexico for so many years I wasn't quite sure who was still with the institute, or in what capacity they worked there. I needed to find someone in a very high position there who would be authorized to request things like police reports from the archives.

I was just a year too late, because one of my former classmates had been the director of the institute under Mexico's last president. If I couldn't find anyone in the institute, then perhaps he could still help me get a look at the reports.

There was no hope of finding anyone I knew there at that hour. No one in of any importance in a government office, or for that matter at the university, or anyplace else, ever comes back to work after lunch. With luck though, I might be able to get a copy of the directory so that I could look it over that evening to see who I still knew there. Even if I could get a copy, I doubted that it would be up to date. But with luck there might be a few names of people I could call to find out who was with the institute.

The offices of the institute were slightly less active than a morgue. There was one bored-looking guard sitting at the entry and no one in the offices, so I decided to see what information I could get out of him.

"Excuse me, sir," I said, "but I am looking for a former student of mine here." I explained that I had been out of Mexico for many years, but that I had worked for the National University.

"Well, not much of anyone here now," the guard said. "You'll have to come back tomorrow."

I explained that I was staying with friends on the far south side of the city and it would be difficult to get back to the institute tomorrow. The guard started to give me the general switchboard number of the institute and I thought I was sunk.

"Wouldn't you possibly have his direct number there?" I asked. "I think he has a direct line."

Having a direct line meant that he was someone of importance in the institute and the guard immediately became more helpful. I explained to him that the person I was looking for had come in under the former director, Raúl Chanticler.

"His name was Miguel, Miguel Mendez, I think," I said, picking a very common last name.

I decided to play the befuddled gringo professor to get a look at the directory. I told him it had been so many years since the young man had been my student I wasn't quite sure of his name and that I always confuse paternal and maternal names since we only use paternal names in the United States. It worked!

I did manage to con him out of his copy of the personnel directory at least for a little while.

As I looked through the directory I planned out just how I would get to look at a copy of the Mad Jesus file. I made a quick list of names of people I knew who were in the directory. I had a couple of former students who worked there, and several students of former colleagues from the National University still worked there.

Phone numbers were essential. The friend I was staying with, Maricela, might be able to help. She was one of the *grandes dames* of Mexican anthropology and knew just about everyone. When I got to her place I asked her if she might have names of several people who might be able to help me. She was a gold mine of information and her black phone book was just what I needed.

I made several phone calls that night to friends and colleagues, asking how I might be able to get the information I needed, sometimes being rather vague about what I was actually after. They were all very helpful, especially Josué Mendel, who was a very astute student of Mexican political anthropology, that is, the politics among anthropologists. His advice about whom to talk to, and how much to tell them about what I was after was invaluable. All night my mind was churning. I needed more information about what was going on at the institute.

The next morning I called Raúl Chanticler, who had been the director of the institute under the last president. Maricela's little black book was the key. Raúl had been one of my classmates at the National School of Anthropology. He had been one of her students there too.

He was one of the young turks of Mexican anthropology at the time, a radical leftist and romantic revolutionary. Mexico's little communist cells were much too conservative for his taste at that time, but Raúl had mellowed over the years. His positions were always very astute, radical, and well reasoned. He had shown himself over the years to be a superb scholar and an adept politician.

The Mexican government has a unique system of co-opting its radical opposition by offering members ever-more-potent political positions. Raúl was now a subsecretary in the Secretariat of Public Education's office. I hadn't seen him in almost twenty years.

I wasn't sure he would even remember me. I explained to his secretary who I was, and she put him on immediately. He was busy all morning, but I suggested that we meet for a drink later. Raúl suggested a favorite cantina we had frequented as students. I wanted to hear what had been going on in Mexican politics and I knew Raúl would be a primary source. I had been almost completely out of touch with Mexico for more than ten years.

I got down to the cantina El Cairo early. The place had changed. The ornate carved painted bar with so many layers of lacquer and enamel on it that there was no telling what color it was, had been replaced with a new Formica one. And two of the turn of the century frescos of dancing Egyptian goddesses were gone. All that remained were their gold art nouveau curlicues along the ceiling. They had been hacked out to make room for the women's restroom. Now that cantinas admitted women, this was a necessity. There was no longer water flowing through the trough under the bar either.

When Raúl walked in I recognized him immediately. His sharp clipped features and short cropped curly hair were recognizable anywhere. He was almost as gray as I was. It gave him an authoritative air. He was dressed impeccably. I noted the gold and lapis cuff links, quite a change from the jeans and shirts that were de rigueur in our student days. We were both very much out of place in a working-class cantina.

"How are you doing, man!" he said to me and gave me a big *abrazo.*

"I'm a chef now," I told him, "but I am looking for some information about some Huichols."

"You and those Huicholes, eh."

"You missed more classes with all those trips up to the Sierra than anyone at the *Escuela.*"

"Well, there is one Huichol in particular I need some information about," I told him.

"He was some kind of Huichol messiah," I said.

I explained to him what I was looking for and showed him the file of newspaper clippings I had assembled about the assassination of Mad Jesus.

He had heard of the incident. It would be difficult to get a look at those files, he said. I asked if Martín Lários, who had been a student of mine, might be able to locate them. Martín Lários worked in the legal bureau at the institute, and I knew that he had been one of Raúl's protégés there. Raúl agreed to give him a call on my behalf, because if anyone could locate the file it was Martín.

Raúl was a font of information not only about Mexican political anthropology, who was in and who was out, who was doing what, and the politics among anthropologists in Mexico, but the unseen side of national politics.

In a way, I missed the Byzantine gyrations of working in the political sphere, but I had been absent from Mexico for so long that it would take me years to learn the ins and outs of the Mexican political maze again. I was spellbound, talking to Raúl after so many years. My radical classmate was now a real player in Mexican politics.

Raúl was an authority on rural peasant movements. We both knew that those movements did not materialize out of thin air. Many of our colleagues in anthropology and rural sociology had been involved with such movements and there were dozens of regions where similar movements could easily crop up. Raúl was doing his best to see that they didn't, moving local teachers and potential peasant leaders around like so many pieces on a chess board.

"You take the ones from Guerrero and move them to Aguascalientes," he told me.

"Then you take the ones from Veracruz and move them to Chiapas. That way none of them become familiar enough with one town or region to cause any trouble. That way they all see aspects of the problems, but none of them see the whole picture."

"It's been the policy since the Revolution," he said.

"That way demands are specific, regional, and easily satisfied. It's all very easy."

"The same way," Raúl went on, "your Huichol may have had a lot of problems, but which one, or which combination of events, may have gotten him killed, you may never know. It may have been everything at once, or nothing at all. Maybe, just some trigger-happy cops!"

We went on talking until quite late, then went out for a bite to eat before I went back to the south of the City.

I made an appointment the next morning to see Martín, assured that Raúl would tell him what it was about.

Martín greeted me with a big abrazo after I made my way through the institute's rabbit warren of offices and ushered me into a little cubicle stuffed with unkempt files.

"You really asked for a hot item," he told me after he had closed the door.

"I can't really let you see this," he said flopping a large legal size file onto the desk, "and I can't get you a copy. This was apparently a rather delicate matter. Even the president's office asked for a summary. That's on the top. The file has all the actas and the complaints as well as the police report. There is a rather poor report by our director in Tepic, but you probably know more about this Huichol Jesus than any of us. Raúl said you had a whole life history from him, and that he was a pretty dangerous type."

"He was," I agreed and gave Martín a quick outline of what I knew about *Jesús*, including the murders and the fact that he had almost thrown me off of a building.

What I really wanted to know, I explained, was what had happened in the nearly eighteen years between when I knew him and his death.

"I don't know if any of this will help you because all of the Huicholes fled after the police attack, and we apparently made no effort to find out anything more about the incident.

The director up in Tepic simply assumed the cult was dead. No one seems to have heard anything about a messianic group since then either, so maybe the director of our center there was right."

"I can't let you see the actual file, and as far as we are concerned it no longer even exists. But I've got another meeting now that Raúl scheduled," he said winking at me.

"Come down to my office when you are finished."

I spent the next four hours poring over the file. There were poor copies of crime-scene photographs, including one purported to be of *Jesús* sprawled on the ground, arms outstretched with ominous black stains that were obviously blood, all over his body. His face was unidentifiable.

He was referred to just as *"El Líder."* The authorities probably never even knew his full name, just as I had never known his Huichol name. The body counts from the newspapers were correct.

According to the report there were no wounded or hospitalized survivors. I wondered if the survivors who didn't escape were simply executed, but there was no way to tell from the photographs, or the cursory coroner's reports that simply said "killed by gunshots."

There were eighteen officers listed as participating in the raid on the compound. I noted each name and identification number. I had hit gold! This was the information that I needed.

The actual police report was only a few pages. Follow-up investigations were equally cursory. No one apparently really wanted to know what had happened there in San Isidro.

The actas, complaints, and denunciations that led up to the incident were far more interesting to me. There were dozens upon dozens of them, beginning as early as 1971. Complaints by local residents usually began in the spring, the time of the Huichol rain festivals, and centered around noise, drugs, drunkenness, all-night ceremonies, and so on. Some of the complaints were absolutely fantastic, like the one filed by a lady who complained that the devil the Indians invoked had caused her cow to quit giving milk, but most of the complaints were probably reasonable.

There were other complaints, however, that were much more ominous. As early as 1972 Padre Cerillo, in the name of the Franciscans, complained to the authorities in Guadalajara about *Jesús* claiming that a false Christ was preying on poor Indians who sought aid in the Franciscan missions. The padre portrayed *Jesús* as a charlatan and a con man who prevented Huichols from entering the church. There was a whole section of complaints by prelates, parish priests, and Catholic laymen about the false Indian Christ, including four more complaints by Cerillo himself.

These may have been what provoked action by authorities. After the revolution the Catholic Church was an anathema in Mexican politics, but for the last twenty years there had been a softening of the hard line between church and state in Mexico. As in any political relationship, the church and state often scratched each other's backs and combed out the mutually bothersome lice, which may have included *Jesús*.

There was a crude map of the compound with x's and numbers where each of the bodies was found. Only one of the men was identified, that was *Jesús, El Líder,* and one of the women, "María Estér Ibañez Calderón, native of San Isidro." The remaining victims were known in the report only as Indian Man one, two, and so on. Both of the children were found near women who were apparently their mothers. It was a gruesome scene to imagine.

At the end of the report was a list of the various government ministries that had been sent copies. The list was quite illuminating.

I closed the cubicle door and walked down to Martín's office. That file was deeply troubling. He was busy for a few moments, the secretary told me, so I waited, walking through the bloody compound in my mind.

Why, after so many years, I wondered, had the police finally decided to act and why had the attack turned so bloody?

Martín finally came out and asked me if I had found everything I wanted. I was lost in thoughts of that sunbaked compound with bodies bloating in the tropical heat.

"Yes," I told him, and he insisted I come into his office.

"The report is pretty gruesome," he said, "isn't it?"

"I just had a few minutes to look it over, but I hope you found what you were looking for."

I had found most everything, I told him.

"But why?" I asked, "Why did they finally go in there after so many years of complaints?"

"I think it was political," Martín commented. Everything in Mexico was ultimately political, so that was no information at all.

"How do you mean?" I asked.

"Well just look at the list of offices that got copies. There is more to this than what is in that report. This is not something that happened just because a band of Indians was causing trouble in a small town. They could have just arrested them all and we would have sent them back to the mountains. Usually it just takes a warning and maybe a little intimidation."

"Maybe it was the money they were after," he said.

"What money?" I asked, "I saw no mention of any substantial quantity of money in the report."

"You know that kind of thing just disappears in reports, then into someone's pocket, but I remember that there were several million pesos involved and a local *cacique,* a strongman, got the house and land."

"Now that is interesting," I said. "Do you know anything more about the incident that might help?"

"Unfortunately, no," Martín replied. "But just remember you never saw that report. If you mention it you will be the next one on the cops' list. They are quite adept at giving people a very hard time. You wouldn't want to be thrown in the can here."

tracing the path of jesus

XXXVI

The report did not bring me any closer to understanding what had happened to Mad Jesus and his cabal of followers. Death visited them so suddenly. How had this little cult aroused such draconian official ire? Was it an accident, or was there something far more menacing about *Jesús* and his band of followers? The only way to find out anything more would be to go up to northwestern Mexico. In preparation for the trip, I started making my lists of people who might be able to shed some light on what had happened to Mad Jesus.

First, there were the Huichols who might know something about the incident. Although I thought I had struck out with the Huichols in Mexico City, perhaps there were some of the followers of *Jesús* who had escaped. Maybe the Huichols in Guadalajara, Tepic, San Blas, or Tuxpan would know some of them. Next, there were the priests and prelates. Padre Cerillo was high on my list. There were so many complaints from him that he probably knew quite a bit about the incident. Then there were the police. I would start on the bottom with the *comandancia* in Tepic and work my way up, I thought. It would probably be easier that way. If I couldn't get any information from the police in Tepic, I could go to Guadalajara, and if I couldn't get any information there I would have to go back to Mexico City, but if they refused me information in Mexico City, I couldn't keep on prying at lower levels either without considerable risk. Then there were the people in San Isidro who must have known something about the incident. There was a lot of digging around to do and not many more weeks to do it in before I had to return to upstate New York for the beginning of the summer season.

Guadalajara was where I would have to begin my search. I took an overnight bus from Mexico City and found a small hotel in the heart of the old city. The old city was just a speck in the vast urban sprawl that was now Guadalajara. *Jesús* and his little band would have meant nothing to the millions in Guadalajara. Why was his little cult singled out?

The Zapopan Mission was my primary goal in Guadalajara. That was where Padre Cerillo was based. I went out to Zapopan almost immediately in the morning. The plaza was immense and recently renovated. The baroque church dominated it completely. This was the home of the Franciscans who had taken over the missions after their archenemies, the Jesuits, had been expelled from Mexico in the eighteenth century.

The Franciscans were the first missionaries in Mexico. They came behind the *Conquistadores* in monk's cloth and sandals to baptize the heathens, atone for the sins of the conquerors, and found a millennial Christian kingdom in this New World. They did not succeed. The politics of European Christendom and the King of Spain intervened.

The Zapopan Mission was a monument to Franciscan persistence through the politics and history of Mexico. The imposing friary had been the hub of missionary work in Mexico for centuries. The store for Huichol folk art was on one side of the church and the cloister on the other.

I went to the cloister and asked about a Padre Cerillo, but at first no one had heard of him. I was invited to wait in the courtyard with its murmuring fountain and fragrant orange trees. Finally a Dutch Franciscan, who spoke excellent English, came out and told me that Cerillo had been transferred to Brazil almost three years ago.

I wondered if his transfer had been due to his predilection for Huichol boys, or his use of pistoleros on his missionary forays. I thanked the Dutch friar and left, wandering the side streets overlooking smoggy Guadalajara.

I spent the evening in the cantinas listening to *mariachis* and took the late bus to Tepic. At dawn the bus pulled into Tepic, and I found a hotel where I could leave my things. There were any number of Huichols in

Tepic who might have known Mad Jesus, but I was more interested in the police. I had the name and I.D. number of every officer who had participated in the final shoot-out at María's compound. Why had federal police been involved in what was a decidedly local matter?

The federal police barracks on the edge of town were forbidding: a complex of low tan buildings with no redeeming features surrounded by a high wall capped with razor wire. It made me shudder.

I went in to the main desk, but there was no one there at first. Finally a hefty woman in a uniform that made her look like a man came out from behind a frosted-glass partition. She was annoyed to have to wait on someone at the desk. Her lipstick and rouge were excessively red on her dark skin. Her thick black short-cropped hair had the look of a motorcycle helmet. I began to explain what I was looking for and showed her some university identification, but she cut me short.

"All right guy, let me see that list and I'll tell ya if they're here." There were no formalities with this lady.

She took a quick look at the list and said, "There's only one of these jerks still here and that's Rodriguez. He's not on duty now but ya can probably find him at the Cantina Paraíso 'round the corner suck'n down a brew. As for the rest of these jokers, some of them were here when I signed on but they're all gone now."

"Any idea where they could be found?" I asked taking a 50-peso bill out of my wallet and putting it into the file folder with the list.

"I can check the records but it's not gonna do ya much good. See, we had this fire 'bout two years ago, but maybe the captain'll know. He's been here longer than anyone else. I'll ask him. Ya wait right here."

She disappeared behind the partition. I heard some doors opening and closing and then heavy footsteps.

"C'mon in, tha Captain'll see ya," she said, motioning for me to come around the desk. She led me behind the partition to a corner office where I could hear an air conditioner groaning to get rid of the early morning heat.

She opened the door and announced, "*Capitán* this is the guy, the professor, or something from the university, a doctor. . . ."

"Nava," I said because my name is almost unpronounceable in Spanish and Nava is the closest approximation.

"A pleasure, Dr. Nava," the white-haired old man behind the desk said, getting up and extending his hand to me. He was quite a contrast to his receptionist, very formal and dignified. His uniform was precise with several decorations I couldn't recognize.

"I am Capitán Miguel Ángel Miriles at your service."

"Now, Carmela here, tells me that you are interested in some men who have served here."

I explained about the incident in San Isidro that had involved some Indians getting shot and told him I wanted to find out just how dangerous those Indians really were.

"Yes, that was that Indian Christ down there. We had plenty of complaints about him, but never any real trouble, then those two from Mexico City came around with the others from Guadalajara. They had orders to get him out of there they said and send him back to the mountains. I gave them about twelve of my men and they sure got rid of those Indians. The Indians wouldn't leave and I think that about four of them got it. That was unfortunate."

The captain put on his reading glasses and looked carefully at my list. "Gomez, Martinez, Fierro, and Santos left the force four years ago. Gonzalez and Aldama are in Mazatlan, and these other two, Corona and Cedros, are bodyguards in Guadalajara. The others, these two," he said pointing to the first two names on my list, "were from Mexico City and these two were from Guadalajara." He said pointing to the next two.

"They were a little trigger happy. Thank God none of my men got hurt."

"Rodriguez is the only one who is still here, and Carmela said that she already told you where you can find that one. You tell him for me that he should tell you everything, it's an order, if he's not too loaded," the captain said.

"And if there is anything else that we can do to be of service, please let me know."

I thanked the captain profusely and asked him if there was anything else he could tell me about the incident, but he confessed that he really didn't know much about it except for the fact that the orders came from Mexico City.

The Indians never caused him much of a problem, he said. Once in a while there were fights among them and there were a few drunks, he said, but in general the Indians were not a problem. It would be better, he told me, if they would stay home in the mountains.

"They are absolutely scandalous when they come to the city," he said.

As I opened the door to leave a wall of hot air almost knocked me down. It was nearly noon, and it was going to be hot. I walked out of the barracks compound and around the corner to look for the Cantina Paraíso.

The cantina was a hole in the wall. It was the only door, knocked rather inexpertly into a long, whitewashed wall that lined the whole block. The name painted in a crude rainbow of colors above a pair of swinging doors was all that signaled its existence.

There were cheap metal folding tables, provided complements of the Cervecería Moctezuma along one wall and the sheet metal bar lined the other wall. There were only a few bottles on the shelf, but under the bar was a big cooler filled with ice and beer. Almost everyone there was in uniform except for the little old man behind the bar and a ten- or twelve-year-old boy wearing a white apron. The floor was littered with bottle caps and cigarette butts. I went up to the bar and asked the old man, whose head barely extended over the bar, if he knew who Sergeant Rodriguez was.

"Yea, he's the one over there sitt'n by the wall," he said, pointing to a short pudgy man seated at one of the tables.

I thanked him and told him to have the boy bring a couple of beers over to the table. There were already two empties on the table, so Rodriguez had been there for a while. I went over to the table and said.

"You're Sergeant Rodriguez, no?

"Your captain told me you might be able to help me. I'm looking for some information about some Huichols." He looked shocked.

I was interrupting the melancholy musings he was trying to drown out with a river of beer. His short, thin mustache was supposed to look debonair like the kiss-me-quick mustaches of Latin lovers from the Mexican cinema of the 1940s and 1950s, but it was too sparse to achieve that look.

Drops of beer were perspiring on his round face. His olive skin was

ready to drip in the heat. It probably took a lot of beer to fill that bul-
bous body to this point.

"Ay, Indians, damned Indians," he said. "So what do you want to
know? We'd all be a lot better off if those shameless bastards would just
stay up in the mountains. They live like animals, so they should stay with
them, in the mountains, and not bother civilized people."

I explained to him that I wanted to know what had happened in
San Isidro. I also made it clear that this was an order from his captain.
At first he just looked at me quizzically, and then he laughed.

Under other circumstances he was probably a pretty jovial soul.

"Those crazy Indians. There was one of them who thought that he
was Jesus Christ.

They were some bad ones.

We went up there with Comandante Elías from Mexico City, his
lieutenant and a few guys from Guadalajara.

They explained to us that this crazy Indian was telling everyone that
he was Jesus Christ. He was training his followers there to kill Mexicans
all over the country.

'Those Indians were all a bunch of drug addicts,' he told us. 'They
made blood sacrifices to their gods. They lived lives of debauchery without any sense, and they had more than one wife, sometimes three or
four women, all at once, together!'

Elías said he didn't know if they were trafficking in drugs, but that
he suspected that they were because there were a lot of foreigners who
hung around with them.

Those Indians had a lot of money," he commented.

"Oh boy, did we find out they had money! We found almost half a
million pesos there, all in cash. Elías got most of it for 'evidence,' but we
didn't make out too badly.

When we got up to San Isidro we went to see the *alcalde* and the
priest.

The padre told us that those Indians were all communists. They never
came to Mass, even on Holy Days.

There were two children abducted in Santiago, and the priest said
he thought the Indians had sacrificed them to the devil, and probably
had eaten them.

We found at least two little ones buried there.

The alcalde told us that the Indians had all been singing and dancing and playing some kind of awful music for the last three days, but other than that they had caused no trouble.

The woman María Ibañez had taken up with those crazed Indians at least ten years ago, the padre told us.

'Such a shame when a good Christian woman takes up with those kinds of shameless Indians,' the padre said. Those were his exact words.

If it hadn't been out of respect for Doña María's father, who had fought with federal troops, everyone would have probably run the woman out of town when she took up with those Indians, the alcalde told us.

They should have done it too!" Rodriguez said, slaming his beer on the metal table.

"A woman like that hanging around with those filthy Indians. They even said she married one of them, but they weren't really married.

She was a frump, a tart, for those Indians.

I shot her trying to escape with the money," he told me with some pride before going on.

"The priest showed us the layout of the compound, but he really didn't know what those Indians had built on the inside. The place was walled in on three sides and there was a steep ravine on the far side. There was only the main gate and the door to the house. The comandante sent two men with rifles around to the other side of the ravine and told them to start shooting as soon as they heard shots. My buddy Manolo and I were to be stationed at the door to the house. We had orders to shoot anyone trying to escape. The comandante and the others all went to the main gate.

The comandante banged on the gate, but no one came.

There was maybe too much noise with all that awful music and singing.

The guys said they shot the locks off the gate and then the riflemen from across the ravine started shooting. They almost got some of our guys!

The chief, the big one with the colorful outfit, came running to the gate with feathers all over him and he was all bloody.

XXXVI | TRACING THE PATH OF JESUS

There was blood everywhere, the men said.

We knew he was the chief because he had all the feathers and tails on his hat and he wore bright Indian clothes.

All the rest of them wore white.

The comandante and the others shot the chief and then the rest of them started to run everywhere.

We stayed at the door, but there was shooting everywhere.

Then that woman and two others came running out carrying big *morales*, big satchels.

We got 'em before they got out the door.

Then we charged in and got a couple more of them on the staircase coming down from the upstairs.

You shoulda seen what we found inside after it was all over.

There was blood everywhere in there. They were butchering a bull. There was one of those Indian houses there with all kinds of things in it, feathers and flowers and arrows, and there was blood all over everything.

It wasn't 'til we dragged the woman in, that we found all the money, then we really tore the place apart. We pulled everything out of the house and those Indian huts too, but there wasn't much there."

Rodriguez finished off his beer, and I ordered two more as he continued to give me all of the gruesome details of the shoot-out. He was proud of what he had done.

I was in a state of shock. I gave him 50 pesos when he finished. We both got up, and Sergeant Rodriguez put on a pair of silvered sun glasses. Dirty Harry, he was not.

He was going to another uptown cantina, he said and asked if I would like to come along. They had great shrimp every afternoon, he said, and I was almost convinced, but I couldn't imagine spending the afternoon with the sergeant.

I took a taxi back to my hotel downtown. I had been riding buses for two nights running and hadn't slept.

I was bone tired, but the image of Mad Jesus dying in a police fusillade kept running through my mind.

I left the hotel and walked the back streets until I found a nondescript cantina and ordered a double tequila, then another. I just kept on seeing reruns of the death of Mad Jesus, but there was more that I was looking for than just the gruesome demise of *Jesús* and his cult. How and why do people become such a threat that they have to be eliminated? Maybe it was just some trigger-happy cops, as Raúl had suggested.

It was late afternoon by the time that I found my way back to the hotel. I finally could sleep, but the cries of a thousand blackbirds vying for space on the one tree in the hotel courtyard wakened me. It was nearly sunset. I knew that I didn't want to stay in Tepic that night.

WHITE ROCKS XXXVII

I paid my bill and took the bus to San Blas. I could feel the sea long before we arrived in San Blas. The moon cast blue shadows through the trees as we snaked our way down to the coast past lagoons filled with sleeping water fowl, black waters, blue shrimp, the moon's pearls shimmering on the waters.

There was a sacred world here of the Mothers, the haiku, the water Snake, the Kuwe Eme, the two Snakes of creation, the clouds, the rushing streams, silent lagoons, and rolling sea. The bus rattled into the station near the market and the mosquitoes began their feast on new flesh as soon as we stopped. It was dark when I arrived. There was barely a breeze.

It was late; there were no boys there at the station to help with my things; the market was abandoned as I walked to the old part of the town. There were few of the colonial buildings left that echoed the heritage of San Blas. Great galleons and coastal ships made this one of the main seaports of Mexico in colonial times. I found an old, heavy-walled hotel and banged on the door.

There were only a few naked bulbs illuminating the rutted dusty street. Finally I awakened the sleepy portero. He gave me a room and some towels. I threw my things on the floor, turned on the lazy fan, took off my clammy clothes, and fell asleep for the first time in nearly three days.

There were two Huichols, San Andreseños as far as I could tell from their costumes, at the bus station when I arrived, but I was simply too exhausted to talk to them. That was something I would do tomorrow.

I wandered the town most of the day, climbing up to the old fort and looking at the few ruins of the colonial grandeur that had once been San Blas.

The white rocks of the Mothers surveyed everything in the port. Few in that ancient port knew that they were perched on sleeping Sea Snakes. Few knew how the waters had boiled at the creation. Few knew how the Mothers had emerged. Few knew that this was anything more than the site of a sleepy port that had seen better days. The site of creation had been lost in the clouds of time.

There were things that I wanted to do on the coast. I wanted to see if I could find the compound where *Jesús* had died. And I wanted to see what people in the town of San Isidro remembered about his demise. The first thing that I wanted to do was to talk to the other Huichols to see if anyone knew anything about Mad Jesus. There were two Huichols on the plaza selling handicrafts. I wasn't sure whether they were the ones I had seen last night. They both looked like San Andreseños.

"Ke'aku," I greeted them.

I asked if they knew any Huichols from Santa Catarina in San Blas. The taller one said no, but the other young man said that perhaps there were some Santa Catarinos living with Don Pepe.

"Where does Don Pepe live?" I asked them.

"Over there," the younger one said, pointing with his lips.

These were typical Huichol directions, but they wouldn't get me to Don Pepe's house by any means. I asked if one of them could take me there and they both agreed to go.

Don Pepe lived on the edge of town on the way out to a couple of old ruined hotels that had once been the finest in the region. Pepe was an unreconstructed child of the sixties who looked like a cross between Jerry Garcia and Andy Weil with a huge bushy beard and glistening pate. He had apparently lived in San Blas for the last ten or fifteen years. Originally from Mexico City, he had found his niche in San Blas with his twenty-five-year-old girlfriend, two small children, and an ever-changing household full of Huichol guests.

He knew the mara'acames who came every year and most of the Huichols who sold folk art in town. He even knew some of the same people from Mexico City who had been involved for years with Huichols. As we sat on his terrace watching the sun set into the Pacific, I decided to ask him what he knew about Mad Jesus.

"There is one Huichol in particular," I began to ask Pepe, "in whom I am interested. He was called *Jesús*. He had some kind of messianic cult in San Isidro and was apparently killed up there not too many years ago. Is there anything you can tell me about him?"

"I never met him," Pepe said "but we all knew when he came every year with that little band of his. He dumped enough stuff in the sea to supply the town for a year. Everyone was trying to fish the stuff out, bolts of cloth, boxes of wool yarn, beads, beans, radios, shoes, clothes, all kinds of things. He wouldn't let any of the other Huichols come to his ceremonies. They camped out near the point and kept to themselves."

"Did any of the other Huichols here ever know him?" I asked.

"I don't know, but I think that Andrés who was out here stringing beads, worked for him for a little while," Pepe said.

"Marta, could you get Andrés?" Pepe asked his wife.

Pepe's Huichol friends, most of whom were Santa Catarinos, had been with us out on the terrace stringing beads and weaving until sunset and then went inside where there were fewer mosquitos and better light.

"I don't know much about this Huichol Jesus," Pepe said, while his wife was looking for Andrés. "There is a rather strange Huichol who lives near the rocks on the point. We don't see much of him here in town, he pretty much stays out there. Fishes, I think. He may have been a part of that band, and I think there are two women living with Don José in Meztitlan, but that's about all I know about the group."

Marta came back with Andrés, who looked rather put off and shy.

"Andrés didn't you know that Jesus?" Pepe asked. "The one everyone called Mad Jesus."

"I knew him. He tried to kill me once," Andrés said.

"Me too," I answered and mentioned the incident on the roof in Mexico City.

"Yea, he was really crazy," Andrés said. "When my wife and I were going to leave he came after us with a machete. He was really a crazy one. He said he was going to bring back Santo Cristo and get rid of all the tewalis, then he would be the president of Mexico.

"I never really believed him but he took care of us all, and we made things for him. He was a real mara'acame; he made offerings for the Mothers, but Santo Cristo never came. The cops got him, we heard. I think it was that brother of his, Matsiwa, that sent them after him. That's what everyone says."

"His brother?" I asked incredulously.

"I knew his brother," I said, "and he always took care of Chucho when he got crazy."

"Yea, but that brother of his is the one who got rich. He takes the airplanes to Los Angeles and to Europe now. He's the one who sells everything to all those people that Chucho used to sell to. He's the one who had Chucho witched, all right. He's the one who placed the evil arrow. That is what sent the cops after him. If you want to really know what happened to Chucho, you talk to that brother of his."

"He did it. He got him," Andrés said and went back into the house to continue working.

I found that hard to believe, I told Pepe, who asked me to explain more about Mad Jesus.

Jesus was a hard man to explain, I said, but I agreed to try. We talked well into the night. It was late when I returned to the hotel.

Walking the town, the port, and the beaches in San Blas provided no resolution. I wondered how many of his followers survived, whether the cult itself survived. There was no real way of knowing. My only hope was the two women in Meztitlan: perhaps they could tell me more, perhaps talking to them could provide some kind of resolution, some kind of perspective. If I could just locate them, perhaps I could begin to understand what had really happened to Mad Jesus.

There was little I knew about the two women. In fact, all I knew was that they were supposed to be living in, or near, Meztitlan with a Don José. Their names, where they were from, their families and relatives, their skills, their faces, all were a mystery to me.

I took the bus to Meztitlan the next day and after considerable difficulty located the two women. They dressed in plain white manta just as the followers of Jesus that I had met in Mexico City did. They

spoke almost no Spanish and there was no one who could really translate well. They told me little about what had happened. One of the
women had lost a child in the melee. They both seemed like frightened does.

san ISIDRO

All the next day, in the town, in the port, and on the beaches I thought about the two scared women. I thought of going back to see the women with a tape recorder and someone who could translate better for me. I was asking myself if there was anything worthwhile that the women could tell me. They fled when the shooting started and managed to survive. How many other survivors there were, I did not know. If there were others, the two women did not know, or would not tell, who they were, or where to locate them.

There was very little that the two women could tell me that really would be important. It might be possible to learn something about *Jesús* and his followers through tedious questioning, but that would be more like torture for all of us. They were better left alone.

In San Isidro there would perhaps be some fleeting memory of *Jesús*; perhaps there was something there of his life, his death, a few memories. To get to San Isidro, I had to go to Tepic. I took the early bus and connected immediately with a bus to San Isidro. Before noon the bus approached the town.

San Isidro was a dusty agricultural town nestled in the low coastal hills about 20 miles from the sea. There were only two buildings of more than one story, one was the town hall and the other was a bank. Feed and grain stores, agricultural equipment stores, and warehouses lined the road into San Isidro. The bus station was a hot, dirty place with two wooden benches where passengers could wait. The town was prosperous, but obviously had few visitors.

I asked if there was any place to stay in town, since I didn't know if I would be able to get back to Tepic before the last bus in the evening, which was listed on the chalk board as leaving at 23:00 hours, eleven P.M. There were no hotels, but down the street was a boarding house, the woman behind the cashier's cage told me, that might have a room. I grabbed my things and trudged out into the heat to find the pension. There were no rooms, but I asked if I could leave my things there in the hope that there might be a room later in the day.

I went out to explore the town under the searing sun. There were already few people about on the streets, and by lunchtime I knew the town would be deserted. I stopped in a few of the general stores and asked about any Huichols living in town. The attitude toward Indians was decidedly antagonistic. There were some Huichols who worked on the surrounding ranches, but I gathered they rarely came to town. In several places I asked about some Indians who had been shot a few years ago, but all I got were blank stares. No one cared about, or wanted to know anything about Indians in San Isidro.

I decided to try the church, but it was locked and there was no obvious nearby rectory. I asked a few people how to find the padre and was told that there hadn't been a priest in town for more than five years. Once a week a priest would come through to say Mass.

Next, I decided to try the police station, and after considerable hassle I was shown into the captain's office.

"Sit down," the captain told me as I was led into his office. "What are you here for and what is this about some of our little Indians? What does a foreigner want with Indians?" He was brusque.

This was going to be difficult, and I explained as simply as I could what I wanted to know about the incident with Mad Jesus without telling him anything about the cult, or Mad Jesus himself. I used the ploy of asking him how dangerous those Indians actually were.

He was finally satisfied, but he was from Tepic and had only been in San Isidro for two years. None of the municipal police, though, had participated in the incident, he emphasized. The federal authorities apparently had little to do with local authorities.

"Where," I asked him "was the compound where this incident occurred?"

"Unfortunately," he said, "I have no idea where those Indians were shot."

Then he asked Officer Torres, who was probably much better informed about local gossip than the captain.

Torres walked over to the captain and whispered something in his ear. The captain scowled and turned to me.

"Well, I think that the compound is now Don Dionisio's home. He was the mayor and now he works for our state legislator. He is a very important man and I don't know if he could tell you about those Indians."

I thought the former mayor might be just the man to tell me about the final days of Mad Jesus. So I pleaded with the captain to at least give this Don Dionisio a call for me. Telling him this was an important matter for the university and implying that there might be more dangerous Indians menacing good, upstanding Mexicans seemed to help.

The captain was not pleased to be asked to give such an important man a call, but finally he picked up the phone and spoke with Don Dionisio. The politician agreed to receive me!

Captain Morales explained how to get to the house and said that Don Dionisio would be there, waiting for me.

I walked block after block in the hot sun. The compound was on the edge of town just as had been described, on the edge of a deep ravine. I walked up to what was obviously the main entry and rang. This was where María was shot, I suspected. After a moment a young man of Indian descent in a white jacket and black pants opened the door. I informed him that I was there to see Don Dionisio, and he told me to follow him. What was obviously the living room was immense with a single stairway on the far wall leading to the upper floor, just as the officer in Tepic had described. The young man led me out onto the terrace where Don Dionisio was waiting.

Don Dionisio was in his early sixties and had mottled white skin and slicked-back silver hair. He would have been a handsome old man at half his weight, but as it was he was an imposing figure dressed in the politician's white guayabera shirt and dark pants. I could see looking around the impeccable gardens that there was not a trace left of the compound where *Jesús* had lived.

I greeted the older man formally and immediately explained to him that I was studying the Huichol Indians and that their beliefs were important for understanding the pre-Columbian heritage of Mexico. He at least seemed a bit interested and asked me to sit down with him in some overstuffed white chairs that looked out of place on the patio. He called the boy and asked if I would like a drink.

"A beer would be fine in this heat," I told him and went on to explain that some of the Huichols I had heard of were rather dangerous. In fact, if I was not in error, some of them had lived in this very place, I told him.

He put his hand to his jowls and said, "Yes, there was some trouble here." He was thinking about how much he really wanted to tell me. "The woman who owned the place, María Ibañez, was an Indian lover. She even married one of them, I heard, but we don't know if she was really married. Those Indians live like animals, you know. They have all sorts of wives and mistresses."

"The Indians that were here were a real problem, dangerous too, but we cleared them out," he said with a nod of self-assurance.

I said that I was interested in the incident that had happened here. I tried to explain to him that it was important to know about the Indians that died here because there could be more like them who might be very dangerous.

"I wouldn't worry about that," he told me. "Here the police know how to deal with those Indians. There are none of them left."

"None!" He guaranteed me.

The case was closed as far as he was concerned, he told me, and if there were any more problems, then the police would deal with them.

I asked him how the compound had looked when he moved in.

"There wasn't much here," he explained, "I bought it after the police got rid of those crazy Indians. They dug the whole place up. Those Indians buried bodies everywhere, even in their houses. It really was quite a scandal. The police took everything apart and took out all of the garbage the Indians left. We tore down their mud huts and started to make this place into a livable home you see now." Don Dionisio made a self-satisfied gesture toward the gardens and continued, "It took a lot, but I am pleased."

"Would you like to see the place?" he asked.

I assured him that I would and he gave me a tour of the compound, telling me just how much he had done to make it the pleasant place it was.

"There are no ghosts lurking here," he assured me. "We had the bishop himself here to bless the house. It was a grand fiesta."

He told me about the dignitaries who had been here for the dedication of the house and then asked me to lunch. It was not a real invitation but more a formal Mexican courtesy.

I was not going to get any more information and told him I had to return to Tepic. With the usual Mexican platitudes about "my house being your house" he bid me farewell, clearly certain he would not see me again.

At the door he told me, "It is a shame I can't tell you more about those crazy Indians, but if you find more like that let the police know. They really know how to take care of those kinds of problems."

The usual formal thanks were given to Don Dionisio, and despite the sun, I was finally pleased to be out of that house. It was lunchtime, and I was the only madman out on the streets. Most of the shops were closed for the midday meal as I walked back to the bus station.

Lunch was being served at the pension when I picked up my bags. The young woman there told me there wouldn't be a bus until four, so I had a long, slow comida while waiting.

Perhaps someone in the pension knew something about the demise of Mad Jesus. I asked the young woman if she knew about what happened to the Indians who were at Don Dionisio's. She didn't, but her mother who was in the kitchen did, she told me.

As I was finishing my lunch an older woman with salt-and-pepper hair tied back in a bun came out of the kitchen. Wiping her wet hands on a long, green apron she came over to my table.

"Good afternoon, sir," she said, formally approaching me. "My daughter has told me you wanted to know about those poor Indians at Doña María's."

Shaking her head and clicking her tongue, she told me, "The police got them all and María too.

Those cops all stayed right here.

They were terrible, didn't even leave descent tips, and all that money they had.

They were in the cantina all night and drunk. It was a scandal.

They came here to get rid of María and those Indians.

Dionisio wanted that house for years, and it looks like he finally got it.

Shame they had to shoot so many, but María should have sold out and left. Once she took up with those Indians no one wanted her around anyhow. Imagine a civilized woman with her father who rode with federal troops, taking up with those savages. It was indecent!

Those little Indians never caused any problems, not like the police did. Everyone said it was a scandal over there with the Indians, but they never caused as much of a scandal as the police. Why we hardly ever saw those little Indians.

They were good little Indians, never caused much trouble and never even spoke to civilized people," she allowed. We talked until just before the bus arrived. It seemed clear that the people of San Isidro knew little or nothing about *Jesús*'s little group. These were Indians, so the residents of the town, who saw themselves as civilized, cared little about the uncivilized savages.

guadaLajaRa XXXIX

At four the bus rumbled off to Tepic, where I spent the night. The next morning I went to the police barracks on the edge of town again to see if Captain Miriles could give me any further help in locating any of the other men who had participated in the shoot-out. I specifically wanted to know about Raúl Corona and Martín Cedros. The captain had said that they were bodyguards in Guadalajara, and that was my next stop.

It was early when I arrived at the barracks, and I went straight over to the comandancia. Carmela was just opening up when I arrived.

"Eh, Dr. Nava, did ya find those little Indians you were looking for?" she called out as she saw me approaching the building and waved.

"No luck yet, Carmela," I told her.

"I was wondering if the captain could help me find a couple of the other men involved with those Indians," I said.

"Well, yer out of luck. He's in Guadalajara until Monday," she said, "but maybe I can help ya. Which ones were you look'n fer?"

"Raúl Corona and Martín Cedros," I told her, "the ones he said were bodyguards in Guadalajara."

"Oh, yer look'n fer Martín, El Guapo, the handsome one. I saw him last week, and let's see," she said, opening up a purse that had probably at one time served as a cartridge case and dumping it on the main desk. Searching through the jumble of miscellany she picked out a slip of paper.

"That's it!" she said, "I thought I had it. Here's his number, his car number and where he works. Wouldn't give me his home, doesn't want me talking to his wife. Corona's probably with him. They're like twins. Ya want some coffee? I was just put'n it on," she said.

"Sure." I didn't have to leave for Guadalajara right away. Carmela even offered to take me out on her motorcycle next time I was in Tepic.

She was a font of information about how the local comandancia actually worked. It was quite clear that what happened in San Isidro was on orders from higher up.

It was nearly midday by the time I finally left for Guadalajara. I wouldn't get anything done there when I arrived, so I decided to get a hotel downtown and start early in the morning. First I would try Martín and then I would head up to Zapopan again. I could probably find Matsiwa through the Huichols there. I wasn't really sure that I wanted to see Raúl and Martín, but I felt that I had to try.

It was already nine thirty by the time I left for Zapopan; I had tried both numbers and left messages for Martín.

The taxi dropped me on the great plaza in front of the Zapopan Mission, and I went over to the folk art shop. They had hundreds of wool paintings in dozens of sizes. I started looking through a group of about thirty leaning against a wall and about the fourth or fifth one I saw was Matsiwa's work.

His style was unmistakable, the arrangement of motifs, the use of multiple colors in backgrounds. I looked at the back of the piece of plywood and sure enough he had signed and dated it. It had been made two months ago, so he must have been around. I pulled out the painting and took it over to the desk.

The lady at the desk apologized saying that she didn't know any of the Huichols but that a Mr. Ruíz, the manager, would be in at ten thirty and surely he would know. I said I would be back at eleven and left my card.

I walked across the plaza to the market, had breakfast, and then went back to the shop. Mr. Ruíz was in, the woman told me as soon as I walked in and she led me to an office around the corner from the main door.

Mr. Ruíz was a small man with the intense look of an accountant about him going over sales slips and checking sums as I walked in. The woman from the desk introduced me.

"Oh, you are the man looking for Señor Sanchez," he said. I was amazed he addressed Matsiwa as Mr. Sanchez.

"Ah, yes I would like to find Matsiwa. I used to know him quite well but I haven't been in Mexico for some time."

"Well, he'll be in later today, but if you want to see him he lives just a few blocks away," Mr. Ruíz told me.

Mr. Ruíz gave me his address and even made a little map so that I could get over to Matsiwa's. Behind the mission heading down the hill from the basilica was a huge old building that had probably been a colonial warehouse. There were four buzzers on the outside but the door was open so I didn't bother to ring. The lower floor was still apparently a warehouse.

I walked up the old stone staircase and saw two Huichols coming down as I went up. This was the right place. The whole upper floor was one huge room with lights hanging from the ceiling and a huge window that ran most of the length of the building. It looked rather like the scene from the Plaza de la Veracruz with dozens of Huichol families each in their own little section working on different types of folk art.

I looked from one end of the room to the other, but I didn't see Matsiwa in the cavernous loft. There were easily fifty people in the room so perhaps I had missed him. On the far end of the hall was a woman who reminded me of his first wife, so I walked over to the group. There was a middle-aged man filling in the designs of a wool painting seated in an uweni with his back to me.

It was Matsiwa. We both stared at each other. Recognition took a moment.

Matsiwa got up from the uweni, singing out my name, "Tiiimooooteeeoooo!"

We both gave each other big abrazos.

We talked most of the morning. Tutuwari was married with two wives and five children, both of Matsiwa's wives were in Guadalajara. He told me about fiestas in the Sierra he had sponsored.

His wives brought us freshly made tortillas and some hot orange chilies from the Sierra and stewed chicken for lunch. Finally I asked Matsiwa what he knew about what had happened to *Jesús*.

"Ay, *Jesús*," he said as if stung by some unseen insect.

"That brother of mine! Chucho Loco, You know how crazy he was."

"You know what he did with that tape recorder you gave him?" He told me, "He took it up to San Isidro and played it in front of the shiriki until it broke. He just kept playing and playing those tapes you made until they broke and the machine broke too. He was crazy! And it got worse, you just saw the beginning. He got in trouble in Mexico City and here in Guadalajara too. There wasn't any place he could go but San Isidro.

He and those apóstoles of his made a lot of money and every year he just dumped it all into the sea there in San Blas. He and that woman of his, María, sold to everyone. They sold plenty, but if I tried to sell anything to anyone he became furious. He wanted me to be like one of his apóstoles.

That wasn't all though, he was really crazy too. Whenever anyone tried to leave him they were 'thieves,' he said 'they betrayed him,' 'they would die,' 'they offended the Mothers and Fathers.' He went after them. I don't know how many he got like Pedro. I'm not disappointed the cops got him. That was what he deserved.

He was just too crazy. He was just too dangerous, that brother of mine. You could never know when he would get crazy. Everyone hated him. Even that priest who called him his 'little bird.'

It was that priest, Padre Cerillo who finally got him. He's the one who went up there with the cops. He's the one who told them where to go.

He came over here with two of those cops and they wanted to know everything about *Jesús*.

Padre Cerillo had been jealous of my brother ever since he left the mission. He just wanted to turn him into a priest like he was. Cerillo always came over to ask about *Jesús*.

We never told him where my brother was or what he was doing, but finally after Chucho was down here—he used to come down here all the time with that woman of his—to buy things. They looked like tewalis when they came down here. Well, she was a tewali anyway even though she sometimes dressed Huichol. That was when I told the padre about him.

Jesús was crazy again. He threatened to kill me if I kept on selling things to the old man in Chapala. The old man was his customer. They were all his customers, as far as he was concerned.

That was when I told the priest. I told him all about how *Jesús* was going to bring back Santo Cristo, how the seas would boil and all of the tewalis would be gone.

I told him what Chucho told all of his apóstoles and how his apóstoles made things for him. I told him how they dumped everything in the sea, and I told him all about Pedro, and his grandfather, and the others.

Later the padre came over with the old man from San Isidro and they said they were going to get rid of *Jesús,* send him back to the Sierra. I told him everything I had told Padre Cerillo.

Finally, the padre came here with a couple of those cops, and I showed them what the place in San Isidro looked like. We didn't think they were going to shoot them all. They said they were just going to send them back to the mountains. That was what they said."

Matsiwa began weeping into the crook of his arm, ritual weeping.

"Then we heard what had happened, we heard from our brothers first, and then it was in all the newspapers. They even got that woman of his, María.

I think that they shot them all. They were all shot.

They were all killed there in San Isidro. They were all dead."

Matsiwa continued to weep. I put my arm around his shoulder.

I told him that this was something that perhaps we all knew would happen to Chucho. Perhaps it was the "Whirlwind" Kieli who had finally caught up with him, the whirling madness that persecuted him.

It was late afternoon by the time I returned to my hotel in downtown Guadalajara. What Matsiwa had told me meant that everyone probably had a hand in Chucho's demise.

There was a message from Martín Cedros. I was to call him after eight at home and he gave me the home number Carmela couldn't get.

I waited until about eight thirty and I called.

A woman answered the phone, and I asked Mrs. Cedros if I could speak with her husband.

"Martín," she called out, "there is a Dr. Nava on the phone."

I explained to him quickly who I was and that I wanted some information about what had happened in San Isidro.

"Whew, I almost got killed there," he said when I mentioned San Isidro. I had just a couple of quick questions for him, I explained.

"First of all who started shooting?" I asked.

"I don't know," he said, "all of a sudden there was gunfire everywhere, there were guns in the compound, but none of the Indians had guns on them when we found them, only the woman and that was in her bag." That was all I needed to know.

Then I said I had heard there was a priest up there with him.

He explained that it was the priest who had told them all about the cult.

I asked if he remembered the priest's name.

It was Cerillo.

I thanked him and said he had been very helpful.

Trigger-happy police, a self-righteous, and perhaps jealous, priest, a covetous politician, and an angry brother all contributed to Chucho's demise. He never saw the fusillade coming that cut him down with his followers.

The next day I returned to the San Blas for a day before heading back to the States. I still hoped the sea would wash away the memories of Mad Jesus.

HOLY, HOLY MADNESS

As I wandered the beaches, looking out at the great white rocks where everything had begun, where the Mothers of the Huichol had emerged, *Jesús* followed me. The sun became a bronze orb and began to dip into the Pacific. Was this where he had been swept out to sea? I swam in the dark waters aware of the current pulling me out to sea.

On the shore there was a lone Huichol crouched on the beach just staring out to sea. Perhaps he was silently chanting the emergence of the Mothers, the creation of the world. The waves lapped at his feet. He didn't move. The current was pulling to the point of *Jesús's* epiphany in the sea. A few strong strokes and the waves pulled me back to the beach. The lone Huichol was still there squatting on the shore as the last glint of light disappeared into the ocean.

Swatting the mosquitoes that were becoming voracious, I stopped to put on some repellent and the man got up. It was time to return to town. He started walking toward me. Pinks and purples illuminated the sky, the sea, and the shore. My footsteps were eaten by tongues of water from the panting sea. The great white rocks of the Mothers were shrouded in shadow.

The man was not old. He walked with a slow, graceful air, his wet Huichol trousers clinging to his muscular legs. His hair was knotted and unkempt, hanging to his shoulders. His white, open Huichol shirt fluttered in the shore breeze. His dark eyes focused in on me.

"Ke'aku," I said as he approached.

"Ah, 'Watermountain,'" he said in greeting me.

He knew my Huichol name, but I did not recognize him at all in the waning light. I apologized in Spanish, saying that I no longer spoke much Huichol.

"You are the friend, the companion, the brother, of our father, our mother, *Jesús,* who walked these sands, these shores, and sang of our Mothers there, sang of the virgin and Santo Cristo, sang of their emergence, of their concern, of their intentions, of the world they had given us, of the world they created for our people, for the Wishalica."

He spoke in a dreamy sort of ungrammatical Spanish with words that flowed and ebbed with the sea, rose and fell on the waves. He crouched down on the sand and continued his monologue, thoughts that broke like waves. I crouched down next to him to listen, intimate words from a man who appeared a stranger. Had he been watching me on the shore, waiting for me to emerge from the sea, rehearsing his words in his language and now transposing them into Spanish, rough irregular Spanish with pauses for thought between phrases?

"I am Huichol, Wishalica. We are the first. The first people, the first created, the first to emerge here on this earth," he began. He talked of what it meant to be a Huichol and what *Jesús*'s vision had meant for him.

He reached over and touched my shoulder, a gesture of sincerity, and I touched his. Brothers and compadres do this in the Sierra.

Venus, as evening star, flickered over the dark waters. The waxing half moon looked down on us. The unadorned outfit told me he had been a follower of *Jesús,* perhaps he had seen me walking about the town, along the beaches. Perhaps he had been awaiting me, watching while I swam, following me, choosing a right moment to speak. Huichols do this. Days will pass without saying a word to someone and then in a single intimate moment all is said which must be said, and has been waiting to be said.

"This is what was given us; this is what was granted us," he told me opening his arms, holding his elbows to his chest stretching his palms from horizon to horizon across the sea.

"Our *Jesús* came forth from the Mothers, from his mother, on the day of Santo Cristo. He came forth to serve the Mothers here; here where they emerged," the man said, emphatically gesturing again to the sea. The evening star had set and the half moon cast a cold blue glow over the silver waters, the great rocks. There was a chill in the breeze and the salt air.

"*Jesús* knew. *Jesús* spoke with them. He spoke with the Mothers.

Our *Jesús* would bring us Santo Cristo. *Jesús* read us the tales, the gospels. He prayed and sang.

He showed us how to make offerings, how to give the Mothers what they needed to dislodge the Virgin, to give us Her Son," his sermon intensified.

"The Mexicans were furious about this and they sent out their police for our Jesus, our Father. They shot him there in San Isidro, but he did not die.

His soul, his iyari lives there with the Mothers. I took the Ulucame to them and there with the Mothers he lives. He is waiting until She is dislodged and all of the tewalis are gone, then he will return to us. We will imprison that Santo Cristo ourselves. We will be rid of all the tewalis.

Jesus will bring us all those things that were not given.

The Mothers will be pleased, the Fathers will be pleased.

We will all dance and sing, because all peoples will have all things, all things, ALL THINGS!"

From where he crouched on the sand the man leapt up and began a dance, a dance like the peyote dance, bouncing up and down alone there on the beach in the blue light of the moon with the breakers rolling in from sea.

"*Jesús, Jesús JESUUUS!*" became his cry.

I watched as he danced off into the distance and slowly got to my feet. His joyous cry echoed through me well into town. There was nothing more. *Jesús*, Mad Jesus, Chucho Loco lived for one man at least, perhaps two. His heart-soul was someplace hidden among the rocks of the Mothers where the sun had set.

AFTERWORD

When I had finished working on the final version of this book, with some fear and trepidation I decided to get in touch with Jesús's brother, who is called Matsiwa in the book. This is a plot-driven narrative, just as my previous book, *A War of Witches*, was. It is ethnographically accurate, based on notes and tapes, but as in any good tale, the plot, tension, and drama of the story take precedence. The events of the life of Mad Jesus have been selectively cut and pared, spliced into the context of the telling of the tale and grafted onto the aftermath of the shoot-out that eliminated his little band on the coast of Nayarit. I wondered how the man I have called Matsiwa would react to my assertion of his guilt in the demise of his brother. In reality none of the players were individually guilty, yet all played a part in the demise of Mad Jesus.

Matsiwa is a very sophisticated artisan with two wives and seven children. He has traveled to Europe and Southeast Asia to sell his work. He has spent considerable time studying English both in Mexico and in Los Angeles. When we finally got together, I explained to him what I was trying to do with the book and I began reading passages to him, sometimes translating, sometimes not, from the first chapter to the end of the book. We reminisced about Chucho. He wept for his brother. Crying is not a demonstration of weakness for Huichol men, but rather a demonstration of emotional power.

When we finished the book he told me, "Well, perhaps, perhaps what you have said is true. It is not what I did, but perhaps in a way it is more true. It is the story of my brother, Chucho Loco." Matsiwa was in the end quite pleased with the tale of Mad Jesus that I had forged out of years of pondering how to tell such a tale.

There were so many people involved in the telling of this tale that it is hard to think of them all. My Huichol friends, some of whom told me of Chucho, and others who would not even mention him, were my prime inspiration. Doris Heyden, Thelma Sullivan, Paul Kirchhoff, Karl Heidt, and Bill Sweezy encouraged me early on. Juan Rulfo was a superb editor. Guillermo Bonfil, Mercedes Oliviera, Arturo Warrman, and Margarita Nolasco showed me an example to follow. All of my colleagues at the Instituto de Investigaciones Antropológicas, especially Ignacio Bernal, Juan Comas, Antonio Pompa y Pompa, and Alfonso Villarojas, the grand old men of Mexican anthropology, and my friends who were becoming grand old men, Alfredo Lopéz Austín and Andrés Medina, as well as our visiting scholars, Bill Bright, Norman McQuown, Claude Levi-Strauss, and Linda Schele were invaluable. Rosa María Blanca, Bob Walls, and Peter Wolfe listened to the tale early on and helped me give it structure while I was working with Juan Rulfo.

Laurence Ferlinghetti, whose comments helped me more than he could ever know, and Jenine Pommy Vega, a very special muse with an ear for the right word and a craftsman's sense of poetry, showed me that a piece was never finished until it was perfect. Gregory Corso, Ed Sanders, and Allen Ginsberg, who always had time to talk, were an inspiration. Claire Ritter, Pedro Lujan, Edwina Williams, Guillermo Contreras, and Barbara Radin in New York listened to many versions of this tale, but it was Peter Shotwell, my collaborator in *A War of Witches*, who, working off of an earlier attempt at telling this tale by Juan Rulfo and myself, developed the thematic structure of the first section of Mad Jesus. His conversations with Francisco Pimentiel and with various mara'acames through Anne-Marie de Badereau during Semana Santa in Santa Catarina in 1995 helped him to integrate tales of Santo Cristo by Benitez and Zingg. Unfortunately, Shotwell's third-person version of the tale had many dramatic problems and at his suggestion I went back to the earlier versions. Shotwell's help was invaluable in earlier versions of Mad Jesus in working out the moral ambiguities of the tale.

Durwood Ball of the University of New Mexico Press made invaluable suggestions, as did an anonymous reader from the Press. My students Juan Olza Coyotzi and Lori Eldridge put together the last version of this book. Ted Coyle made substantial suggestions on the final version of this tale, many of which I have incorporated into this final version. Dennis and Barbara Tedlock, Gary Gossen, Peter T. Furst, and

Jill Leslie McKeever Furst, as well as Phil Weigand, provided constant encouragement in this project. Duncan Earle and Jeanne Simonelli have urged me many times to finish this book when I was about to abandon the project, and I thank them for that. My colleagues at the Universidad de las Américas, Bob Shadow, John and Guadalupe Carpenter, Patricia Plunket, Gabriela Uruñela, and Manuel Gandara, have constantly provided encouragement and advice in this long project. The Universidad de las Américas has also provided the institutional support I needed to finish this project. Paul Rich's gardens at the Universidad de las Américas provided the place to contemplate this work. My students have avidly read and commented on this book in courses on Northwest Mexico and Myth, Magic, and Religion, despite the fact that it is in English. But it is to my children, Philippe and Michèle, that I dedicate this book, in the hope that they, as well as the students and scholars for whom it is intended, will read it and learn from the tale of Mad Jesus.

Timothy J. Knab
November 3, 2001
Universidad de las Américas–Puebla
Cholula, Puebla
México

GLOSSARY

A donde vas joven?: Where are you going young man?

Abrazo: A hug used as greeting among men in Mexico.

Actas: Official documents such as birth and marriage certificates but also officially lodged complaints.

Aguapura: Pure water, or drinking water.

Aguardiente: A strong distilled alcoholic drink made from agave, sugarcane, corn, or potatoes.

Ahuehuete: *Taxodium mucronatum,* "the great old man of the waters," great pinelike trees that graced swampy areas throughout Mexico but that have generally fallen victims to pollution in recent years.

Akieli: A child who participates in Huichol rituals as a messenger for the gods because of his or her purity, or virginity.

Alcalde: The mayor, or official in charge of a town.

Alemanes: Germans.

Alguacil: A constable, or peace-officer.

Americanos: Americans.

Amigo: Friend.

Ancianos: The elders or ancient ones.

Archivo histórico: Historical archive.

Arrieros: Muleteers or itinerant traders in remote, roadless regions of Mexico.

Artesanía: Folk art.

Artesanías muy finas: Very fine folk art.

Artista: Artist.

Así era: That was how it was.

Atole: A hot corn gruel usually flavored with chocolate spices or fresh fruit.

Ay indio, no toques nada: Hey Indian, don't touch anything.

Ay, este tonto no habla: Hey, this fool can't even speak.

Ay, Indio, que tonto, tienes vuelto: Hey, dumb Indian, you've got change!

Ay, pobre: Oh, poor guy.

Barbón: Man with a large beard.

Barranca: A steep ravine.
Bebé: Baby.
Borracho: Drunk.

Cabrón: A large male goat used as an expletive to describe the sexual proclivities of such a goat.
Cacique: Indian chief, or political boss.
Calle Nueva York: New York Street.
Calzones: The white cotton pants of indigenous people and peasants in Mexico taken from the Spanish term for undergarments.
Camionero: A truck or bus driver.
Cañada: A glen, dell, hollow, or cattle path.
Canela: Mexican cinnamon.
Cantador: A cantor, or singer. In Huichol ritual the shaman, or *mara'acame*, who sings the mythic origin of the ceremony.
Cantinas: Traditional Mexican-style bars for men.
Capitán: Captain.
¡Carajo! : A rather strong expletive in Mexican Spanish.
Carnitas: Potted pork for tacos.
Casa Huichol: The Huichol house.
Castillano: An alternative term for the Spanish language.
Centavo: Cent.
Certificado: Certified.
Charro: Spanish type of wide-brimmed hat that accompanies the typical horseman's outfit used in the last century in Mexico; the type of outfit normally worn today by mariachi bands.
Chicharrones: Pork cracklings.
¡Chingao! : A very strong Spanish expletive equivalent to the "F" word in English
Chinos: Chinese.
Chucho Loco: Spanish term, Chucho is a diminutive for Jesus; Loco is crazy or mad. This was one of the common names for Mad Jesus.
Cilantro: Fresh coriander leaves.
Ciudades perdidas: The slums on the outskirts of the city.
Cobrador: Money collector, or ticket taker.
Comandancia: The police station.
Comandante: A police commander, or chief.
Comida: A long, multicourse Mexican lunch.
Compadres: A term for the relationship between parents and godparents; coparents.

Comunidades: Communities.
Conquistadores: The Spanish explorers or conquerors.
Coyotes: Low-paid assistants who wait in lines for official documents; a general lawyer's gofer.
Cristeros: The right-wing opponents of Federal troops after the Mexican Revolution who supported the traditional rights of the Catholic Church in Mexico.
Cuadros: Square pictures.
Curandero: A healer or shaman in rural Mexico.

Datura: A dangerous, intoxicating plant; associated with Kieli, the evil sorcerer.
Diablo: Devil.
Dios: God.
Don Timoteo: Mr. Timothy.
Dos tequilas de lo mejor para mi amigo: Two tequilas, the best for my friend.
Dueña: Landlady.

¡Eh! ¡Indio! Pinche borracho. ¡Vete pendejo! : Hey! Indian! Damned drunk. Leave asshole!
El Chueco: The crooked one.
El Guapo: The handsome one.
El Líder: The leader.
El Rey de los Rayos: The King of the Peyote Thunderbolts.
Eso es un lugar para gente de razón. ¡Vete Indio!: This is a place for decent people. Get out, Indian!
Evangelios: Gospels.
Ex votos: Votive offerings, usually small paintings with a specific intention written on them.

Federales: Federal marshals.

Gachupine: Those who are from Spain, degrading term.
Galería: Gallery.
Gobernación: Governing secretariat, or Home Office.
Gobernador: Governor.
Gorditas: A corn tortilla made with a thin layer of refried beans in the center covered with salsa and grated cheese.
Gordón: A big fat man.
Grabadora: Tape recorder.

Grandes dames: Great ladies.
Gringo patrón: An American patron, employer, or host.
Guitarita: A diminutive guitar played by the Huichol.

Haiku: Huichol for water snake.
Hewi: Huichol for "The Ancient Ones"; ancestors and revered elders.
Hikuli: Huichol for peyote, the sacred cactus of the Huichols.
Huaraches: Sandals.
Huey Yohualli: Aztec for great night rituals.
Huicholes: Spanish for "The Peyote People," an indigenous group from Northwest Mexico.

Ikuri Nesha: Huichol for the festival of the First Rains.
Indígenas: Indigenous people, a term preferable to Indian.
Inditos: Little Indians.
Ingleses: The English.
Instituto Indígenista: The Indigenous Institute, or Indian bureau.
Iromali: Huichol for the night-half of Kauyumali.
Italia: Italy.
Iyari: Huichol aspect of the soul.

Japoneses: Japanese.
Jesús: The name for Jesus, a relatively common Latin American name.
Judios: Jews, who are equated with devils in rural Mexico.
Juzgado: Law court, or tribunal.

Kakauyali: Huichol for the Ones that were once Mothers and Fathers, referring to Kieli.
Kaliwey: A term for the traditional Huichol temple borrowed from Náhuatl.
Kawiteros: A term for the Huichol council of elders, also a borrowing from Náhuatl.
Kauyumali: Huichol deity, the Deer, messenger to and from the gods, the shaman's patron and the first peyote pilgrim, good brother of the evil Kieli.
Ke'aku: Huichol greeting.
Kieli: The Huichol deity who is the evil brother of Kauyumali, also called "Tree of the Winds," patron of sorcery and maleficence existent in the form of a plant with dangerous hallucinogenic properties, *Datura* or *Solandra*.
Kieli Tewiali: "Tree of the Winds," a variety of Kieli.

Kielisha: The bad little kielis that become horns like the deer; the Evil Little Ones, referring to Kieli.

Kielitshate: Huichol for the Dwarfed Little Ones, referring to Kieli.

Kupuli: A Huichol aspect of the soul.

Kuwe Eme: Huichol for the green, poisonous sea snakes.

Los Santos Apóstoles: The Holy Apostles, a term used for those who followed *Jesús.*

Manta: Coarse cotton fabric.

Manteca: Pork lard.

Mara'acame: Huichol term for shaman.

María Santísima: The Most Holy Mary, one of the descriptive names for the Virgin Mary.

Mashakwashi: Huichol deity, the older brother of Kauyumali; the Deer Tail.

Matón: Someone who kills others; a hit man.

Médico: Doctor.

Mitote: A big festival, or dance ceremony.

Morales: Satchels, or shoulder bags.

Mordelones: Police; cops; those who put the "big bite" on someone.

Movieli: Huichol wands of power (with eagle and hawk feathers).

Mozo: Servant.

Nawa: Huichol corn beer, also called Tesgüino by the Tarahumara.

Nealika: Huichol wool painting made by pressing yarn into wax.

Negocio: A business.

Negros: Blacks.

Niwetuka: One of the Huichol Mothers.

Norte: A cold air mass that sweeps down from the northland then in from the coast bringing chilling damp clouds.

Norteamericanos: North Americans; Americans.

Notat: "My father" in Huichol.

Nunutsi: Huichol for a little one, or baby.

Ocote: A type of pine tree, pitchpine, or fatwood used for kindling.

¡Oyes chamaco, llévate éste a tres estrellas a Guadalajara! ¡Su camión se va! : Did you hear, kid? Take this guy to the three-star bus to Guadalajara. His bus is leaving.

Padre: Priest; father.

Patrones: Patrons; employers; hosts; masters.

Perico guapo: A handsome bird.

Peseros: Mexican communal taxi cabs similar to buses.

Peyotero: Peyote dancers, or pilgrims.

Pinche Indio: Damned Indian!

Pinche indios mentirosos: Damned lying Indians.

¡Pinche ladrón! ¿Dónde está mi mujer?: You damned thief! Where is my woman?

¡Pinche! : Spanish expletive; Damn!

Pistoleros: Hired gunmen.

Plata: Silver, or money.

Pobrecitos: Poor little ones.

Ponche: Punch, the drink.

Portera: A woman doorkeeper.

Procuraduría General: Mexican Attorney General's Office.

Pues, vete indito! El camión sale a las ocho: Get moving Indian! The bus leaves at eight.

Puestos: Food stands.

Quechquemitls: A triangular blouse worn over the neck.

Ranchería: Widely separated ranches of extended family groups, typical of Huichol settlement patterns.

San Pedro: Saint Peter.

Santiago: Saint James; symbol of the conversion of the indigenous population to Christianity.

Santo Cristo: The Holy Christ.

Santo Entierro: The Holy Grave, or Burial.

Santo Salvador: The Holy Savior.

Sargento: Sergeant.

Semana Santa: Holy Week.

Shiriki: Huichol shrine for the gods and the ancestors pertaining to particular families.

Shokolis: Huichol for the bowls that carry their messages to the Mothers and Fathers.

Shuliku. Shuliku! Shitimen! Shutiali nica, nica, nica. Nica! : Common Huichol nonsense words.

Sierra: A jagged mountain chain.

Solandra: A botanical species with similar pharmacological action to *Datura*.
Solicitud: A specific written request.
Suiza: Switzerland.

Takutsi Nakawe: Huichol "Grandmother Growth," the goddess of creation, one of the principal deities of the Huichols.
Takwatsi: Huichol for the sacred bundle each Huichol carries on a pilgrimage.
Taquitos: Small tacos.
Tatei Nieli: One of the Huichol Mothers for whom a special fiesta is held each year.
Tatematinieli: Huichol "Spring of our Mothers" in Wilikuta where they collect their sacred water.
Tatewali: Huichol "Grandfather Fire," one of the principle deities in Huichol cosmology.
Tatoani: Náhuatl for speaker, or governor.
Tatsiotewiali: Huichol for the Rabbit brother of Kauyumali and Mashakwashi.
Taweakame: Huichol for the Whirlwind, the father of Kieli.
Te mato: I'll kill you.
Teakata: Huichol place name near Santa Catarina for the Huichol center of the world.
Tesguino: A type of corn beer.
Tewalis: Huichol term for Mexicans, foreigners, outsiders to the Huichols.
Teyau: The Huichol sun deity sometimes associated with Santo Cristo.
Tierra caliente: A place with a warm climate.
Tlacuache: Opossum.
Toloache: A Náhuatl borrowing into Spanish for a dangerous intoxicating plant, same as *Datura*.
Toloatzin: The original Náhuatl term that was corrupted into Toloache in Spanish.
Tomin: Money.
Tortilladora: A woman or a machine that makes tortillas.
Tostadas: Crisp fried tortilla with refried beans, lettuce, and hot sauce on top.
Tuche: A Huichol alcoholic drink not as strong as aguardiente made from agave.
Tuki: Huichol for the Kaliwey, or Huichol temple, which is a term borrowed from Nahuatl, meaning "great house."
Turcos: Turks.

Turistas: Tourists.
Tutakuli: Huichol alternative term for Kieli.
Tututsikipa: Huichol for the home of the five kielis of the five colors.

Ulucame: Huichol aspect of the soul.
Ulus: Huichol for the arrows that carry their messages to the Mothers and Fathers.
Ulusha: Huichol for a sorcerer's arrow.
Upali: Traditional Huichol chairs for women with no back, more like a stool.
Urashi: A screeching bird.
Usha: Huichol for the face paint sought on peyote pilgrimages.
Uweni: Huichol shaman's chair.

Vecindad: A slum or neighborhood housing unit in urban areas.

Wealica: Huichol for the two-headed eagle.
Wewia: A type of Huichol wool painting.
Wilikuta: Huichol place name for the Magic Peyoteland.
Wishalica: Huichol term for "The People"; Huichols.
Witsi: Huichol for a hummingbird, borrowed from the Nahuatl *huitzitl.*

NOTES

I

1. When *Jesús* is set off from the text in italics and has an accent, I intend that the Spanish pronunciation of the name be used, *heySOOS*. This is done to avoid unintended allusions to Jesus Christ for the English-speaking reader.

III

1. Schaefer and Furst 1996, 2.
2. Lumholtz 1900, xx.
3. Ibid., xi.
4. See, Furst 1978; Schaefer 1993a, 1993b; Valadez 1978.
5. See Grimes and Grimes 1966.
6. The term *Kaliwey* is derived from the Nahuatl (Aztec)-language term *huey calli*, meaning "great house."
7. See Schaefer 1996.
8. Neurath 2000, 84.
9. Diguet 1911, 25.
10. Velazquez 1961.
11. Lumholtz 1902, 2:24.
12. Ibid., 2:22–23.
13. Liffman 2000, 129.
14. Lumholtz 1902, 2:272.
15. See Weigand 1981.
16. Schaefer and Furst 1996, 24.
17. In an analysis in 1971 of more than four hundred individuals from the community of Santa Catarina listed in kinship networks, Huichol friends identified 80 percent of the men as mara'acames, or men having entered the path of shamanic training. This does not mean that these individuals have become shamen, or completed their training; in fact, friends who have accompanied me on the peyote pilgrimage will often refer to me as a mara'acami. This means that these men are on the path to becoming mara'acames.

18. Zingg 1938, 741.
19. Schaefer 1989; Weigand 1972.
20. Malinowski 1948, 74–90.
21. Zingg 1938, 742.
22. Ibid., 61.
23. Ibid., 67.
24. Ibid., 60.
25. Furst 1997, 265.
26. Zingg 1938, 61.
27. Angiano Fernández, and Furst 1978.
28. Knab 1972.
29. Gutiérrez del Angel 2000, 112.

IV

1. Huichol men believe that they are born with a limited quantity of semen and that as this semen is exhausted an individual becomes progressively weaker. Women in Huichol society are seen as the sexual aggressors who seek to exhaust a man's supply of semen.

IX

1. It is not unusual for a Huichol shaman or teller of tales to use multiple voices. His grandfather used a different voice for the god Tatewali, and Chucho used different voices for his grandfather as well as Tatewali.
2. Mashakwashi is also known as Great Grandfather Deer Tail.
3. There is a unique system for the classification of hallucinogenic experience in the Sierra. To be on the "path of the flowers" is to be intoxicated by peyote. To be "in the center of the flower" is to be quite intoxicated, to the point that everything becomes part of the multicolored swirling hallucinogenic reality. To be "beyond," or "on the other side of the flower" is to have what many aficionados of hallucinogenic drugs in the 1960s called a "white-light" experience.

X

1. Zingg 1938.
2. Weil and Rosen 1983, 132.
3. Furst and Myerhoff 1966.
4. Furst 1989, 1996.
5. Knab 1977.
6. Yasumoto 1996.

7. Valadez 1996.
8. Fikes 1985.

XI

1. When I asked old Pablo, my Huichol father, what the mirrors were in many of his wool paintings, he explained, "When you look into the mirror, what do you see? You see yourself but you don't see what is on the other side of the mirror. What is on the other side of the mirror is the god. It is so that the gods can see you when you are seeing your-self; they are the Ones on the other side of the mirror."
2. Lumholtz 1900, 84.
3. Chaumiel 1995, 21.

XII

1. Lumholtz, Sierra Notebook, 4, 1898, p. 15, and Sierra Notes, 1902, p. 73.
2. Lumholtz, Huichol Diary, Sunday, May 8, 1898, p. 14.
3. Lumholtz 1902, 2:163.

XIX

1. Diáz 1986, 26.

BIBLIOGRAPHY

Angiano Fernández, Marina, and Peter T. Furst. 1978. *La endoculturación entrelos Huicholes.* 2d ed. México, D.F.: Instituto Nacional Indigenista.

Chaumiel, Jean Pierre. 1995. Del proyectil al virus. El complejo de las flechas mágicas en el chamanismo del oeste amazónico. In *Chamanismo en Latinoamérica: Una revisión conceptual,* ed. Isabel Lagarriga, Jacques Galinier, and Michel Perrin, 21–44. México, D.F.: Editorial Plaza y Valdés, La Universidad Iberoamericano and El centro de Estudios Mexicanos y Centroamericanos de la Embajada de Francia.

Díaz, José Luís. 1986. Plantas mágicas y sagrados de la medicina indígena. *México Indígena* 9: 26–29.

Diguet, León. 1911. Idiome Huichol. Contribution a l'Etude des Langues Mexicaines. *Journal de la Societé desAmericanistes de Paris* 8: 23–54, n.s.

Eger, Susana (Valadez). 1978. Huichol Women's Art. In *Art of the Huichol Indians,* ed. Kathleen Berrin, 35–53. New York: Fine Arts Museum of San Francisco, Harry N. Abrams.

Fikes, Jay Courtney. 1985. *Huichol Identity and Adaptation.* Unpublished Ph.D. dissertation, Department of Anthropology, University Microfilms, University of Michigan, Ann Arbor.

Furst, Peter T. 1969. Myth in Art: A Huichol Depicts His Reality. *The Quarterly Publication County Museum of Natural History Los Angeles* 7, no. 3: 16–26.

———. 1978. The Art of "Being Huichol." In *Art of the Huichol Indians,* ed. Kathleen Berrin, 18–34. New York: Fine Arts Museum of San Francisco, Harry N. Abrams.

———. 1989. The Life and Death of the Crazy Kiéri: Natural and Cultural History of a Huichol Myth. *Journal of Latin American Lore* 15, no. 2: 155–79.

———. 1995. Kieri and the Solanaceae: Nature and Culture in Huichol Mythology. *Acta Americana, Journal of the Sweedish Americanist Society* 3, no. 2: 43–57.

———. 1996. Myth as History, History as Myth: A New Look at Some Old Problems in Huichol Origins. In *People of the Peyote: Huichol Indian History, Religion and Survival*, ed. Stacy B. Schaefer and Peter T. Furst, 26–60. Albuquerque: University of New Mexico Press.

———. 1997. Assimilation and Transformation of Some Catholic Icons in Huichol Myth and Ritual. *Journal of Latin American Lore* 20, no. 2: 249–74.

Furst, Peter T., and Barbara Myerhoff. 1966. Myth as History: The Jimson Weed Cycle of the Huichols of Mexico. *Antropológica* 17: 3–39.

Grimes, Joseph B., and Barbara Grimes. 1962. Semantic Distinctions in Huichol (Uto Aztecan) Kinship. *American Anthropologist* 64: 104–16.

Gutiérrez del Angel, Arturo. 2000. Blood in Huichol Ritual. *Journal of the Southwest* 42, no. 1: 111–18.

Knab, Timothy. 1972. *Kinship, Marriage and Incest among the Huichol*. Unpublished manuscript.

———. 1977. Notes Concerning the Use of Solandra among the Huichol. *Economic Botany* 31, no. 1: 80–86.

Liffman, Paul. 2000. Gourdvines, Fires and Wixarika Territoriality. *Journal of the Southwest* 42, no. 1: 129–66.

Lumholtz, Carl G. 1898a. *Sierra Notebook*. Manuscript, American Museum of Natural History, New York.

———. 1898b. *Huichol Diary*. Manuscript, American Museum of Natural History, New York.

———. 1900. Symbolism of the Huichol Indians. *Memoirs of the American Museum of Natural History* 3, no. 1.

———. 1902a. *Unknown Mexico*. 2 vols. New York: Scribner's and Sons.

———. 1902b. *Sierra Notes*. Manuscript, American Museum of Natural History, New York.

Malinowski, Brownislaw. 1948. *Magic, Science and Religion*. New York: Free Press.

Neurath, Johannes. 2000. *Tukipa*. Ceremonial Centers in the Community of Turapurie (Santa Catarina Cuexcomatitlan): Cargo Systems Landscape and Cosmovision. *Journal of the Southwest* 42, no. 1: 81–110.

Schaefer, Stacy B. 1989. The Loom and Time in the Huichol World. *Journal of Latin American Lore* 15, no. 2: 179–94.

————. 1993a. Huichol Indian Costumes: A Transforming Tradition. *Latin American Art* 5, no. 1: 70–73.

————. 1993b. The Loom as a Sacred Power Object. In *Art in Small Scale Societies, Contemporary Readings*, ed. Richard Anderson and Karen Field. Englewood Cliffs, N.J.: Prentice Hall.

————. 1996. The Crossing of the Souls: Peyote, Perception, and Meaning among the Huichol Indians. In *People of the Peyote: Huichol Indian History, Religion and Survival*, ed. Stacy B. Schaefer and Peter T. Furst, 138–68. Albuquerque: University of New Mexico Press.

Schaefer, Stacy B., and Peter T. Furst. 1996. Introduction. In *People of the Peyote: Huichol Indian History, Religion and Survival*, ed. Stacy B. Schaefer and Peter T. Furst, 1–25. Albuquerque: University of New Mexico Press.

Valadez, Susana Eger. 1989. Problem Solving in a Threatened Culture. In *Mirrors of the Gods, Proceedings of Symposium on the Huichol Indians*, ed. Susan Bernstein, 17–32. San Diego Museum of Man Papers No. 25.

————. 1996. Wolf Power and Interspecies Communication in Huichol Shamanism. In *People of the Peyote: Huichol Indian History, Religion and Survival*, ed. Stacy B. Schaefer and Peter T. Furst, 267–305. Albuquerque: University of New Mexico Press.

Velázquez, María del Carmen. 1961. *Colotlan: Doble forntera contra los bárbaros*. México, D.F.: Cuadernos del Instituto de História 3, UNAM.

Weigand, Phil C. 1972. *Cooperative Labor Groups among the Huichol Indians in Jalisco, Mexico*. Carbondale: University of Southern Illinois Press.

————. 1981. Differential Acculturation among the Huichol Indians. In *Themes of Indigenous Acculturation in Northwest Mexico*, ed. Thomas B. Hinton and Phil C. Weigand, 9–21. Anthropological Papers No. 38. Tuscon: University of Arizona Press.

Weil, Andrew, and Winifred Rosen. 1983. *Chocolate to Morphine: Understanding Mind Active Drugs*. Boston: Houghton Mifflin.

Yasumoto, Masaya. 1996. The Psychotropic Kiéri in Huichol Culture. In *People of the Peyote: Huichol Indian History, Religion and Survival*, ed. Stacy B. Schaefer and Peter T. Furst, 235–63. Albuquerque: University of New Mexico Press.

Zingg, Robert M. 1938. *The Huichols, Primitive Artists*. New York: G. E. Stechert.

SELECTED READINGS
ON THE HUICHOL

The following are some of the ethnographic classics on the Huichol, works by important authors, and general reference works on the Huichol.

Benítez, Fernando. 1968. *En la Tierra Mágica del Peyote.* México, D.F.: Ediciones ERA.

Diguet, León. 1911. Idiome Huichol. Contribution a l'Etude des Langues Mexicaines. *Journal de la Societé des Americanistes de Paris* 8: 23–54, n.s.

Furst, Peter T. 1972. To Find our Life: Peyote among the Huichol Indians of Mexico. In *Flesh of the Gods: The Ritual Use of Hallucinogens,* ed. Peter T. Furst, 184–236. New York: Praeger Publishers.

———. 1995. Kieri and the Solanaceae: Nature and Culture in Huichol Mythology. *Acta Americana, Journal of the Swedish Americanist Society* 3, no. 2: 43–57.

———. 1996. Myth as History, History as Myth: A New Look at Some Old Problems in Huichol Origins. In *People of the Peyote: Huichol Indian History, Religion and Survival,* ed. Stacy B. Schaefer and Peter T. Furst, 26–60. Albuquerque: University of New Mexico Press.

Furst, Peter T., and Barbara Myerhoff. 1966. Myth as History: The Jimson Weed Cycle of the Huichols of Mexico. *Antropológica,* 17: 3–39.

Hinton, Thomas B., ed. 1972. *Coras, Huicholes y Tepehuanos.* México, D.F.: Instituto Nacional Indigenista.

Lumholtz, Carl G. 1900. Symbolism of the Huichol Indians. *Memoirs of the American Museum of Natural History* 3, no. 1.

———. 1902. *Unknown Mexico.* 2 vols. New York: Scribner's and Sons.

Myerhoff, Barbara G. 1974. *Peyote Hunt: The Sacred Journey of the Huichol Indians.* Ithaca, N.Y.: Cornell University Press.

Reed, Karen B. 1972. El INI y los Huicholes. *Colección de Antropología Social No. 10.* Instituto Nacional Indigenista, México, D.F.

Schaefer, Stacy B., and Peter T. Furst, eds. 1996. *People of the Peyote: Huichol Indian History, Religion and Survival*. Albuquerque: University of New Mexico Press.

Weigand, Phil C. 1981. Differencial Acculturation among the Huichol Indians. In *Themes of Indigenous Acculturation in Northwest Mexico*, ed. Thomas B. Hinton and Phil C. Weigand, 9–21. Anthropological Papers No. 38. Tuscon: University of Arizona Press.

———. 1992. *Ensayos sobre El Gran Nayar: Entre Coras, Huicholes y Tepehuanos*. México, D.F.: Centro de Estudios Mexicanos y Centroamericanso de la Embajada de Francia en México, Instituto Nacional Indigenista, and El Colegio de Michoacán, A.C.

Zingg, Robert M. 1938. *The Huichols, Primitive Artists*. New York: G. E. Stechert.

INDEX